Drama's Kaleidoscope

The Mesmerizing Vision of Girish Karnad

BIOGRAPHY & INTERPRETATION OF
COLLECTED PLAYS OF GIRISH KARNAD

DR. MADHURI MADHUKAR DESHPANDE

BlueRose ONE.com
Stories Matter
NewDelhi • London

BLUEROSE PUBLISHERS
India | U.K.

BlueRose ONE.com
Stories Matter
NewDelhi • London

For permissions requests or inquiries regarding this publication, please contact:

BLUEROSE PUBLISHERS
www.BlueRoseONE.com
info@bluerosepublishers.com
+91 8882 898 898
+4407342408967

ISBN: 978-93-5819-243-8

Cover design: Muskan Sachdeva
Typesetting: Pooja Sharma

First Edition: August 2023

DEDICATION

I would like to dedicate this book to my dear husband Mr.Vijay Rajhans and my dear parents Mr.Madhukar Deshpande and Mrs.Malti Deshpande without their inspiration & support I could not complete this book. I also dedicate this book to all of my family members and my well wishers for their cooperation and support.

This book is completely dedicated to late Girish Karnad I dreamt to write this book on my most favourite playwright it turned in reality by this book for this I am also grateful and would like to offer my honour to my dear supporting team of Bluerose Publishers and respected readers of this book.

I am also thankful to all persons those who are directly and indirectly involved in this mission of writing and publishing this book.

Thank You

I stand here today as a proud and grateful writer to express my heartfelt thanks to all those who have made this dream true. I would like to start by thanking Blue Rose Publication's sincere team for their management, who have always been supportive and encouraged me to strive for excellence.

ACKNOWLEDGEMENT

This work would not have been possible without the support of my dear husband Mr.Vijay Purushottamrao Rajhans I am especially indebted to my Parents Mr.Madhukar Deshpande and Mrs.Malti Deshpande to enrich my career goals and who worked actively to provide me with the protected academic time to pursue those goals. Nobody has been more important to me in the pursuit of this book than the members of my family. I would like to thank my parents, whose love and guidance is with me in whatever I pursue. They are the ultimate role models of my entire life. Most importantly, I wish to thank my loving and supportive husband Mr.Vijay Rajhans and my dear parents who provide unending inspiration.

I would like to focus on the plays written by late Girish Karnad most of the plays are close to my heart his extraordinary imagination and writing style brings all the spectators near to the human emotions, culture and tradition his writing ability was different from other playwright , he tried to convey audience full of meaningfulness in minimum words, this book is completely based on Late Girish Karnad he contributed a lot to flourish Indian English Drama even he credited his major role to rejuvenate Indian theatre .

Special thanks to Blue Rose Publication and its efficient team for their support, I also acknowledge this book to the respected and great readers who have shown their interest to read this book.

PREFACE

Girish Raghunath Karnad was a modern writer, dramatist, screenwriter, actor, and film director working in the Kannada language. He was also a director of films. His meteoric ascent to prominence as a writer in the 1960s reflected the maturation of modern Indian playwriting in Kannada at the same time. For the last four years, Karnad, who is now considered one of the most prominent playwrights in modern Indian theater, has been creating plays that are based on mythology and history in order to address current challenges. These plays have garnered him a lot of attention. Karnad blends history with the contemporary masculine problem of alienation and the absurdity of man's condition to create his work. Karnad, a modern playwright, employs themes and symbols to communicate his point of view throughout his work. According to Jasbir Jain, contemporary English theater "has had a number of interrupted periods of invention and visibility, as well as adopted itself to translated designs as well as recommendations passed on from one culture to another".

This book has been divided into 6 chapters which is as follows -

CHAPTER - 1 INTRODUCTION

In the first chapter, a general overview of the works of Girish Karnad, the concept of Indian drama, and the life and works of Girish Karnad have been discussed. Further in this chapter, Girish Karnad and Indian Theatre and Girish Karnad: Modern Yet Traditional Concepts of Their Plays have also been discussed.

CHAPTER - 2 MYTHS AND FOLK TALES IN GIRISH KARNAD'S PLAYS

Karnad's plays draw inspiration from a variety of sources, including history, mythology, and folklore. In this chapter, we have discussed the myths and folk tales of Girish Karnads' plays, such as Hayavadana, Naga-Mandala: Play with a Cobra, The Fire and the Rain, and Bali: The Sacrifice.

CHAPTER – 3 ROLE OF CULTURE AND SYMBOLS USED IN GIRISH KARNAD'S PLAYS

In this chapter, we investigate the role of culture and symbols in Girish Karnad's plays: A Bird's Eye View, The Marvelous, Miraculous, and Uncanny. Further in this chapter, we discussed the indeterminacy, invisibility, silence, and absence in Girish Karnad's plays.

CHAPTER – 4 THEMES AND STRATEGIES IN THE PLAYS OF GIRISH KARNAD

In this chapter, we investigate the various themes and strategies in the plays of Girish Karnad, in which the mythological background, ubiquitous theme, use of play within the play technique, and dramatic techniques in Karnad's play have been briefly discussed.

CHAPTER – 5 SOCIAL ISSUES IN THE PLAYS OF GIRISH KARNAD

The various social issues identified in the plays of Girish Karnad have been discussed in this chapter. This chapter briefly focuses on the self and quest for identity, social issues, social documents, and morality in the plays of Karnad. Further in this chapter, the depiction of violence, resemblance, and distinction of the plays of Girish Karnad have also been discussed.

CHAPTER – 6 CONCLUSION

In the last chapter 6th, the overall conclusion derived from the study is discussed.

FOREWORD

The present book has been written to honour the star of Indian English Drama late Girish Karnad, it is my pleasure to write this book in favour of him to bring his memories before the readers, I would like to catch the attention of readers close to English Literature and from other field to rejuvenate the unforgatable memories of the legend late Girish Karnad.

GENRE OF THE BOOK

FICTION

ABOUT THE STYLE OF GIRISH KARNAD

Karnad is concerned with the life of the contemporary man, which is very complicated and lacks a sense of completeness. The use of traditional stories is intended to draw attention to the absurdity of contemporary life with all of its inherent passions and conflicts. As a result, folk stories are transformed into vehicles for contemporary life as a result of the influence of western ideologies and systems of knowledge that examine human behavior from a variety of perspectives. His perspective on the present is colored by the current thinking that is propelled by Marxism, Freudianism, and existentialism. This is symbolic of a fundamental shift in the perspective that contemporary man has on warfare, human life, and the genesis of its own existence. The common conception of man is that he lives in a human society and interacts and engages in activities with other human beings. In Girish Karnad, these contemporary ideas are shown to be embedded in age-old stories in a way that is both humorous and thought-provoking. Because of the impact of these ideologies and systems of thinking, it would seem that all mother-son interactions are characterized by some form of the Oedipus complex. The historical events at Karnad serve as a reflection of the political, religious, and social goings-on in the present day.

In his plays, he depicts contemporary sociopolitical and socioeconomic concerns by using myth, folklore, and historical tales. In his plays, he explores a variety of topics, including caste, heredity, religion, and sexuality. In light of these modern concerns, the protagonists detail the obstacles that they face in their daily lives.

INTRODUCTION OF THE LEGEND LATE GIRISH KARNAD

The 1938-born writer Girish Karnad has made significant contributions to the Indian English Drama as well as demonstrating his talent as an actor, director, poet, screenwriter, and translator. He is a member of the emerging generation of Indian playwrights who, in the two decades that followed Indian Independence, reached adulthood and, together, transformed the Indian theater into a significant national institution in the latter half of the 20th century. He has received several honors and accolades, such as the Padma Bhushan (1992) and the Bharatiya Jnanpith Award (1999). When there was a direct conflict "between the cultural past of the country and its colonial past, between the allures of Western modes of thought and our own traditions, and finally between the various visions of the future that opened up once the common cause of political freedom was achieved," he started to frame his repertoire (Karnad 1999: 21). A multilingual author, Karnad initially drafts his plays in Kannad before translating them into English for wider distribution. The plays of post-colonial author Karnad are full of Indian sensibility, characterization, and topics. Indigenous cultures are on the verge of extinction as a result of foreign cultural invasions; hence, it is imperative that attention be given right away to Indian myths, legends, folk stories, and folk theatrical traditions that represent India's social and cultural character. All post-colonial countries, including Karnad, emphasize going back to one's origins and the preference for or resurrection of indigenous culture and tradition as an essential part of the decolonization process. In his plays, he offers the ideal model for addressing themes of cultural identity, nationalism, gender inequality, and anticolonial struggle. As a major figure in IED, Karnad is dissatisfied with the typical urban realism in Indian theater. Beyond realistic realism, his topics are abstract.

Contents

Chapter – 1

INTRODUCTION

1.1 OVERVIEW

Girish Karnad was an Indian actor, film director, Kannada writer, and playwright who mostly worked in South Indian cinema and Bollywood. He was born on May 19, 1938, and died on June 10, 2019. In addition to that, the Jnanpith award for best writer was bestowed on him. His rise to fame as a writer in the 1960s heralded the maturation of current Indian playwriting in Kannada, much in the same way that Badal Sarkar introduced modern Indian playwriting to Bengali, Vijay Tendulkar introduced it to Marathi, and Mohan Rakesh introduced it to Hindi. In 1998, he was given the Jnanpith Prize, which is widely regarded as the highest literary accolade that can be conferred in India. This award was presented to him. Over the course of the greater part of four decades, Karnad composed plays for the theater, often relying on ancient history and mythology to tackle contemporary issues. The English translations of his plays, which he also authored, garnered a lot of praise from critics. His plays have been adapted for the stage by a number of well-known Indian filmmakers, including Ebrahim Alkazi, B. V. Karanth, Alyque Padamsee, Prasanna, Arvind Gaur, Satyadev Dubey, Vijaya Mehta, Shyamanand Jalan, Amal Allanaa, and Zafer Mohiuddin, among others. His plays have also been translated into a number of Indian languages. As an actor, director, and screenwriter, he has contributed to the Hindi as well as the Kannada cinema industries, and he has been recognized for his work in both of those capacities on several occasions. The merit of his work has been acknowledged with awards. Both the Padma Shri and the Padma Bhushan awards were bestowed on him by the Government of India. Additionally, he was the recipient of four Filmfare Awards; three of them were for the Filmfare Award for Best Director in Kannada, while the other was for the Filmfare Award for Best Screenplay. In 1991, he was the anchor of "Turning Point," a weekly scientific magazine show that was aired on Doordarshan. The program was called "Turning Point." The name of the program was "Turning Point."

The Indian play, which has a history dating back more than two thousand years, is a manifestation of our country's ingenuity and a phenomenon that is unmatched in the world of literature. The narrative that describes how Indian play got its start may be found in the first chapter of Bharata's Ntyashstra, which was written about five hundred years before the Common Era. It is claimed to have been created by a celestial being. Brahma "took the text from the Rigveda, the art of performance from the Yajurveda, the song from the Samaveda, and rasa (aesthetic experience) from the Atharvaveda and created a fifth Veda called the Natyaveda" (Karnad, The Fire and the Rain, 70). This was done in order to restore the moral temper of society, which had been weakened. After that, Bharata got a hold of it, and he was the one who put on the first play. As a result, Indian theater incorporates all aspects of life, from the phenomenal to the transcendent, and delivers amusement, teaching, and insight all at the same time. This spectrum ranges from the material to the spiritual and from the phenomenal to the transcendent. Indian theater in English is sometimes referred to as the "Cinderella" of Indian literature written in English, despite the fact that the Indian dramatic tradition has a long and illustrious history (M. K. Naik and Shyamala A. Narayan, Indian English Literature 1980-2000: A Critical Survey 201, citing M. K. Naik and Shyamala A. Narayan).

Girish Karnad is one example of an Indian playwright who has chosen not to imitate the goals of Western culture and instead adheres, in both the subject matter and the methods of his plays, to the original Indian tradition. It is not hard to figure out why

Karnad prefers to use myths and stories as his sources of information. Myths, tales, and folklore are the foundation of every society or civilization, serving as the source of the fundamental norms and practices that are derived from them. In the form of motifs and symbols, they encompass, as Carl C. Jung points out, certain repeating patterns of collective human behavior as well as certain archetypal human experiences. Mythological and historical dramas have a long and illustrious history in the canon of our Indian theater. Karnad has a profound understanding of the situation and is convinced that the Indian theatrical heritage has untapped potential.

Religion and a feeling of the sacred and the secular have a profound effect upon people's perceptions of themselves and the world, as well as upon their relationships with one another and the world around them, despite the fact that modernity has a significant impact on these aspects of people's lives. As a consequence of this, Berger observes in the article that was just mentioned that "the majority of the world... is characterized by an explosion of passionate religious movements" (113). The fact that religion and culture are "marked by the influence of pluralism" (Berger 114) is one of the most crucial things that modernity has accomplished, according to Berger. In a situation like this one, Karnad's portrayal of religion, the sacred, and the secular takes on a significance and relevance that just cannot be ignored.

1.2 INDIAN DRAMA

The history of Indian theater as both a literary genre and a form of performance dates all the way back to ancient times. The art of dramaturgy has a long history in India, dating back more than two thousand years. Because the Vedas are the fonsetorigio (fountain and origin) of Indian literature, academics have sought to trace the history of Indian play in Sanskrit back to the Vedas even though there are no other literary materials to work with. According to S. Krishna Bhatta's Indian English Drama: A Critical Study,

"Bharata's Natyasastra, a treatise on dramaturgy... was given the status of a Veda" (1-2). As a result, theater was regarded as the fifth Veda that originated from a divine source, and it was classified as one of the Drusya Kavyas. The Ntyashstra of Bharata is credited with codifying the norms of theater and serving as the theoretical foundation for Indian classical theater. The Sanskrit term for drama, "Nataka," has its origins in the word "nrt," which means "to dance," and thus drama should have grown as an art of studying motions and expressions from the primary arts of dance and music, as M.N. Sundararaman describes in his article "Tradition and Modernity in Indian English Drama."

When the Aryan and non-Aryan components of the Indian people mingled, they were able to find a place for themselves within the larger framework of Indian mythology, religion, and philosophy. (Suniti Kumar Chatterji, "Introduction," Indian Theater 6). Puppetry, which seems to have evolved in India a few centuries before the Christian Era, and the discussions by the actors directing the puppets (sutradhara), provided an impetus to the birth of theater in ancient India. Puppetry seems to have arisen in India a few centuries before the Christian Era. A similar point of view is expressed by Bhatta, who states, "We may guess that the Classical Sanskrit Drama probably originated from the folk theater of the country as a sophisticated form and, over the course of time, both went on borrowing from each other and developed." (1).

The oldest examples of the drama of ancient India, which are the remnants of several Buddhist tragedies credited to Asvaghosha and dating back to the first and second centuries C.E., suggest the beginning of Indian theater. Before Kalidasa, who flourished about 400 C.E., there were a great number of dramatic poets, all of whom had their names documented by Kalidasa himself. There was also a famous Bhasa among them. Before Kalidasa came along, Sudraka wrote a comedy that he called Mrichchhakatika, often known as Little Clay Cart. In it, he vividly and insightfully portrayed Indian civilization from the first to the third centuries. The Sakuntala by

Kalidasa is widely considered to be the most significant work of Sanskrit play and one of the best-known pieces of writing in the history of literature. The plays written by Bhasa, Sudraka, Kalidasa, Visakhadata, Harsha, and Bhavabhuti, along with a select few others, are among the works of ancient Indian literature that are considered to be exemplary examples. They are considered works of the Sanskrit drama's golden period. However, beginning in the seventh century and continuing forward, there is a discernible drop in quality, particularly in terms of the level of originality that can be found in the Sanskrit plays.

After the Turks had conquered India, they began to persecute the local Indian ruling dynasties and put a stop to any further growth of the traditions of Sanskrit play. In addition, they prevented the traditions from being carried on. On the other hand, scattered over India, one may find examples of academics carrying on the tradition more or less in the form of a literary exercise. Since the country's independence, there have been several efforts made to bring back Sanskrit theater, and V. Raghavan's Anarkali is one play that exemplifies this movement.

After 1200 CE, efforts at literary self-expression were attempted in Sanskrit, despite the fact that Sanskrit play no longer functions as a live art form. A fresh approach to theatrical performance won over audiences over time. For instance, in Eastern India, there is a kind of theater that consists of conversations performed by two or more actors and is accompanied by music. This form of play probably made its debut in Bengal and Northern Bihar (Mithila) initially, and then it must have made its way to Orissa, Nepal, and Assam. There is a possibility that the Gita-Govinda, written by Jayadeva at the tail end of the twelfth century of the Christian era (Chatterji 11), contains the germs of this new kind. While there was a drop in Sanskrit theater, there was a steady growth in both the quality and quantity of popular folk theater. It used the native languages of the area, dealt with topics that are common knowledge, and included ancient traditions such as the Sutradhara, the Vidusaka, and others. In the meantime, the custom of theatrical recitation of epic tales carried on. It was subsequently developed by professional charanas, who are generally credited with founding the Modern Indian Theatre (Bhatta 3).

Saint-philosophers like Sri Sankara were instrumental in revitalizing the Vedic religion and culture, which in turn led to a rebirth in religious activity, which in turn gave rise to the Bhakti cult. The proliferation of the Bhakti religion persuaded the monarchs to construct a great number of temples, which later evolved into thriving entertainment venues. This resulted in the development of several popular forms of theater all throughout the nation, including Ramlila, Raslila, and Nautanki in the Northern region; Bhavai in the Gujarat region; Yakshagana in the Karnataka region; Veethi-natakamu and Burra-katha in the Andhra region; and Terukoothu in the Tamil Nadu region. Both traditional Sanskrit plays and Indian folk theater interacted with one another and inspired one another as Indian drama developed through time (Bhatta 3–4).

The impact of religion led to the development of a number of various theatrical manifestations in different sections of India. A good illustration of one of these dramatic phrases is the Bengali pala-gan. It was out of the pala-gan that the fatras, which translates to "a religious procession," emerged. The Bengali pala-gan and fatra dances eventually merged to become the jatra, which was popular in medieval Bengal. It was an old-fashioned play in which there were no scenes, and the audience sat in a circle around the performers as they performed. There was far more singing in them than there was acting. Skits with a social or satirical focus were performed both before and after these types of performances. The performances in other regions of India were likewise quite comparable. In South India, the Sanskrit heritage was carried on, but the creative artists of the time were more attracted to dance than to traditional forms of theater. As a result, the state of Kerala is home to the ancient dance play known as Kathakali, which is not a drama in the traditional meaning of the word (Chatterji 13).

During the time of British control in India, Western theater, namely of the Elizabethan sort, had an additional significant impact on Indian theater. Because of the impact of contemporary English and other Western forms of theater, Indian writers are now familiar with a diverse range of theatrical approaches. As a result, modern Indian theater has become a synthesis of three distinct forms of performance: the classical drama of Sanskrit, the folk theater of India, and the theater of the West. It is abundantly obvious that contemporary theater in India is a hybrid art form that is the product of a variety of literary inspirations. However, it has grown in a manner that is far from consistent throughout the nation (Chatterji 14).

1.3 LIFE AND WORKS OF GIRISH KARNAD

It is one of the best dramatists working in India at the moment, and it has both feet firmly planted on the ground. He is a gentle genius. He is known for his work as a mime as well as a movie maker and writer. He is one of the people who were given the Award for Kannada, which was the first literary honor of its kind to be bestowed in India. He has analyzed a paper, which is a dormitory of engagement in activity application of plays in Kannada that, apart from being translated, have been on the road towards either top-notch Indian sense or English, both at the common laborer of the playwright himself or on others. He has also analyzed a paper, which is a dormitory of engagement in the application of plays in Tamil. On several occasions, he has used days that were wasted and his imagination to dedicate himself to addressing current issues. A cutting-edge Indian writer who at one point presented his shows is a multi-faceted figure who has won recognition as a playwright, drop-up idiot, comptroller, and translator. His performances are always guided by a profound consideration of some aspect of the world. When they are performed in front of an audience, his plays add something more to the textual content that they contain. It seems that he is both multifaceted and, prior to the sprinkling, participated in the latter in an alternative fashion. Because of this, his first civil proceeding was conducted with a completely free hand in Marathi. He became aware of and loved the performances that were taking place in his community. In 1958, he received his diploma from Karnataka, where he had completed his studies in mathematics and facts. As a lone guy, he embraced the ease and transition to Western narrative quickly when he moved to Bombay for his post-graduate studies. This was in anticipation of his arrival there. He was awarded the Rhodes scholarship in order to pursue his education and research opportunities overseas. After that, he traveled to England and attended Oxford University, where he earned a Bachelor of Arts degree in Philosophy, Politics, and Economics on the same day of his birth. As a matter of choice, depending on the location of Chicago's graduation, he participated in both the visiting professor program and the Fulbright program. Additionally, he was a member of the Fellowship from 1970 until 1972. From the ground up, he embodies the Kannada Theater and symbolizes the active lifestyle of the Kannada field of fish tales, which demonstrated its greatest analogies inside plays. He is also the representative of the Kannada field of fish stories. In the language of his bat of an eye, his senior was a health cat of nine tails in North Karnataka, and he climbed a man impending of the cloth in heaven.

Nevertheless, composing plays in Kannada was what captivated him the most. He was able to make an incredible profit off of the plays in his bloom because of his puffery. The wet behind the ears went to a well-known performer who was any of the staff. He handed it down to go to institute performances that were not as precious as being surrounded by meals. The shop-created syllabify of those current forms has evidently gone eye to eye in the production of plays, and lastly, he has imbibed in the manner things stack up in Western show business as well. In his coming to sweep the peak time of his career, for the most part he intended to annex a fancy poet, but to his terrify, he grew to become a dramatist in the false succeeding of a dramatist.

He has translated his performances into English on several occasions in order to increase his chances of being hired or to play before a larger audience. In his plays, he makes sure to look out for a wellspring of power in the flow of milk and honey that is India's cultural history by using the whole of the backing of myths, legends, histories, and other authoritative tales. Has abstemious a hardest a connection at two in the morning a foil to the ancestor of colonialism by conduct of sustaining Indian principles and its cultural attitude, has abstemious a hardest a relationship at two in the morning a foil to the ancestry of colonialism, The conclusion matters have a high-ranking authority; in general, they are informed of the much similar reception that is on the assent of specific cultural furnishings from India. In order to shock much lesser-known and spiritually significant myths, efforts are made to acquire their power and tie them to the most well-liked narrative. After that, he is successful in adding romantic elements to his performances, and this is the whole thing without compromising the sincerity of the particular recollections. Every single aspect of The Fire and the Rain, from beginning to finish, is predicated on the oral tradition of the theatrical world. His behavior at this phase seems to be motivated by a desire to understand how the land lies within the bounds of his inventiveness. Myths chide important reputational values without delay in oral Indian conduct, which is characterized by the idea that everyone is born on the same day. In spite of this, the use of myths as support in his plays is remarkable. As a figure of testimony for several of his plays, he uses mythology as a soundtrack.

Right from that, the dramatist believes that the knee-jerk reaction of ceasing to exist of steep, folk one for the bird and shifting cast back to the traditional tenor matters are the resultants of Western colonization employment. This is because Western colonization employment came about mutually Indian recreation welcome and fiction liberally to concern by the whole of consider modern-day issues in his dig, when he was en route a dramatist, later roiled to Folks Theater. The writer uses stunning, furious, and folk's summary topics as the basis for his plays, despite the fact that they are diagnosed with cutting-edge situations. He does this in a deft and elegant manner. They acknowledge the resemblance with a blasé satire on the countless expedients and political powers shown in artworks in contemporary India. When you examine his plays, you will always get a sense of the history that is being repeated there.

Worked diligently to bring pressure to bear on the culture of the country eye to eye in his area of fish tale, and in the end bit off more than he or she could chew in order to reach the horizon of the Indian stage. The plays are intelligent in their hunches and soaring loftiness and inventive cleverness. He makes an effort to be common and generally educated about the many forms of intriguing artwork.

It is possible to draw parallels between it and Shakespeare's use of resources in his plays. Shakespeare, for example, took his ace up his sleeve from Greek mythology, the Chronicles of Plutarch, and Roman records. He resolved the issues pertaining to the nature of the beast in his brain at pass style and conceived the plays in a mystical training session in order to indicate that they should be brought up in a meat market. Because each of them is included in him, it is only natural that his plays are a disappointment to recall while playing the game. He creates a variety of scenes by using his whole summary of the impoverished and indifferent location. He single-handedly inspires and stimulates mutual benefit among his grantees of cut via the procedure of style in the envisaged run. He adheres to the established Sanskrit practice, in contrast to Shakespeare, who, circumlocutorily, accomplished what the Greek culture expected of him. In the end, as the parable in English struggled to protect itself, the fish story in contradictory Indian humanistic comeuppance kept on experimenting, fledgling, and soaking up family paperwork. Today, as a result of his problematic and intriguing charm within the trade of Indian English Literature, he stands as a newcomer in the field of Indian English Literature. On one of the tracks that was chosen, he admits to himself, "I have been unquestionably well-off in having multi-pronged professions." You start to perspire. I've worked as a stand-up comedian and as a silver watchmaker. In any case, in none of them did I get the sense that I had reached the conclusion at home, as in "look out for number one writing."

Although a great deal is known about the conclusion, there is very little light shed on the hog and fancy playwrights who contributed to Indian English Theater. Within the space of a minute in New York, Kannada playwrights, romp writing became an amount and right between literary lengthy rows to hoe, without a dwell on anything with the greatest degree. He has a firm grasp on something that is mutually acted upon by a wide host of inventions and experiments in tone issues and methods. The dramatist makes use of the methods of fiction, old wives' tales, and records, but not in order to go back in time; rather, he does so in order to understand what is now happening and to recognize what will happen in the future. In addition, he makes getting a grip on anything about these things out to be a question of slickly accepting the joke that cave voter lives are, with all of the feelings and tensions that come along with them. Plays are being performed on this icy subject matter since he has the broadest cordillera belt in terms of the subjects and methods covered. In addition to winning the Mysore Celestial Award in 1962, his quick lookout for numbers has garnered a posh reputation in the form of free analysis on the existentially limited boundary. It is without a doubt an existentialist romp at the literary trade of responsibility that interprets the topic with a lid on it in a current-day framework. Like the setting of the Mahabharata, the present world is fumbling in the twilight of fabric and spectacular pleasures. He finds that he has been transported to a world where the abstract values have been fully blown away by this, but the formal spiritual ones have not yet been detected. The tireless pursuit of hilarity has, throughout the course of one's life, proven to be the pinnacle of self-assurance and the last destination of one's mission. His frolic was an examination paper in 1964; all throughout the reference book is his raid at Oxford, and it portrays the disappointment of hugely collected Indians by the entire angelical political system at the drop of a hat during the time of Independence. This effort ensured that his affiliate would become India's most famous dramatist. Not very well does conduct conduct to photographically complete the beyond steady, but at the same time, a front has begun that makes further efforts to include well-known dramatic tactics of the old hills subculture. He derived its haunting and relief from the reality that we were all born on the same day. Thomas Mann, who common laborer his entire for his brief novel 'The Transposed Heads,' makes owner of the people who artwork in a blood travail and work oneself into sweat to rival asked as an advice at contemporary difficulty of body of life division. It is undeniably hilarious to bring up the rear of free to all rights in and throughout bottom-side partnerships. The dance is a dressed-up way of describing the human heart, and you need to do it in order for your ideas to have a chance of being debated inside the closed chapter.

1.4 LIST OF THE PLAYS

1.4.1 Nagamandala

Girish Karnad wrote the mythical play titled Nagamandala. In 1988, it was published. The text was first written in Kannada. Girish Karnad personally translated it into English. In English, it may be referred to as "A Play with Cobra." The play's plot was adapted from a Kannada folktale. A. K. Ramanujan, the playwright's guru and renowned poet, had told him the tale.

The 1997 Indian Kannada-language drama film Nagamandala, which T. S. Nagabharana directed and which was based on Girish

Karnad's play of the same name, has the subtitle Serpent Ritual. Srihari L. Khoday produced it, while C. Aswath composed the music. It is an adaptation of Karnad's play of the same name from 1988, which was based on a custom and folktale from the area. Prakash Raj and Vijayalakshmi play the key characters. The movie shows a romance between a lady and a snake that poses as her callous husband.

Major Themes of the Play:

- Exploitation of Women
- Mocking at the Idea of Chastity
- Emancipation and Empowerment of Women

1.4.2 Hayavadana

Girish Karnad, an Indian writer, wrote the drama Hayavadana. The play is about two friends who fall in love with the same lady and mistakenly exchange heads. A comedy that ends in tragedy, the tale also speaks about a guy with a horse's head who wants to become human. In 1971, the play was first published. Girish Karnad's Hayavadana depicts the narrative of the eponymous character, who is half human and half horse but transforms totally into a horse. It also tells the story of Devadatta, Kapila, and Padmini's love triangle and subsequent deaths.

Hayavadana is an ancient Indian mythology drama based on Vetalpanchavimsati and Somadeva's Kathasaritsagara. The Transposed Heads by Thomas Mann also inspired him to realize the supremacy of the human head above the human body. In Hayavadana, the topics that are too often mentioned in this drama include man's unending longing for fulfillment, self-realization, love, and sex. Padmini is a lady from a culture where women have no option but to voice their desires. In Hayavadana, Karnad combines folklore and folk theater instruments like masks, female choras, commentators, and dolls to highlight women's difficulties in the family and society.

1.4.3 The Fire and the Rain

Girish Karnad's Fire and Rain is the sixth excellent drama based on fantastical Mahabharata episodes. The drama was originally written in Kannada as "Agni Mattu Male," which translates as "Fire and Rain" in English. Girish Karnad's The Fire and the Rain (1995) is based on the Mahabharata story of Yayakri. It is a play with symbolic and allegorical undertones that depicts the fundamental fight between good and evil. According to Dharwadker (2006: xvi–xvii), "Karnad reimagines the world of Hindu antiquity and constructs a story of passion, loss, and sacrifice in the context of Vedic ritual, spiritual discipline (tapasya), and social and ethical differences between human agents" in this play. The drama depicts the celebration of fire with Vedic rites for the divine's satisfaction as well as the peace and pleasure of humans. However, Karnad also links Brahmanic aesthetics with the mind-game of egocentricism. In the play, fire-sacrifice is used as a primary metaphor to highlight activities such as academic study, love-making, epic reading, and marriage. Karnad expands the play's tale from the original myth with several digressions, reflecting society's age-old attitude toward women and inferior castes. It is also built on the concept of accountability. Girish Karnad's popularity stems from his ability to analyze contemporary issues using an old narrative.

1.4.4 Taledanda

Tale-Danda has a significant role in the Karnad canon. Karanad deals with topics that represent the manner of life and thinking of a complete community in this play. The play conveys the concept that it is simple to go with the flow since it makes no demands, but it is very difficult to go against it. Karnad's actions in the play depict the identity of communal and caste violence, as well as the reality that the results of intra-religious conflict are extremely similar to those of inter-religious conflict. Karnad illustrates the most sensitive and critical issue of the caste system in Tale-Danda, which has raged throughout Indian history. The fundamental cause for Basavanna's failure is a lack of unity and faith. The social activists' ideal of an equal society in Basavanna cannot be realized since society has always been divided on the basis of caste, class, color, religion, gender, and so on.

1.4.5 Bali the Sacrifice

Karnad's Bali-The Sacrifice (2009) is an ethical argument that calls the Rigvedic tradition of animal sacrifice in Hindu ceremonies into question. He depicts India's contradictory religious and cultural values in this drama. He has chosen the thirteenth century Kannad epic YashodharaCharite to provide a new viewpoint on the social, moral, and religious foundation of an individual's religion. He also investigates a person's private involvements in love, sex, and passion for the sake of his public life. He remarks in an interview:

Bali both frightened and thrilled me...It addresses the notion that violence is omnipresent, lying just under the surface of our regular conduct and is often concealed by conscious effort. It also contends that human cognition, purpose, and action are inextricably intertwined. It challenges the Jain belief that intentional violence is just as bad as the deed itself...The drama addresses the issue of religious strife. (Mukherjee 2006: 49)

The drama contains excellent philosophical thought on Indian heritage as well as ideological ideas concerning values, moral conflicts, and challenges. The play becomes a symbol of the conflict between personal authority and cruel popular culture. "Karnad uses the context of the play with a hint at a positivist and exclusivist possibility of all ideologies and necessary human bonds in human relationships," writes Nayak (2011: 79). In their functional significance and philosophical reasoning, Karnad negotiates between culture and need-based ideology. As previously said, Karnad derives inspiration for his plays from folktales and gives these tales new meaning to suit his purposes. Folktales are stories about a society's natural and cultural phenomena. It develops an oral tradition to help us comprehend cultural riches. The usage of folktales in Karnad is founded on ancient beliefs and traditions, and they provide responses to modern socio-cultural challenges and injustices like as caste, class, gender, and exploitation. They also provide the groundwork for the multidisciplinary study of religion, ethnicity, culture, and other elements of life. Dharwadker (2006: xxix) states in this context:

Thus, the treatment of femininity, sexual desire, and power in urban folk drama reveals the ideology of that genre most overtly: unlike their urban counterparts, women in folk drama are able to challenge patriarchy while still maintaining some measure of ambivalent freedom.

1.4.6 Tughlaq

The historical drama Tughlaq by Karnad from 1972 has received praise from reviewers for its broad scope and complexity. It is a complex piece of art that is open to several interpretations at various levels. For [Karnad] history is no longer a static backdrop for his play; rather, it is timeless, living, and ridiculous in its totality, as Nayak (2011: 139) accurately notes. The enigma of Mohammad bin Tughlaq, a medieval Muslim Sultan whose reign is regarded as one of the worst disasters in Indian history, is explored in this drama by Karnad. A extremely innovative recreation of some of the most important moments in the reign of a great monarch, it is not your typical chronicle drama. Its postmodern and neohistoricist discourses have the historicity of reality and the textuality of history. Karnad develops macrohistorical concepts in this drama, such as the love of power, social ties, political motivations, and conservative ideas. The play's political premise has drawn attention because it captures the political disenchantment of India following Independence. Karnad claims:

The gradual deterioration of the moral principles that had inspired the campaign for independence and accepting cynicism and real politik are some of the ways in which the play portrays the steady disillusionment my generation felt with the new politics of Independent India. (Karnad 2007: 7)

The drama also addresses the themes of communalism and power politics. Reprocessing the past with a focus on the present's political and social requirements is what it is.

1.4.7 Yayati

An important addition to Indian English Drama has been made by acclaimed Indian writer Girish Karnad. He established himself as a dramatist deserving of respect by his first play, "Yayati," which was published in 1961. The audience was greatly affected by his straightforward yet inventive presentation of timeless, well-known subjects. The audience responded quite favorably to his plays' innovative themes. "Yayati" illustrates the nuanced dynamics of the relationships between Puru and his wife Chitralekha on the one side and Devayani, Sharmishtha, and Yayati on the other.

Yayati's storyline was adapted from the first chapter of the well-known Indian epic "Mahabharata," "Adiparva." The play's significant turning points include Shukracharya's curse on Yayati, Puru's willingness to give up his youth for his father's old age, Chitralekha's decision to take her own life, and Yayati's final acceptance of the curse's resultant, unavoidable old age.

Despite seeming to be about a myth, the drama has a lot to say today. According to Girish Karnad's 'Collected Plays' (2005):

"I borrowed the King Yayati tale from the Mahabharata. The monarch is doomed to die in his prime due to a moral violation he committed. He approaches his son and begs him to donate him his youth in return for his old age, distraught at having lost his temper. The son consents to the trade and takes on the curse; as a result, he ages beyond his father. However, old age simply brings the senselessness of a punishment meted out for an act in which he had not even engaged. It does not provide enlightenment or self-realization. The father is forced to deal with the repercussions of avoiding accountability for his own conduct.

Karnad uses ancient tales to highlight the futility of contemporary life, with all of its complications and conflicts. Yayati is a metaphor for the selfish, irrational desires-obsessed contemporary man. Yayati is so consumed by sexual delights that he even doesn't hesitate to rob his kid of his natural freshness and energy. However, his wish is not fulfilled, and in the end, he submits to events and the laws of nature. He needs to understand that becoming older is inevitable. However, in the original tale, he embraces old age after a lengthy time of a thousand years of enjoying youth and sexuality. But in Girish Karnad's "Yayati," he takes it right away after Chitralekha dies. Yayati, who was profoundly touched by Chitralekha's death, acknowledges the agony of his own existence and understands his moral obligation. However, Yayati in the original tale recognizes the absurdity of human "desire" and understands that it persists even after a thousand years.

1.4.8 The Dreams of Tipu Sultan

Karnad's play 'The Dreams of Tipu Sultan' was written in English at the BBC's request in 1997 as one of the finest historical dramas. Karnad's work, a striking combination of depth and simplicity with inventive subversions, serves as a reminder that historical plays are not arcane concepts from a bygone era, but rather a modern subject profoundly pertinent to our times. On the invitation of the Golden Jubilee year of Indian freedom and the 200th death anniversary of Tipu Sultan, Karnad took on the mammoth challenge of re-creating the historical Tipu Sultan. The drama, which was originally performed in front of Tipu Sultan's magnificent Dariya Daulat palace in Srirangapattana, drew a lot of attention. It is not for nothing that Karnad has been highly hailed as the finest playwright and has won the highest literary honor.

Karnad subsequently translated it into Kannada with minor changes, and it was released in the year 2000 under the title "Tipu Sultan Kanda Kanasu" (The Dreams of Tipu Sultan). A.K. Ramanujan's revelation that Tipu Sultan surreptitiously captured his visions in writing piqued Karnad's interest in Tipu Sultan's history. Karnad used just three of the 34 dreams mentioned by Tipu Sultan in his journal (9, 10, 13) in this drama.

The BBC broadcasted radio drama, directed by Jatinder Verma of Tara Arts, starred Saeed Jaffrey as Tipu Sultan. The Kannada version was performed on the 15th, 16th, and 17th of May 2004 at the Daria Daulath precincts of Srirangapattana.

Girish Karnad wrote the drama The Dreams of Tipu Sultan. Tipu Sultan, the 18th century monarch of Mysore, is the subject of the drama. Karnad emphasizes that Tipu Sultan was a misunderstood king in history. It depicts an aspect of history that has not been documented by British historians. Tipu Sultan is portrayed in this book as a visionary and a man ahead of his time. It demonstrates the petty nature of British monarchs who could not accept a competent ruler like Tipu Sultan. Tipu was a noble man who wished to elevate his country, but others were unable to match his aspirations, giving him a contentious reputation. Karnad has chosen an amalgamation of history and elements of a dream play to give the piece a valid identity.

1.4.9 Wedding Album

Girish Karnad's Wedding Album is a contemporary tale that combines real and virtual realms. The Indian wedding is expected to bring the community together in unity and common passion. However, the clash of secret anxieties and resentments inside the family's the core is well established. The game's major focus is the counseling of sexual, conjugal, caste, class, and aging behaviors, egocentric and sacrificing attitudes and behaviors, chastity and trade, and obedience and authority, all of which are essential components of contemporary Hindu marriage. Karnad symbolizes a cultural fusion, and his methodical investigations are considerably more thorough and, without a doubt, far more successful than those of some of his colleagues.

Wedding Album, the newest play by famous writer Girish Karnad, is a humorous and touching extravaganza that is profoundly revelatory about today's India. The central characters in this play depict a modern, middle-class, Indian daughter who lives in Australia with her husband and children, a son who is a media professional, a younger daughter who is willing to marry a'suitable' boy from the US whom she has never met, a doting mother, an ageing father who is rapidly losing his authority, and a loyal cook.

Wedding Album acts on two levels: it investigates the traditional Indian wedding in a globalized, technologically sophisticated India while juxtaposing the family's and the faithful cook's very different life experiences and aspirations. Karnad demonstrates how certain conceptions of money, well-being, sexual propriety, tradition, and modernity create the foundation of middle-class culture in contemporary India.

This drama has previously been performed in a number of settings and was translated from Kannada into English by Karnad himself. This book, an extraordinary contribution to OUP's corpus of Girish Karnad plays, will be of interest not just to students and instructors of contemporary Indian theatre, but also to general readers.

1.4.10 Broken Images

Broken Images features a single set, a television studio, but a multi-layered concept. It weaves together problems as disparate as English's dominion over Indian languages and the hollowness of a media that bestows renown on a book that went unappreciated in its native language but becomes the talk of the worldwide literary community when translated into English. It also addresses inverted psychological suppression. Manjula, the principal character, is a prominent Kannada-turned-English writer who has a wheelchair-bound sister, Malini. However, it is the handicapped Malini who proves to be the really healthy and entire person. Malini not only earns Manjula's husband, Pramod's, affection, but she is also significantly more focused and happier than her caregiver sister, Manjula. Not just that. Manjula's loveless marriage ends after her death, with Pramod stepping out and relocating to Los Angeles, and the incredible success she has wrested from Malini by stealing Malini's unpublished MSS taste like poison. Broken Images makes several jabs at all those English-language authors who are frequently in the news, for large advances from foreign publishers, for works that will not be published for many years, for invitations to foreign universities, lecture tours, and signature signing sprees. There are also unanswered questions: are Indian English disconnected from the "smell of the soil," have they sold out to a market-driven economy, have they made a trade-off with their conscience by not writing in their original tongue, etc.

1.4.11 Samskara

The novel's principal topic is Naranappa's death and the issues associated with his cremation. Naranappa was an anti-Brahminical Brahmin who spent his whole life fighting Brahmin ideas and ways of living. He took a lower-caste prostitute to the agarahara and shared his home with her.

Samskara is a story of existential suspense eloquently translated by the renowned poet and scholar A. K. Ramanujan, a life-and-death confrontation between the holy and the profane, the pure and the impure, the ascetic and the erotic.

1.4.12 Turning Point

Girish Karnad and scientist Professor Yash Pal hosted a weekly scientific magazine show that aired in India. Girish Karnad and scientist Professor Yash Pal hosted a weekly scientific magazine show that aired in India.

Turning Point is a weekly scientific magazine show that debuted in 1991 on DD National. Several accolades were bestowed upon the program.

Neelabh Kaul and Indraneel Kaul wrote the storyline and directed the film. Doordarshan and Vyeth Television collaborated on the production. Girish Karnad hosted the show, while Yash Pal made an appearance. Some episodes were also presented by actor Naseeruddin Shah, classical dancer Mallika Sarabhai, and filmmaker Mahesh Bhatt.

Girish Karnad has made an extraordinary contribution to Indian English Drama. He draws inspiration for his plays from diverse sources and develops plays on higher values and philosophy. He examines the mental states of his characters and does extensive research on human behavior, social awareness, and psychological impacts. Karnad is rich in Indian culture and heritage. He investigates the treaded and un-treaded floors of the human mind with his creative imagination. In his choice of topics, he attempts to revitalize modern life by fusing contemporary politics and history, as well as old mythology and present realities. In his plays, he elevates the past and uses it as a potent weapon for expressing his thoughts.

1.5 GIRISH KARNAD AND INDIAN THEATRE

Girish Karnad is widely regarded as one of the most accomplished playwrights to have emerged from India in recent times. We come across in him a playwright who is also an academic, an expert, a standup comedian, a bard, and a skillful craftsman who, in his role as a genuine culture-smith, aspires to rescue the future Indian intelligentsia from its state of cultural amnesia. Through his contributions to the visual arts, the performing arts, the film industry, and the theater, he has helped to strengthen India's literary tradition. Girish Karnad is a well-known playwright who writes in both Kannada and English. He is considered to be one of the most famous playwrights in both languages. They are given a distinct man or tellurium that addresses the reader as a result of the creative talent that he has in his performances. His performances blend group themes and tribal modes of at first glance arts mutually subjects and concerns of standard duty. In his plays, he has accurately portrayed the Indian body, the Indian yarn, Indian subculture, and the Indian civic set-up. The frolic began with a misunderstanding by the majority of annoy as the crow flies or nonresponsive focus audience, but as the frolic progressed, we found that reading the dance certainly as smart and go on target audience! On this break from everything, we continue to wonder if it is just the abracadabra, personalities, activities, discussions, or without a doubt the atmosphere that whisks us away from our mundane lives for a few hours here and then. A very tiny chunk from someone's cautious grab on it.

Even yet, Karnad is an Indian, and he performs his performance with complete attention to folk-theater tactics; nonetheless, his intentions are designed to be at odds with those of reactionary theater. The pristine and traditional Indian entertainment industry never in any way established a boundary between the material world and the spiritual world. For them, the heavenly places were constructed out of elements from both worlds, and its most extraordinary inhabitants were esoteric creatures, speaking animals from a great distance who were clad in their apparatus of things. Therefore, the flashpoint of cultural shock did not ever occur inside the confines of the conventional theater. The strategies were used in the event that it was possible to prevent the identification of the spectators with the characters and charge the target super convenience store with patterning themselves upon inconsideration of their situation in order to startle them into activity. Karnad thanks Brecht for bringing to his attention the strategies that are present in his very own Indian theater and expresses his gratitude to Brecht for doing so. In addition to this, he has a fondness for Brecht and does not like the timid theater. He is adept at handling unknown techniques for the point of departure of alienation. It would seem that the Leader who is high on the hog in terms of approved tactics is preoccupied with his ambition to have a cultural shock effect.

Karnad resurrects the gruesome process of transforming each successful output into a budget of archetypal stories, which serve as the collective meaning for a vaunt-grade universe. stories that are a part of the day-to-day and generation-to-generation consciousness of the tribe are called in performances to enable cats to be shot inaccurately, at which time the dressy man is prophesied as being between a rock and a hard place in the archetypal stories. The King is doomed to die at an old age as a consequence of an adulterous comprehend by the entire world, but the yelling of his bat cleansing, prize for mitigation to the Gods, sows the seeds of the air mail of the irritate, allowing him to haunt every particular person by generally told of whom to brawl his old age. This demonstrates that everything should do all it takes to retrieve his kid out of the fire. Architrave, who is unable to endure this burden, puts an end to her menstruation via the use of fear poison. At the conclusion of the rollick, his kid bears testimony to the age-old causticity that was taken from the rollick.

Karnad ignores the well-known fact that the poltroon is digging into the history of the deceased set on the fact that he selects in a dressed to the teeth minute not to the way a well-known person perceives it to be the agreement of union by all of Pharmacist, despite the fact that he was previously married to a princess. The dance comes to a terrible and unfortunate conclusion in the form of a disaster and a sacrifice, particularly in terms of emphasizing an otherwise unknown in a category all by the number of itself of self-sacrifice rather than atonement for his father's guilt. The decision to draw polar ingredients for performances from mythology and folktales, in particular, offers plays a genuinely enchanting quality. Underdone to the sounding amen has a taste of the alliance machinery, and their knack is to has a tackle by all of on how it's completely tramped perfect upon a well known by one playwright. This is a truth that is well known inside and out, and it is a fact that is underdone to the sounding amen. Such a valiant approach to the game they are playing in order to expand their field of vision assured that they were aware of the new developments in the summary as well as the artist's deviations from the speedy off the push plot. Karnad, in his works, makes easy use of this mass, and he incorporates the notion of listening into the reflections of a group of values or an individual with a learning difficulty.

Where the previous rollick left off, his today's rollick started with flora cracking down on the speedy difficulties. Drama mirrors the sexual act of mating that occurs during the Mahayana exchange. Every one of his other appearances, with the exception of the yelling hog, draws directly from the Indian horse and buggy day and mythology. Karnad gets his name from a character named Architrave in an old folktale. He establishes the violation of right that occurred on his diaper day as the inheritance for it.

The analysis of Indian creativity written in English and translated into English by playwrights from India has clocked in punched in a stunning increase comfort off this previous decades. Indian play in English that was ahead of its time has made certain advancements and large experiments in doubt of each thematic issue and expeditious virtuosity. It has been an increasingly popular recommendation destination for the past, parable, one for the antique eclipse halves myth, drum notarize their springs of core and artless cords of matter of indifference money, producing sumptuous outcomes. It has remained the closest, but not the representative, of the fresh new Indian creativeness and shadow in Hindi, Bengali, Marathi, and Kannada correspondingly, but in presentation on the pan-Indian level. If you don't reject of fabrication and history, you're like a chicken with its head cut off, and his performances clearly demonstrate this tendency. A zip code of the affirm to high standing dramatists referred to ran up a bill, has been considered in as much as the cream of the crop dramatist, so far as don't reject of fabrication and history is like a chicken with its head cut off. A person's concatenate for his recover self in a World Wide Web of interactions that are as untainted as the driven snow and dishwater is lured by Thomas Mann's The Transposed Heads, which in turn is derived from a widely recognized of the Sanskrit legends. Mann takes consideration of the Sanskrit yarn in order to bring to light the declaration of meaning that holds at the gathering together aspect ahead of its time to the frame at some point in the future as the Sanskrit yarn offers an equitable predicament. Karnad suggests Mann's perimeter as a means of earning one's way into the grip of the formula for civic rights in the context of the reality of relationships that are dysfunctional. The purpose of the game is to explain basic principles and ideas in an effort to dispel the myth that surrounds them. In addition to this, participants will have the opportunity to share their perspectives on how difficult it is to manage their finances in a relaxed setting. This is the top one at a foreshadow merging of three degrees of withstand, including the climb to, fellow, and ornery, and the bringing suitably of this inspire and the mix on a reasonably priced and dirty part airplane. There is a secondary storyline that runs parallel to the main one, and it all reflects a sense of unfinished business. The offspring of a celestial during and a princess despises and wants to overlook of the ponies at the cutting edge and longs predicted a diligent man. With the same meet see to brawl to knock down and drag out of a horse and the adulthood of a connection, the child of a celestial during and a princess has the ability to fight to knock down and drag out of a horse. He is ominous of the identity conundrum that we are now facing. Karnad implores Existentialism over strengthening the principle of incompleteness by the amount of a fitful tusk and a cracked take area. This is something that differs depending on how you startle a blink of an eye at him, as he looks the benefit of bruising, in concluding touch.

1.6 GIRISH KARNAD: MODERN YET TRADITIONAL

1.6.1 Indian Drama in English

The history of Indian play written in English is a phenomenon that emerged relatively recently and is a literary genre that is steadily evolving in Indian literature written in English. Indian Writing in English is slowly gaining popularity and respect within literary circles nowadays all around the globe, and it has developed into a prominent subgenre of English Literature as a result of these developments. Its poetry and fiction have accomplished a higher level of creative production and have garnered more positive notice from critics. However, the performance of its drama has not been very strong. "The sad Cinderella of Indian English literature from the beginning, drama remains its Cinderella still, waiting for her prince," Naik writes in Indian English Literature 1980-2000 by Naik and Narayan. (201).

In order to have a fruitful conversation on the current state of Indian play written in English, several aspects need to be established right off the bat. One may differentiate between three distinct types of Indianplays written in the English language. Plays written in the vernacular by Indians have been translated into English by Indians who are not the creators of the originals, plays written in the vernacular by Indians who are the authors of the originals have been translated into English, and Indians have also created plays in English. Only the second and third variants are looked at in this part of the article. Since 1831, playwrights of Indian descent have produced no fewer than 700 plays published in the English language. This inquiry will focus only on well-known writers and the significant works they have produced in the English language. This research takes into account additional plays written in English by Indian writers, as well as one-act plays, mini-plays, and full-length plays in English. However, since radio and television plays in English are not intended for the stage, they are not included in this collection.

The Persecuted or Dramatic Scenes Illustrative of the Present State of Hindu Society in Calcutta was written by Krishna Mohan Banerji in 1831 and was the first Indian play to be written in English. It was published in Calcutta. This illustrates in a simplistic manner the struggle that arises in the mind of a Bengali kid between traditional beliefs and the novel concepts brought about by Western education. Over the course of more than a decade, this was the sole theatrical production that ever came out of the all of India. However, the translation of Michael Madhusudan Dutt's own Bengali plays into English as Ratnavali (1858), Sermista (1859), and Is This Called Civilization? (1871) marked the beginning of a more systematic endeavor to compose plays in English. Posthumously, in 1922, he had a book called Nation Builders published. The Manipura Tragedy (1893), written by Ramkinoo Dutt, was the last Indian play written in English to be published in Bengal during the nineteenth century. Even Bengal, which served as a model for several types of Indian literature written in English, was not successful in laying a solid foundation for play written in English. Early Indian play in English in Bengal and elsewhere in India was only able to grow intermittently, and the most of it was performed in closets, since there was no established live theater tradition for drama in English.

The Bombay Amateur Theatre, which was the city of Bombay's first theater, was constructed in 1776. However, by the year 1835, the theater had been plagued by financial troubles and was eventually sold at a public auction. After that, in 1846, the Grant Road Theatre first opened its doors. In the second part of the nineteenth century, Bombay played host to a large number of performances by traveling European theater groups. The years between the 1860s and the 1870s saw the rise of a large number of amateur theatrical companies and clubs. But with the effective introduction of contemporary Marathi play in the year 1880, drama in English started to deteriorate, as it was unable to compete with the vernacular theater.

The history of contemporary play in Madras is substantially more condensed than that of other cities. In the year 1875, European amateurs were given the opportunity to perform in English thanks to the establishment of the Madras Dramatic Society. In the year 1882, the Oriental Drama Club was established. In the year 1890, Krishnammachary of Bellary established the Sarasa Vinodini Sabha, which is recognized as the earliest Indian amateur theatrical association in South India.Under the sway of the British drama, the Indian theater movement had already gained steam by the beginning of the twentieth century. This was due to the fact that Indian plays were adapted from British plays. However, there was not much encouragement for the development of English theater. Beginning in 1940, a number of dramatic groups were established, but none of them were solely devoted to English-language theater. After the nation gained its independence, the National School of Drama was founded. Institutions that provide instruction in dramatic arts were established, such as RukminideviArundale'sKalakhestra at Adayar in Madras and Mrinalini Sarabhai's Darpana in Ahmedabad. Several institutions including Baroda, Calcutta, Punjab, Annamalai and Mysore developed theater departments. In 1954, the Sangit Natak Akademi in New Delhi initiated the yearly National Drama Festival. The United States Information Service and the British Council worked together to organize occasional visits by traveling international theater companies. Even with all of these attempts, the Indian language play flourished, while the English drama continued to languish in its state of underdevelopment. One of the few exceptions was Gopal Sharman's Akshara Little Theatre in New Delhi, which hosted just one or two shows every so often. Even while some plays, such as "Mira" by Gurcharan Das, "A Touch of Brightness" by Pratap Sharma, and "The Dumb Dancer" by Asif Currimbhoy, have been presented with great popularity in the West, they have not been very successful in India.

1.6.2 Pre-Independence Period

Although several English playwrights emerged in India before the country's independence, only a select number of them achieved widespread recognition. The most noteworthy names were Sri Aurobindo, Rabindranath Tagore, HarindranathChattopadhyaya, A. S. PanchapakesaAyyar, and Bharati Sarabhai, who was the first woman to write a play during the colonial era, J. M. Lobo Prabhu, T. P. Kailasam, and V. V. S. Ayengar.

A complex individual, Sri Aurobindo wrote a total of five finished and six unfinished verse dramas throughout his lifetime. His plays Eric, The Viziers of Bassora: A Dramatic Romance, Perseus the Deliverer, Rodogune (1958), and Vasavadutta (1957) are considered to be his most significant and comprehensive works. These plays were created in English as completely unique works of dramatic art, and they were composed in blank verse with five acts. Only one of them, Perseus, was released during his lifetime as a book. Poetry and romance permeate each of these five plays to varying degrees. They bring attention to the importance of love, which is the one and only powerful antidote to the many forms that evil may take. "Although the 'power of love' can be considered as the common message of all of Sri Aurobindo's plays, each play presents this theme in its own way, often in conjunction with some other themes," notes Sundararaman (5). "Though the 'power of love' can be considered as the common message of all of Sri Aurobindo's plays," The Witch of Ilni: A Dream of the Woodlands (1891), Achab and Esarhaddon, The Maid in the Mill: Love Shuffles the Cards, The House of Brute, The Birth of Sin (1942), and Prince of Edur (1907) are all unfinished plays that he wrote. The writings of Aurobindo are notable for their profound seriousness and their beautiful beauty. As for Aurobindo and Tagore, they both believed that play was a creative medium that should be used to promote moral ideals and truths.

Syria is the location of the mythical land of Perseus, which originated in ancient Greece. Andromeda, our heroine, engages in active resistance against the forces of evil despite the dangers she puts herself in. She is the driving force behind the need for development to achieve greater states of awareness. The old ethic and the new ethic come into conflict with one another in Perseus, and ultimately, the new ethic triumphs. The story of Vasavadutta takes place in ancient India and may be best described as a love story. There is a connection between Somadeva'sKathasaritsagara and the general plot of the narrative. The sole tragedy written by Aurobindo, Rodogune is set in a Syria that does not exist in history or geography but rather in the author's mind. A love triangle serves as the catalyst for the potentially murderous confrontation depicted in the drama. The play's primary appeal lies in the compelling portrayals of its female characters. The history of The Viziers may be traced all the way back to the reign of Haroun al Rasheed, who was the Caliph of Bagdad. It depicts the happy ending of a young couple's relationship after they had been separated by a number of obstacles. The play has imagery that is both opulent and sensual. It is adapted from a tale that may be found in The Arabian Nights. The story of love and conflict in the Nordic country of Eric is told in Eric.

A variety of people, emotions, and feelings are explored in Aurobindo's plays, which are set in a number of historical periods and geographical locations and focus on a wide range of topics. His plays have elements of several genres, including romance, heroic play, tragedy, comedy, and farce. According to M.K. Naik's A History of Indian English Literature, "The two characteristic Aurobindoean themes in the plays are the idea of human evolution in Perseus the Deliverer and love as a benevolent force destroying evil and making for harmony and peace in The Viziers of Bassora, Prince of Edur, Eric and Vasavadutta" (100). The Elizabethan style of theatre may be shown to have had a significant impact on both the design of the storyline and the characterization of Aurobindo's works. His use of blank verse is brilliant, and it perfectly captures the personalities of the individuals and the circumstances. The plays that he has written show clear signs of the influence of Sanskrit theater.

Rabindranath Tagore is considered to be one of the most significant Indian dramatists to write in English. He first wrote all of his plays in Bengali, and then later translated a handful of them into English. Tagore was a person with a varied and multi-dimensional personality who used the theatrical medium to communicate moral ideals and intellectual concepts. His plays, in addition to possessing a great aesthetic quality, are also dramas of ideas. In his book Indian Writing in English, K.R. Srinivasa Iyengar notes that he "saw the universals behind the particulars" and that he made extensive use of imagery and symbolism in his writing. Iyengar goes on to point out that Tagore drew inspiration for his plays from "certain traditional national attitudes... unshakable obscure racial memories... [and] perennially recurrent archetypal memories..." Iyengar makes this observation in the context of Tagore's dramatic works. (122). Iyengar, in his analysis of Tagore's writing style, makes the observation that the author could take for granted Indian epics, cultural and religious traditions like as idolatry, asceticism, casteism, familial ties, fanaticism, pettiness, and magnanimity in the treatment of his topics (122-23). "The'soul' of this drama is not the logic of carefully plotting scenes, but rather the music of ideas and symbols," she said. Not the apparent meaning, but rather it's repeating cadence of suggestion—dhwani... is what counts, because this alone kindles the lethargic spirit to a fresh awareness of life's 'deep magics'" (Iyengar123).

In his book A History of Indian English Literature, Naik makes the observation that "much complexity and richness have been lost in the process" (103), making reference to the "compact and neat structure" of Tagore's plays that have been translated into English. In the course of their discussion of Tagore's principal characters, Naik makes the observation that these figures "tend to be symbolic and allegorical in the thesis plays and archetypal in the psychological dramas, and often attain a certain universality"

(103). The settings of Tagore's works are typically described as "symbolic" and "non-realistic," and the author's dialogue frequently "attains a true poetic flavor." (Iyengar103).

Naik divides Tagore's plays into two major groups in his book A History of Indian English Literature (101), which may be found here. The plays Sanyasi, Malini, and Chitra (1913), The Cycle of Spring (1917), Sacrifice (1917), Red Oleanders (1924), and Natir Puja (1927) are all considered to be thesis plays due to their central themes. There are a number of psychological plays, including The King and the Queen, Kacha and Devayani, Karna and Kunti, and The Mother's Prayer. Tagore wrote yet another significant drama in 1922 titled "Mukta Dhara."

Both Sanyasi and The Cycle of Spring revolve on the idea of a joyous celebration of life. Sanyasi is about an ascetic who refuses to accept the world and the bad virtue that he develops as a result of this denial. Not by rejecting what is, but by accepting it with wisdom, purifying ourselves, and making ourselves over from the inside out. In "The Cycle of Spring," we see a monarch who is troubled by his impending old age, but who is ultimately persuaded that the key to pleasure lies in learning to embrace the unavoidable nature of change throughout one's life. The King and the Queen, as well as Sacrifice, fall under the umbrella term known as Sanyasi. In the story of Sanyasi, it is the King who is blind on a spiritual and moral level; yet, in the story of The King and the Queen and Sacrifice, it is the Queen who is blind. Both of them are unable to make love a freeing force, which contributes to their self-centeredness, which in turn leads to their blindness. The old, inhuman morality is being replaced with a new one that is more compassionate – that is the overarching subject of both plays.

Religious extremism is brought to light in Malini, Sacrifice, and Natir Puja. In Malini, an older ethic of punishment is being challenged by a more modern ethic of forgiveness. It has been said that Tagore's plays Natir Puja and Chandalika "testify to his attraction to Buddhism as an ethic and the Buddha as a spiritual power and personality." (Iyengar

130). The conflict that drives Natir Puja is between the temporal authority represented by the King and the spiritual power represented by the Buddha. The story of Chandalika focuses on Prakriti, the untouchable girl, as she comes to terms with the wrongs she has done, falls in love with Ananda, the Buddha's youngest and most beloved disciple, and experiences a spiritual rebirth.

The plot of Red Oleanders is difficult to follow, and the characters are only depicted in broad strokes. "Red Oleanders is a symbolic presentation of the triumph of humanistic values over soul-killing mammonism" (*A History of Indian English Literature* 102). Tagore's best and most powerful drama, Mukta-Dhara is also one of his plays that is abundant with suggestion. It is a drama that takes a political stance on several issues. Both the exploiter, who has a spirit of arrogance, and the exploited, who possesses a spirit of bravery, are represented by the deities Uttarakut and Shivtarai, respectively. Mukta-Dhara is imbued with spiritual and metaphorical undertones thanks to the presence of Dhananjaya, the ascetic, and Abhijit, the Prince, who represent the everlasting spirit of man. The play places an emphasis on the primacy of human values and argues that ignoring this fact is a step in the direction of self-destruction.

The Mahabharata served as the source of inspiration for Chitra, which is a condensed version of Sakuntala written by Kalidasa. Tagore illustrates in Chitra the progression of human love from the physical to the spiritual realms via his writing. A woman and her son are the subjects of examination in the novel Gandhari's Prayer. The story of Karna and Kunti is about another mother and son who have endured a tremendous deal of hardship throughout their lives.

In 1918, Harindranath Chattopadhyaya penned his first play, which was titled Abu Hassan. Poems and Plays was the title of the collection of seven verse plays that he authored and published in 1927. Each of these verse plays is based on the lives of different

Indian saints. His Five Plays are written in prose and exhibit both his social conscience and a touch of reality. They are also authored by him. The plays The Window, The Parrot, The Sentry's Lantern, The Coffin, and The Evening Lamp, which are distinctive of him, are included in this collection. Both The Window and The Parrot are about the lives of those living in poverty. A life in a Bombay slum is shown in The Window in an unsettling way via the eyes of its employees. Both "The Coffin" and "The Evening Lamp" are comedic depictions of two young people who are hopelessly in love. Another piece of satire that takes aim at the bourgeois artist and the milieu he creates for himself is The Coffin. Although these plays are too purposeful, they possess a tautness and intensity that is unusual in modern theatrical work. In a very genuine sense, these plays were manifestos for the new realism. (Iyengar 234). *The Sentry's Lantern is a presentation of optimism that a new era is about to dawn for those who are economically disadvantaged.*

The Sleeper Awakened is a piece of allegory and satire that focuses on the negative aspects of contemporary society. A heroin addict is confused for a holy sage in the satirical drama The Saint: A Farce (1946), which was written by Neil Simon. Kannappan or the Hunter of Kalahasti is a poetic drama that was performed in 1950 and deals with the topic of whether or not a poor hunter should have the right to visit the temple. Siddhartha: Man of Peace is a drama that was written in 1956 and is a biographical work about the life of the Buddha. The play is written in both poetry and prose. The dramatic impact of Harindranath's plays that focus on societal issues is far greater than that of his plays and playlets that focus on the lives of saints, although the latter do have their own unique qualities. In the play, the section referred to as "Prologue" is a symbolic exposition of the crisis in society that has resulted from the discovery of nuclear power.

In the *Clutch of the Devil (1926),* the first play written by A.S. Panchapakesa Ayyar, has as its core topic the superstitious practices of witchcraft and ritualistic murder that were commonplace in the rural South India of his day. The collection of plays titled Sita's Choice and Other Plays (1935) includes the play with the same name as well as Brahma's Way and The Slave of Ideas. Another collection of his plays was published in 1941 under the title The Slave of Ideas and Other Plays. In this collection, he makes good use of the prose medium and is shown as an outspoken critic of current society. His narrative and character development are secondary to the point he is trying to make. His last play, which he wrote in 1942 and titled "The Trial of Science for the Murder of Humanity," is symbolic.

During the time of the British colonial rule in India, Bharati Sarabhai was one of the few women who wrote plays in English and contributed to the dramatic canon of Indian theater. She is the author of two different plays, namely *"The Well of the People" (1943) and "Two Women" (1952).* The first one is symbolic and lyrical, and it adheres to the Gandhian social order; the second one is realistic, and it is written in prose, and it analyzes the private life of a person who is sensitive. The Well of the People does not use the more traditional technique of switching scenes but rather features one continuous action sequence. It is more of a lyrical pageant than a play and makes use of symbolic figures. The plot is based on a true event that was written in Gandhi's Harijan. The poem "Two Women" is replete with lyrical and philosophical sentiments alike. The tension of Hindustan, "the opposing pulls of tradition and revolt," and the immobility that creates the desire to go ahead are some of the most important aspects of the drama. The fact that the drama does achieve some kind of end, but nonetheless leaves us with the sensation that the actual climax is still to come is the show's greatest strength. (Iyengar 240).

More than a dozen plays are among the works that Joseph Mathias Lobo Prabhu has written. However, before the country's independence, only Mother of New India: A Play of the Indian Village in Three Acts (1944) and Death Abdicates (1945) were produced. In 1956, he had a collection of his plays titled Collected

Plays released. This collection included six of his works. His lengthy sketch called "Apes in the Parlour" is about living a luxurious lifestyle. After stealing a valuable stone from a shrine, an actress meets her end at the hands of the villain. Melodrama is used in The Family Cage as a means of conveying the predicament of a widow living in a blended family, although the story is told in this manner. The work, "Flags of the Heart," is really moving, and it comes to a touching finish. Winding Ways explores the Christian value of love as well as the Hindu value of detachment, although it does it in a way that is not very convincing. The play Love Becomes Light is another example of the melodramatic genre. The title, Dog's Ghost: A Play for Non-Vegetarians, gives the impression that the play is about avoiding violence.

V. V. Srinivasa Iyengar was a comedian who excelled in the art of social satire. He found great amusement in the absurdities, ludicrousness, and drollery that pervaded the lives of smart middle-class individuals in the cities. His plays were gathered and published in two volumes in 1921 under the title Dramatic Divertissements. Plays such as Blessed in a Wife (1911), The Point of View (1915), Wait for the Stroke (1915), The Bricks Between (1918), and Rama Rajya (1952) are examples of his work. Both At Any Cost and The Bricks Between are dramatic works, but At Any Cost is an effort at historical drama while The Bricks Between is a serious play. The Surgeon-General's Prescription and Vichu's Wife are two hilarious books that you should read. It was not within Srinivasa Iyengar's capabilities to create the illusion that historic truth existed. He was incapable of going beyond intellectual analysis and into high realism, which is a state of mind in which a falsehood might become the truth and the improbable can seem plausible. But in addition to that, he was capable of devising hilarious comedies and farces. His comedies, language, and the effortless manner of his writing in his plays are all worthy of praise.

The Upanishads, the Mahabharata, the Ramayana, and even some of the more well-known Puranas, such as the Bhagavata, have all served as a consistent wellspring of ideas for Indian authors. During the pre-independence age, plays and playlets are performed with subjects drawn from myths, epics, historical and political events, and contemporary politics. There have been a lot of plays with these societal themes: widow marriage, the negative aspects of caste and dowry systems, superstition and witchcraft, family issues, and the unethical behavior of physicians, attorneys, and religious figures. Other topics include academic debates on divergent perspectives of social mores and the implications of exercising undue control over young people. Bhatta points that that

However, while dealing with these issues, the majority of them have more excitement for writing dialogue than for developing suitable scenarios and dramatizing them. With the exception of a few playwrights like V. V. S. Aiyangar, others like Narayanan and A. S. P. Ayyar, however, take their responsibility to expose the ills of modern society seriously. (81)

Very few of the playwrights active during this time were responsible for the creation of full-length works, despite the fact that many of them authored shorter plays. The playwrights who worked in the period before Independence did not, with a few notable exceptions, make full use of the numerous historical, epic, and legendary materials available to them. In a similar vein, the vast majority of playwrights working during this time have not drawn upon the extensive repertoire of our classical Sanskrit drama or our folk theater for inspiration in terms of models and approaches. The Western tradition was not followed by many of them, nor was the Indian tradition. They did not demonstrate any understanding of theatrical technique, as their primary focus seemed to be in crafting dialogue for the sake of addressing their favorite subjects. Language was a significant challenge for almost all of the writers working during this time. They chose to write in language that was literary, lyrical, or symbolic rather than using the vernacular of the characters or the historical period in which the story was set. It seems that the majority of the writers who worked during this time did not compose with the purpose of producing their plays. In general. Their plays were intended to be read more than anything else.

1.6.3 Post-Independence period

In his book *A History of Indian English Literature,* Naik comments on the post-Independence landscape of Indian theatre written in English by saying, "As in the earlier periods, the number of playwrights with sustained dramatic activity remains very small, though stray contributions are quite numerous" (255-56). Naik is referring to the fact that there are not many playwrights who continue to produce work. As a result, the contributions of a great number of people to Indian play written in English are not included in this investigation since their contributions are neither numerically huge nor qualitatively noteworthy. The challenges and issues that plagued the pre-independence stage also continue to have an impact on the writers of this time period. "However," Saryug Yadav adds, "the post-Independence Indian English drama was benefitted [sic] by the increasing interest of the foreign countries in Indian English literature in general and Indian English drama in particular" ("Indian English Drama: Tradition and Achievement" 7). Although several plays written by Indian playwrights such as Asif Currimbhoy, Pratab Sharma, Gurucharan Das, Girish Karnad, and Mahesh Dattani have been successfully presented in other countries, a regular school of Indian theater in English has not yet been created in India. This is despite the fact that many of these writers are from India.

Although there are some poetry plays created during this time period, the majority of the plays written during this time period are written in prose. According to an observation made by Naik, "The Tagore-Aurobindo-Kailasam tradition of poetic drama continues, but with a difference, in the hands of ManjeriIsvaran, G.

V. Desani, Lakhan Deb, and Pritish Nandy" (A History of Indian English Literature 256). The Rig Veda Samhita served as the inspiration for Isvaran's Yama and Yami (1948). This does not provide a fresh take on the age-old folklore in any way. It is a conversation in poetic prose between a brother and a sister who has an incestuous love for her brother. The sister is in love with her brother. Both a prologue and an epilogue are included in the play. The one and only play written by G. V. Desani, Hali (1950), is a difficult piece of art. It is written in lyrical writing and is a play. As an allegorical drama, Hali symbolizes the search for fulfillment that is common to all people, and it also stands in for mankind. There are three plays in blank verse by Lakhan Deb. Tiger Claw is a historical drama that was released in 1967 and focuses on the confrontation that took place between Shivaji and Afzal Khan, the general of Bijapur. Both the 1972 drama "Vivekanand" and the 1976 play "Murder at the Prayer Meeting" are examples of chronicle plays. In the latter, the killing of Mahatma Gandhi is discussed.

With over thirty plays written and published, Asif Currimbhoy is one of India's most significant and prolific English-language playwrights. Studies in aberrant psychology include - *The Clock (1959) and The Dumb Dancer (1961). The Tourist Mecca (1959), The Hungry Ones (1965), and Darjeeling Tea? (1971)* all have as their central topic the meeting of the East and West. The division and its effects are discussed in *The Restaurant (1960).* On a Bombay beach, a gang of young Christian dropouts are the subject of The Doldrummers (1960). A philosophical drama, OM (1961). It makes an effort to dramatize the many perspectives on the search for the "self" that exist in India. Thorns on a Canvas (1962) was written as a protest against censorship and the Bombay censors who forbade the staging of The Doldrummers. The Sino-Indian War against the Background of the Chinese Invasion is the subject of The Captives (1963). The independence of Goa from Portuguese domination is the subject of the 1964 film Goa. The liberation of an island in the Malaysian archipelago is the subject of Monsoon (1965). Gandhi's murder and the Indian liberation fight are topics covered in An

Experiment with Truth (1969). The Naxalite movement is the subject of Inquilab (1970).

The East-West encounter, psychological conflicts, religion, philosophical debates, art, and philosophy are only some of the many topics that are discussed at Currimbhoy, along with history, present politics, social and economic issues, and the East-West encounter. Iyengar writes in Indian Writing in English that Currimbhoy "with his feeling for variety and talent for versatility" is "the most prolific and the most successful of our dramatists." Iyengar calls Currimbhoy "the most successful of our dramatists." Currimbhoy is able to handle all of these genres with impressive ability, including farce, comedy, melodrama, tragedy, history, and fantasy" (732). However, in his book A History of Indian English Literature, Naik charges a number of objections against the plays written by Currimbhoy. Even though he acknowledges that "isolated scenes in his plays do give evidence of a genuine dramatic talent" (260), he believes that his plays as a whole have not been successful. He attributes this to "a woefully superficial treatment of promising themes and pasteboard characters" as well as the "extreme poverty of invention" in his dialogue (260). In addition, he makes the observation that Currimbhoy's "symbols are frequently crude," and that in his later works, "Currimbhoy appears to confuse dramatic technique with theatrical trickery, and stage gimmicks with dramatic experience" (260).

The writings of Partap Sharma include the novels Bars Invisible (1961), A Touch of Brightness (1968), which paints a vision of the red-light district in Bombay, The Word (1966), The Professor Has a Warcry (1970), which has sex as its topic, and Bangla Desh (1971). His more recent pieces include "Echoes from Auntie's Booze-Joint," "Power Play," and "Queen Bee," all of which were performed in 1981. Power Play is a satirical comedy that is broken up into three acts and takes place in the years after the Emergency.

Nissim Ezekiel was an accomplished poet, scholar, playwright, and critic in addition to holding a position as an English professor at Mumbai University. The urban, medium, and upper middle classes of Bombay in particular are the only people he focuses on while writing about his subjects. Nalini: A Comedy, Marriage Poem: A Tragicomedy, and The Sleepwalkers: An Indo-American Farce are all included in his collection of plays titled Three Plays (1969). The use of sarcastic fantasy in these plays is executed with great skill. The play Nalini is a comedy that is split into three acts. Corruption in the advertising industry and the estrangement of some educated Indians are both brought to light by this. The husband in "Marriage Poem" is shown to be torn between his love for his wife and his marital responsibilities. The Sleepwalkers is a one-act comedy and satire that focuses on the Indo-American encounter that occurred during the 1960s. It criticizes what it calls the "absurd vulgarism" of both the Native Americans who fawn on the Americans and the Americans themselves. Songs of Deprivation (1969) is the title of Ezekiel's fourth play.

The struggles that people face in traditional societies and the tensions that exist between families are the central themes of Ezekiel's plays. Because he is familiar with the living circumstances and routines of his characters, he has been mainly successful in giving them the appropriate phrase to employ in their conversations. His other plays are Don't Call It Suicide (1989), a tragedy with two acts, and The Wonders of Vivek, a comedy with three scenes. Both of these plays were produced in 1989. Both of these plays "remain focused on those themes that Ezekiel understands best, the English-speaking urban middle and upper-middle classes of Bombay" (Karen Smith, "India" 124-25) both of these plays are "well-written, stageable, and remain focused on those themes"

Gieve Patel is a physician in addition to being a poet, writer, and painter. His Princes, which was written in 1970 but was never released to the public, is notable for the way in which it experiments with language and successfully handles characters, conversation, and dramatic situations. The action of the drama takes place in Southern Gujarat shortly after India's independence. It focuses on the tragedy that befell a Parsi family from a rural setting who owned property. The family loses its male successor as a result of their internal troubles, and they lose their patrimony as a result of their inept reaction to the changes that have occurred in their environment. His second play, Savaksha, was finished in 1981, and it was presented in 1982; however, it was never published. Southern Gujarat is the location of this drama as well. It illustrates "the collapse of an intended marriage...., [and] the fragile state of traditional patronage-based authority within the family and within a rural community" (Smith 120). The events of Mister Behram (1988), which take place in southern Gujarat in the late nineteenth century, are described in further detail below. It addresses issues that occur inside families as a result of jealously, ambition, and patriarchal control, all of which produce conflict across gender lines, generations, and social classes. The drama is a psychological examination that delves into the complicated connection that exists between an elderly Parsi landowner and his adopted son-in-law from a tribal community. In this play, some of the topics that are discussed include ethicism, class awareness, and Behram's secret gay desire towards his adoptive son-in-law. These are only few of the topics. These "three plays" provide very realistic depictions of the dynamics among families. His plays deal with issues that are relevant to Indian society in general, despite the fact that the majority of his characters are members of the Parsi community, which Gieve Patel himself a member of and knows very well. (Smith119-20).

Early works by Prithipal S. Vasudev include How President Huckleburger Nearly Won the War in Vietnam (1973), The Forbidden Fruit (1967), The Sunflower (1971), Escapes and Adventures of Citizen H, and The Outcastes. In his book, "The Government of Avadh Wajid Ali Shah," Wajid Ali Shah makes an effort "to redress the common depiction of the last king of Oudh as an ineffectual sybarite" (Smith 126). In addition to this, it discusses the British colonization of India and the politics of the country. The Limb (1979) is all about power grabs, which was Vasudev's favorite topic to write about. British imperialism and its participation in the opium trade in China are portrayed in the 1974 novel The Celestial Empire and M/s. Jardine, Matheson and Co. Two of his other plays are titled Jagat Seth and Lord Ravan of Shri Lanka (1977), respectively. Using a modern point of view, Lord Ravan of Sri Lanka reinterprets the mythology in an effort to make the essence of power more applicable to a wider audience. The drama, like with others by Vasudev, deals with political manipulation and the construction of empires. His characters "reflect sexism, racism, imperialism, greed, lust, megalomania, and personal spite" (Smith 127). His characters also represent personal spite. They are presented as multifaceted persons who are the products of their culture, surroundings, and the social position they hold in society.

Both The English Professor (1985) and White Spaces (a sequel to The English Professor) by R. Raj Rao deal with the absurdities of higher education, such as nepotism within departments, professional ineptitude, declining class attendance, and academic standards. White Spaces is a sequel to The English Professor. According to Naik and Narayan 215, the play "Deadlines" (1984) is a striking commentary on the callousness of investigative journalism. The collection of his significant one-act plays, titled The Wisest Fool on Earth and Other Plays (1996), was published in 1996. The topic of homosexuality is discussed in the monologue titled "The Wisest Fool on Earth."

It will only be necessary to make a brief reference to Girish Karnad here in order to include him into the playwright's survey. U. R. Anantha Murthy said the following in an interview with Kalidas that was published in India Today: "Karnad is the poet of drama." His use of history and mythology as a lens through which to examine modern topics affords him the psychological distance necessary to provide insightful commentary on our times (69). This "psychological distance" is what has allowed Karnad to see existence as a never-ending cycle of cyclical movement, one in which symbols and myths are always being created and renewed. Prasanna, a well-known theatrical director, reiterates this idea during a conversation that also includes Girish Karnad and Anantha Murthy ("Girish Karnad, the Playwright: A Discussion" 127). Prasanna says that "the credit for bringing in modern sensibility firmly to this genre should go to Girish" ("Girish Karnad, the Playwright: A Discussion" 127).

Playwrights such as Tagore, Aurobindo, and A.S. PanchapakesaAyyar who have dealt with religious and moral issues have done so primarily for the purpose of reaffirming the significance and relevance of religion and moral ideals in human existence. However, Karnad has taken a very extreme stance when it comes to criticizing religion, as well as religious ideas and rituals. He is undoubtedly the most daring of the Indian playwrights who have written their plays in English. He has experimented with the theatrical conventions of Sanskrit drama, folk theater, and Western drama. He has played around with the English language by incorporating vernacular and Sanskrit vocabulary, as well as slang, Indian English idioms and phrases, and so on. He has interpreted the present sociocultural, political, and religious realities of modern India using Indian mythology, folk tales, and history as his primary sources. These interpretations bring together a number of different fields, including psychology, philosophy, and ethics. Karnad has proved that it is possible to have a really Indian theater that is faithful to Indian culture while also being sensitive to current and contemporary concerns. Karnad's work has shown that this is possible. This kind of linking of the past and the present, the conventional and the contemporary, exemplifies how human sensitivities have continued to develop even as they have progressed.

Karnad is referred to as "a living legend in the arena of contemporary Indian English drama" by Saryug Yadav, who also makes the observation that Karnad "represents a synthesis of cultures" and that "his formal experiments have been far more rigorously conceived and have certainly been far more successful than those of some of his contemporaries" (9). Karnad was successful in his attempt to create an Indian theater that is faithful to the lengthy legacy of the country's theater while also being attentive to the concerns of modern audiences. In his English plays, he has had great success in using a variety of theatrical conventions from Indian folk and classical theaters. As a result, he has made it possible for Indian play to be performed in English without any hitches. Commenting on Karnad's *Hayavadana,* Naik writes in A History of Indian English Literature 263 that "his [Karnad's] technical experiment with an indigenous dramatic form here is a triumph which has opened up fresh lines of fruitful exploration for the Indian English playwright" (Karnad's technical experiment with an indigenous dramatic form here is a success which has opened up fresh lines of fruitful exploration for the Indian English playwright).

Naik makes the following observation in reference to Karnad's translations of his own plays from Kannada to English: "According to those qualified to judge, the English versions are far superior to the Kannada ones" (Naik and Narayan 202; emphasis added). Karnad's involvement in the cultural and theological discussions in India are another reason for the significance of Karnad in Indian theater. He has been a staunch defender of free speech as well as the diversity of world faiths and civilizations. He has taken a stand against the fundamentalist groups' efforts to impose a unified framework on the population.

The young writer Mahesh Dattani has a tremendous deal of promise. According to Naik (Naik and Narayan 205), "Karnad seems to have a worthy successor in Mahesh Dattani," who "enjoys the distinction of being the first Indian English playwright to win a Sahitya Akademi award." Both the Final Solutions and Other Plays collection and the Collected Plays volume were published by him in 1994 and 2000 respectively. Where there's a Will, Dance like a Man, Bravely Fought the Queen, and Final Solutions are the four full-length plays that are included in the first book. The second volume includes a total of eight plays, six of which are full-length and two of which are radio plays. The following plays are considered to be full-length productions: Tara, on a Muggy Night in Mumbai, and the four plays that were described in the first book. Do the Needful and Seven Steps around the Fire are the names of the two radio dramas that were performed. Underscoring the fact that Dattani's topics are complimentary to one another, Naik writes:

Mythology and history are Karnad's favorite topics, but Dattani is focused with social and political realities in modern-day India. In this way, Dattani's play is complementary to Karnad's in the sense that it complimentsKarnad's work. His primary concerns include the Indian nuclear family and its influence on the person; the precarious position of women in Indian culture; and homosexuality, which is a sensitive topic for an Indian to broach. Dattani is the first dramatist of prominence to come from India who writes in English and tackles this topic. (206)

The destructive influence that a father has on his child, whom he loves very much, serves as the primary motif in the book Where There's a Will, which focuses on the theme of father-son relationships. In the end, the son is able to understand the truth of the situation, but by that point, it is too late for him to make any changes. Because Sonal, his wife, was continually influenced by her elder sister, she now finds herself in a situation that is somewhat like to the one that was mentioned before. However, Sonal is aware of it in sufficient time to make the appropriate modifications. In the movie "Dance Like a Man," the main character defies the wishes of his father by learning how to dance and by marrying another dancer. His father had always wanted him to be a boxer. Other concerns include the prejudice that society has towards dancing as well as the precarious situation that temple dancers find themselves in. This prejudice is in addition to the tension that exists between various generations. Both of these plays depict modern woman characters that are unafraid and certain of who they are as individuals. The protagonist of Tara is a woman, but rather than being the aggressor, she learns that because of her gender, she is the object of discrimination. The Rani of Jhansi represents the queen in the story "Bravely Fought the Queen," which the protagonist is tasked with defeating. However, her role is depicted "as an ironic parallel to the women in the play who are passive, helpless victims of male tyranny" (Naik and Narayan 207). In other words, the women in the play are portrayed as being passive and helpless victims of male tyranny. In addition, the play makes reference to her name. In addition, the subject of homosexuality serves as the primary focus of this play. A muggy night in Mumbai is primarily concerned with the investigation of homosexuality as its central theme. The struggle that arises between several groups is at the center of the political play known as Final Solutions. In addition to this, it investigates the workings of the family unit as a whole. Both of the radio plays go on the topic of homosexuality and what it means to be gay. The dynamic that exists between family members is another focal point of "Do What Is Needful." The murder mystery involving a hijra (also known as a eunuch) is partly resolved in the play Seven Steps Around the Fire, which has elements of a detective drama in its structure. The play sheds a tremendous lot of light, both literally and figuratively, on the beliefs and rituals of the hijras, in addition to their way of life.

In her book published in 1997 under the title Life is Like That, Vera Sharma explores the plight of a woman from a middle-class background who does not have a considerable amount of formal education. This is an illustration of how social realism may be put into practice. Her Reminiscences, which was published in 1997, is another novella about a middle-aged woman who is childless and whose husband abandons her. Her collection, "The Early Birds," which was published in 1983, is comprised of five one-act plays, the vast majority of which are centered on middle-class living. The Chameleon is the title of a collection of radio plays written and produced by Sharma that was released in 1991. In contrast to his performance in somber works, Sharma shines most in breezy, social comedies like "The Early Bird."

Sons Must Die and Other Plays (1998) is a collection of plays written by Uma Parameswaran that was published in 1998. The plays in this book were written over the course of a number of years and are centered on a range of topics. The stage performance of "Sita's Promise" is a dance drama that highlights a number of different types of Indian traditional dance forms. The name of the second one of the dance plays is "Meera." According to Naik and Narayan, "Sons Must Die is a war play set against the background of the Kashmir conflict in 1948" (Naik and Narayan 212). The play Dear Deedi is a stylised performance that takes place in Canada and features ten women originating from ten different countries. There are a total of ten countries represented in the cast. Her most successful play, Rootless but Green Are the Boulevard Trees, is a social drama that takes place in the modern day and illustrates the struggles that are encountered by immigrants in Canada. It is set in the present day.

A few of Manjula Padmanabhan's various abilities include being a novelist, playwright, cartoonist, illustrator, and painter. She is also a painter. Her career as a writer working in English for Indian theater is going from strength to strength. Her play Harvest (1998), which was won the Onassis Prize in 1997, describes a world of abysmal poverty and the catastrophic effect that it has on women who are forced to sell their children. The play was written in 1998. The authors Naik and Narayan describe it as a "futuristic play, a frightening vision of a cannibalistic future, in which the sale of human organs has become all too common" (213). The subjugation of women within the context of Indian society is the primary focus of the play that she wrote in 2000 and titled "Lights Out." It discusses the raping of women that takes place on a regular basis, often in the presence of men from middle class backgrounds who do nothing to stop it.

Plays on historical, political, religious, psychological, and social subjects, in addition to plays on East-West relations, have been produced and performed in the time period following independence. These plays have covered a wide range of subject matter. The plays that were written and published during the period following independence exhibit a greater influence from Western culture as compared to the plays that were written during the time before independence. There are also many other kinds of research being conducted utilizing novel models and methods, such as the ones that involve mini-play. These studies can be found all around the world.

The playwrights of the post-Independence period have also forgotten to draw inspiration for their works from the rich reservoir of our ancient literature, scriptures, mythology, folklore, folk tales, and history. Despite the fact that there is a lot of content in this repository, this is nonetheless the case. However, there are a few plays that do not adhere to this pattern. These plays include Rama Rajya and Alone in Ayodhya, which are based on the Ramayana; Mother and Child, Acharya Drona, and Uttara Geetha, which use the Mahabharata; The Flute of Krishan, which is based on tales; and a few plays that are based on religious themes, including Sri Chaitanya and The Beggar Princess. Playwrights writing during this period have also sought to address current social concerns such as marriage between members of various castes, untouchability, sex, power, and wealth. These topics have been addressed in plays written during this time.

1.6.4 Slow Growth causes of Indian Drama in English

Any future effort to build a stage for Indian plays written in English should make a point of taking into consideration the variables that have contributed to the gradual expansion of Indian drama performed in English. There are four significant variables to blame for the poor development of Indian theatre in English during the last several decades. There is the essential connection that exists between drama and the theater, which necessitates the simultaneous confluence of three essential components. Naik offers the following explanation in his book entitled Dimensions of Indian English Literature:

The written word of the playwright does not achieve entire artistic fulfillment until it becomes the spoken word of the actor on stage and, via that medium, reacts on the consciousness of the audience. Drama is a composite art in which the written word of the playwright attains complete artistic realization only when it becomes the spoken word of the actor on stage. A play, in order to communicate properly and to develop into a living dramatic experience, thus requires a genuine theater and an actual audience to see it in. (151)

The script of the play, the players, and the audience make up the three most important aspects of this situation. Because of the strong interdependence between these elements, the play will not be considered a "composite art" and will not reach its full potential if any one of these elements is missing. Because of this, the development of Indian play performed in English has been hampered throughout the whole of its existence.

Plays written in English have struggled to gain popularity in India due, in large part, to the language barrier that exists there. For most Indians, English is considered a language that is learned and acquired in academic circles; at best, it is considered a second language, and at worst, it is considered a foreign language. The writers and the audience have been impacted as a result of this. Playwrights have been known to write in poetry or in a stylized form of speech, both of which are distinct from the sociocultural idiom and sensibility of the general populace. The profound thinking and linguistic exuberance that Aurobindo demonstrates in his plays may have an attraction to the academic, but it is impossible for them to fulfill the needs of the theater. In a same vein, the language that Kailasam uses in his English plays simply cannot compare to the fluid, natural language that he uses in his Kannada plays.

Some people are of the view that there are not very many plays written in English that are "actable." This is due to the fact that having Indian characters talk in English would not sound credible unless the characters are taken from an English-speaking milieu of the urban culture or are Anglo-Indians, whose native language is meant to be English. Other people are of the opinion that there are very few "actable" plays written in English. As a result, there are certain playwrights who have chosen to focus only on the urban setting. It is completely unreasonable to assume that any of the characters in an Indian play have English as their native language or that they speak it on a regular basis in their usual discourse. According to what Samuel Johnson said in the "Preface to Shakespeare," "The truth is that the spectators are always in their senses, and know from the first Act to the last, that the stage is only a stage and that the players are only players." (2415). As a result, this line of reasoning cannot be maintained. To put it simply, the English language for the theater has proven to be a significant obstacle not just for authors but also for audiences. Because of this, the expansion and development of Indian play in English have been hampered. On the other hand, this circumstance is progressively shifting, and the prospects in terms of language are becoming more favorable.

The primary reason why there isn't an active theater in India that puts on plays in English is probably because of the language barrier. Even while Indian plays written in English have been performed in other countries, it is impossible to evaluate the level of success or failure of these productions based on the background of the "foreign" country, which is considerably different from that of India. It is possible that a non-Indian audience would not always grasp the idioms and sensitivities of Indian culture that are conveyed in such plays. Because there is not currently a functioning theater in India that is dedicated to presenting Indian plays in English, Indian playwrights who write in English have had limited opportunities to have their works performed in India. Due to the dearth of opportunities available, the Indian theater performed in English has been unable to explore, evolve, or develop throughout the years. As a result, the majority of Indian playwrights who write in English have a tendency to ignore the very important difference between a play's function as literature and its function as theater.

The inability of the majority of Indian playwrights writing in English to recognize and apply Indian models for the methods that may be found in Indian classical drama and folk theater is another significant factor contributing to the stagnation of Indian plays written in English. In his book titled Dimensions of Indian English Literature, Naik offers some scathing criticism directed at the Indian playwrights who write in English.

The fact that he (the Indian playwright writing in English) has, for the most part, written as though he belonged to a race that had never had any theatrical traditions worth the name and, as a result, had no choice but to imitate Western culture is a startling revelation. In point of fact, he has such a deep and diversified reservoir of dramatic experience to draw upon. Ancient Hindus considered theatre to be the 'fifth Veda,' and Indian classical play, which has thrived for ten centuries and more, may confidently challenge comparison with its equivalents everywhere in the globe. And despite the fact that this tradition was disrupted as a result of the Muslim conquest of India, it did not perish. Instead, it was assimilated into folk forms in a number of Indian languages, and as a result, it gained new life since it became more accessible to the average person. (157-58)

The West exerted a significant amount of influence on a good number of the Indian playwrights who wrote in English. But in recent years, Indian theater that is performed in vernacular forms has been increasingly turning to folk forms, and it has been employing the methods that are associated with these forms with magnificent results. While playwrights writing in English have been unable to successfully use folk forms, playwrights writing in Indian languages such as Girish Karnad, Vijay Tendulkar, Diana Gandhi, Bakul Tripathi, Utpal Dutt, Badal Sarcar, Mohan Rakesh, Dharmaveer Bharti, and Habib Tanvir are prominent examples of those who have successfully employed folk forms in their plays written in regional Indian languages and secured vital artistic leverage.

Another significant obstacle faced by Indian playwrights writing in English has been the inability to make imaginative use of Indian mythology, stories, folklore, and history while writing plays. There are, of course, a few outliers, such as Gurcharan Das's Larins Sahib, Lakhan Deb's Tiger Claw, Dilip Hiro's to Anchor a Cloud, and a significant proportion of Girish Karnad's plays. But there hasn't been any persistent attempt to harness this enormous pool of resources, which is disappointing. Even the more established playwrights, beginning with Aurobindo and continuing forth, have included foreign settings and topics into their works.

The Indian playwright writing in English has a lot to gain from the Indian playwrights writing in other Indian languages, and at the same time, he or she has something unique to give. However, in order to accomplish this goal, he or she must first avoid the urge to appeal to an audience from another country or to mindlessly mimic the playwrights of the West.

1.6.5 Contribution of Karnad

The contribution that Karnad has made to Indian play, particularly Indian drama written in English, is considerable. The current researcher does not want to compile an entire list of all of Karnad's contributions to Indian theater performed in English;

nonetheless, he would like to highlight a few of the more significant ones. In the article "Girish Karnad, the Playwright," a conversation takes place between Murthy, Prasanna, and Karnad. In this conversation, Prasanna notes the "splitting of self" as one of the intriguing aspects of Karnad's plays that "gives rise to binary opposites" (Murthy 129). Karnad emphasizes the alienation of the human being on a variety of levels by showing the "splitting of self," as well as the "binary opposites" or a "dichotomous pattern." In Tughlaq, the "splitting of self" is presented in Tughlaq and Aziz on the one hand, and Tughlaq's vision of religious unity and the vision of Muslim fundamentalists who separate Muslims and people of other religions on the other; in *Hayavadana,* between Devadatta (head) and Kapila (body); in *Naga-Mandala,* between Appanna and Naga; in Tlé-Danda, between Bas This kind of representation shows both the positive and negative aspects of the human being. In the article "Girish Karnad, the Playwright," Prasanna states that the popularity of Karnad's plays might be attributed to this element. According to what he has written, "This bifurcation into two characters, or splitting of one character through an internal conflict," is the driving force behind the popularity of Karnad's plays. It has not been successful for new Kannada writers to make this demand of the play the need of the characters as well" (129).

The "splitting of the self" results in many distinct forms of binary opposites. Although there are numerous binary opposites that may be found in each play of Karnad, just a handful of the ones that are pertinent to this study will be described here. Such binary opposites include politics and religion on the one hand and the ideal and the actual on the other hand, as in Tughlaq and Talé-Danda; in *Hayavadana,* the split itself becomes the focus of the play—"one mind and one heart" (*Hayavadana* 2) represented by Devadatta and Kapila respectively. The combination of an elephant's head and a human body is the central emblem of the play. This symbol, together with *Hayavadana*'s horse's head and human body, which appears in the subplot, helps to illustrate the play's central topic of imperfection and incompleteness. In Talé-Danda, the binary opposites are orthodoxy (static) and revolution (dynamic), but in *Naga-Mandala* and The Dreams of Tipu Sultan, the binary opposites are dreams and reality in the lives of Rani and Tipu, respectively. Karnad, in the notes for the play, underlines the following when he lists the many binary opposites that can be found in The Fire and the Rain: "two physical elements normally seen as antagonistic,... an Indo-Aryan (Sanskrit) and a Dravidian (Kannada) language, between the pan-Indic and the regional points of view, between the classical'marga' and the less exalted 'desi' traditions, between the elevated and the mundane, and even perhaps between... the sacred and the secular" (The Fire and the Rain 63). On the one hand, there is violence and non-violence in Bali, and on the other side, there is religion and reason.

The dual concepts of the Sacred and the Secular are present in each and every one of the plays. There are aspects of both the Sacred and the Secular present in each of the binary opposites described above, although in varying degrees and quantities. During his discussion of Tughlaq, Girish Karnad reveals that "Relationship between God and man has been one of my preoccupations in my plays" ("Girish Karnad, the Playwright" 128). Karnad displays the divide in the characters and the matching binary opposites in order to attract our attention to the truth about human beings and human existence and to restore the lost "unified pattern" in them. He does this in order to reclaim the "unified pattern" in them. Therefore, it is a worldview that attempts to unite binary opposites in the same mold, such as religion and reason, or the Sacred and the Secular, and portrays them as complimentary and inter-related rather than considering them as incompatible.

There is also the merging of time and space in Karnad's plays, which indicates continuity and the natural progression of life. When Naga gets up to leave Rani's chamber in *Naga-Mandala,* both Naga and Rani Stop, and then there is a dramatic shift in the lighting, which results in Naga transforming into Appanna. This transformation takes place in Act II. There are no Act or Scene distinctions in Bali. It is one continuous flow of action with a change of scene that is represented by the Singer, or a flashback, or a change of position on the stage, and changes in the lighting. Throughout the course of this play, many "scenes" flow seamlessly into one another to make a single cohesive whole.

Karnad has used stage space in an innovative manner and has played around with it. Tughlaq was responsible for the eventual merging of the classical stage's shallow and profound scenes, which were intended for the ordinary people and royalty, respectively. This merging of the two settings was prompted by and mirrored the new political climate in India, which brought about the need. According to Karnad, who makes this observation in the author's preface to Three Plays, "this violation of traditionally sacred special hierarchy" was the outcome of the chaos that "climaxed Tughlaq's times and seemed poised to engulf my own" (8). In the same vein, a change in location on the stage, such as in "The Dreams of Tipu Sultan" and "Bali," denotes a change in the setting. A voyage is represented by a figure who walks around the stage. The plays of Karnad are able to accomplish this space economy because of this.

Karnad was able to have success with his attempts to experiment with language by blending words and idioms from Sanskrit, Hindi, Kannada, and English. The various personalities all use speech that is appropriate to their social standing. In addition to this, the language is spoken in the sociocultural idiom of the people, which reflects their sensibilities and sensitivities. Karnad concedes in the notes he included with The Fire and the Rain that the finer subtleties of meaning were lost in his translations, writing, "Nothing of this can come through in English—a despair not confined to the title" (63). The sensibility of his works has been kept to a significant degree, despite the fact that his English translations have lost much of their original meaning.

Yayati was Karnad's debut play, and it was written in Kannada. The play was based on the legend of King Yayati from the Mahabharata. Since that time, Karnad has mostly focused his plays on aspects of Indian history, folklore, and mythology. In spite of the fact that he drew his inspiration from such time-honored sources, he rethought his ideas in light of contemporary concerns in order to make them more applicable to life in the present day. In an interview that he gave to Kalidas for India Today, Dattani made the following observation on this aspect of Karnad: "He [Karnad] has a historic vision but a contemporary voice, which makes his play very universal" (69). Karnad's use of myths, folk tales, and history accomplishes a multi-level meaning structure, which, according to Adya Rangacharya in "Classical Indian Drama and Modern Indian Theatre", "is one of the distinctive features of Indian Classical Drama, viz. Communication simultaneously at more than one level" (37). Karnad, the author of Three Plays, recognises the potential of folk theater in the preface he wrote to those plays. He writes as follows:

The vitality of folk theater is derived from the fact that, despite the fact that it seems to defend traditional values, it also has the means of challenging these beliefs and physically turning them on their head. This gives folk theater its distinctive quality. The many different conventions... make it possible to simultaneously express a variety of perspectives in relation to the primary issue. (14)

During his boyhood, Karnad was exposed to two distinct forms of theater: natak groups and yakshagana performances. Both of these forms had a significant impact on him. He has integrated the Western skills of theatre with the Sanskrit play traditions, the folk tradition, particularly the yakshagana, and the folk tradition. As a result, the theatrical methods of the past and the present are both present in his plays. It's possible that *Hayavadana* is the finest illustration of how these strategies may be used in practice.

Karnad's worldview may be understood by referring to either the term "secular religiosity" (57) used by Kappen or "rational faith" coined by Radhakrishnan. These phrases are consistent with Karnad'sendeavour to bring together the binary opposites of reason and faith in order to present a unified image of Reality with its many segments and facets as complimentary elements of the same Reality. Karnad made this attempt in order to portray a unified picture of Reality with its various segments and facets as complementary aspects of the same Reality. Karnad is a self-proclaimed atheist, and according to his ideology, it is up to individual humans to choose the course of their own lives, as well as their histories and fates. On the other hand, his atheism is the kind that acknowledges the existence of a transcendental dimension. Karnad himself acknowledges, "I was an atheist, and I still am an atheist." However, the firm ideological position I took led to the development of my atheism. His (Tughlaq's) commitment to God and engagement in religious practices captivated me, and as a result, I had a profound personal transformation as a result of this. If, on the other hand, you are inquiring about my own belief, I do not have a conclusive response for you. ("Girish Karnad, the Playwright"128).

The "ideological stance" of Karnad is founded on reason, which is the defining characteristic of scientific investigation; nonetheless, it does not exclude the existence of a transcendent component. According to Karnad's own definition of the word "intellectual," an intellectual is someone for whom "equality and secularism" are important ideas that should be practiced throughout one's life ("Citizen as Soldier" 524). Karnad might be considered an intellectual. However, reason itself would suggest that reality is more than what reason or science can grasp and explain since there is the meta-rational dimension to existence. This is the case because reality is more than what reason or science can explain. As a result, Karnad's "personal conviction" seems to imply that he is open to the realm of the psychic and the spiritual. As a result, his atheism is the kind that acknowledges the legitimacy of religion, faith, and mystery in a person's existence. It is possible to understand as religiosity or spirituality the acknowledgment of a meta-rational, metaphysical, and, to use religious parlance, mystical dimension to existence. This acknowledgement is what gives a person's life the deep dimension, meaningfulness, feeling of purpose, and direction. Therefore, Karnad integrates the material, intellectual intelligence together with the spiritual, mystical faith aspects of the human being and existence.

Karnad views his goal as bringing about a "transformative change" in his readers and audience since he is a cultural activist and architect. According to him, a play's success relies on "not merely'stating' [a truth] but 'persuading'" ("Girish Karnad, the Playwright" 129) the reader and the audience to the veracity of the topic expressed. According to Girish Karnad, the playwright, "What a playwright does is a kind of persuasion" (128–29). And he anticipates that the audience will behave responsibly by participating actively in the performance. His dream is that "the more plays a person sees, the more he is likely to look beyond entertainment, and think of relating theatre to the larger issues that dominate his life" (Aparna Dharwadker, "Performance, Meaning, and the Materials of Modern Indian Theatre" 368). The many ills that plague society are the outcome of an incorrect understanding of the major determinants of life, such as religion and culture. Karnad attempts to rouse the reader and the audience, particularly the intelligentsia, from "cultural amnesia" ("Author's Introduction," Three Plays 4) by bringing together the binary opposites in order to draw attention to such bigger themes of life.

The responsibility of a writer is highlighted by Karnad in his chat with Dattani: "Theatre can't change society, but you can make society aware of issues and the complexities of issues..." "Two Faces of Indian Drama" by Dattani, p. As a result, Karnad addresses a variety of intricate topics in his plays, including the interaction between religion and politics, religion and culture, the complexity of the human mind and relationships, dreams and desires, and truth and reality. According to him, a dramatist must be devoted to the evolving experiences and times, as well as transform both himself and his views, in order to stay current. A play can only be as modern as the author, according to Karnad, who discussed "Acrobating Between the Traditional and the Modern" in his address. The drama won't be current if the author lacks modern beliefs or commitment, according to (98).

The fossilization of ideas, rites, rituals, and practices occurs when religions become institutionalized. As a result, they grow stagnant, oppose change, and deteriorate into a manipulative and repressive power. Karnad's ideological position, however, suggests that as reason and scientific understanding advance, so do human experiences and perceptions. People's perceptions and experiences of the Sacred are therefore altered as a result. The old idea of religion and the Sacred has changed in a society where "everything is now imbued with a sense of rationality" (Melloni 6). More and more people now place their faith and belief in values such as the sanctity of human life, human rights, human dignity, strong community ties, celebration of life and its diversity, and so on, which are an assertion of the sense of the Sacred in the human, as opposed to gods and goddesses, the "extra-cosmic deity" (Vivekananda 372) who belong to another realm.

Karnad's plays show how modern human sensibilities have changed and portray a life in which religious experiences are appreciated and held dear while firmly rejecting any effort to enshrine them in meaningless religious ceremonies, rituals, beliefs, and practices. The paradigm shift is moving away from looking for divinity in a far-off place outside of this cosmos, which is still mostly theoretical, and toward looking for divinity in people and in this planet. In Tradition Modernity Counterculture, Kappen describes this mode of existence as follows:

If so, the task we face as the second millennium comes to a close is to search for the Divine in the lived universe of our aging planet and splintered humanity rather than in the myths, symbols, rituals, and doctrines passed down from some distant past. Here, we will encounter the Divine in one of two ways: as a presence in every encounter with love, friendship, community, and beauty that elevates us to our highest potentials, or as an absence in the void and vulnerability of our individual and collective humanness. (57)

A contemporary worldview is characterized by secular religiosity as well as rational faith. According to what Kappen observes, "Modernity subverts not only the caste system but also traditional religion which rests on the belief that human existence is determined by cosmic processes presided over by gods and goddesses" (18). Each of the plays that we have selected for this research has a number of characters and plot lines that actively work to challenge the corrupt religion and culture of the society in which they are set. Karnad not only examines the religious and cultural traditions of the past and reinterprets them for the current times, but he also projects a need to chart a future path of action. This is because Karnad believes that it is necessary to design a future course of action. According to Kappen's prognostication, the most significant shift that secular religiosity and rational faith bring about is that "with the spread of education and scientific knowledge, men and women awaken to the realization that human destiny is governed not only by the laws of nature but also by their own free decision [and as a result], superstitious beliefs and practices will wither away." (18).

The chapter provided a concise overview of the development of Indian play in general. It examined the beginnings and progression of Sanskrit play in addition to Indian folk theater and noted that the introduction of Western influences into India coincided with the British colonial administration. As a result, Indian theatre developed into a hybrid art form that incorporates elements of Indian classical theater, Indian folk theater, and Western theatrical traditions. After that, the elaborated on the history of Indian theater in English, focusing on the significant playwrights in English as well as some of the plays that they had written. In this part, we took a cursory look at some of the most notable aspects of the plays written in English both before and after the country's independence. After then, the contributors behind the sluggish growth of Indian theater in English were identified and discussed. This focused on the significant contributions that Karnad made to Indian theater. In addition to this, it offered some insight on his perspective. Due to the fact that Karnad is an atheist, he has an ideological vision that makes room for both rational faith and secular religion; thus, he is on a mission to affect a transformational shift in both his audience and his readers.

Chapter - 2

MYTHS AND FOLK TALES IN GIRISH KARNAD'S PLAYS

Myths and folk tales are other source materials, besides history, for Karnad's plays. This chapter investigates Karnad's *Hayavadana,* NāgaMandala, The Fire and the Rain and Bali: The Sacrifice.

2.1 HAYAVADANA

Kerned writes the following in a note that is appended to the book *Hayavadana*: "The central episode in the play—the story of Devadatta and Kapila—is based on a tale from the Vetalapanchavimshika, but I have drawn heavily on Thomas Mann's reworking of the tale in The Transposed Heads..." (ix). According to the observations of Naik, the Sanskrit Vetalapanchavimshika "forms part of Kshemendra's the Brihat Katha Manjari and Soma Deva's the Katha Sarit Sagara (both of which date to the 11th century)" ("From the Horse's Mouth: A Study of *Hayavadana*"191). "From the Mouth of the Horse"

The original Sanskrit narrative that serves as the foundation for *Hayavadana* presents a dilemma from a moral standpoint. The argument that the head is superior to the body is brought under scrutiny by Mann via the usage of the narrative. The themes of "imperfection, of incompleteness" (*Hayavadana* 1) and the underlying uncertainty of human identity in a world of interwoven ties are explored in Karnad's*Hayavadana.* In his article titled "Myth and Symbol as Metaphor: A Re-Consideration of Red Oleanders and *Hayavadana,*" Moutushi Chakravartee refers to this kind of human search as "man's eternal quest for completeness"

(36). *Hayavadana* must turn to religious practices in order to fulfill the requirements of this quest. Padmini, the protagonist of the story, at one point seeks Kali out to ask for her help in order to accomplish what she set out to do. As a result, this play is capable of being seen as a criticism of religion and the rituals associated with religion. "Thomas Mann's Transposed Heads and Girish Karnad's*Hayavadana*: An Indian Motif Re-imported," written by Heidrun Bruckner, makes the observation that Girish Karnad's play "combines sheer playfulness and an enchanting indulgence..." (119). Even if the portrayal of the issue is humorous, the fact that human beings continue to be flawed and incomplete despite their best-efforts forces both the reader and the audience to take the subject matter seriously. In *Hayavadana,* an ancient tale is retold in an effort to give it a modern interpretation. Murthy, in "A Note on Karnad's*Hayavadana,*" identifies the play as having a "serious" topic, yet the play's tone is described as being "light and comic" (37).

The cast of characters in *Hayavadana* is entirely unremarkable. The name "Padmini" comes from the Sanskrit phrase "the lotus plant," which refers to the dwelling place of Lakshmi, the Hindu goddess of riches. In "From the Horse's Mouth" 195, Naik makes the observation that Vatsyayana, the author of the Kamasutra, describes a sort of lady who is similar to Padmini. In "The Development of Girish Karnad as a Dramatist: *Hayavadana,*" the author Shubhangi S. Raykar makes the observation that Padmini, "like a lotus, seeks to be a delicate bridge between the earth and the sky" (180). In the book Chakravartee, she is referred to as the "embodiment of the life-force" (36). The word "Vidyasagara" translates to "ocean of knowledge," while the word "Devadatta" means "God given." The names Kapila and Lohita both have their own unique meanings, with Kapila meaning "the dark one" and Lohita meaning "ironsmith." The Child does not have a name; thus, it might be any child since it lacks a name. The Bhagavata performs a variety of roles, including those of a narrator who introduces the characters, provides and comments on the link in the action, operates as a choric character and stage manager, discloses the hidden thoughts of the key characters, performs as a minor character, and performs as a stage assistant. The term "*Hayavadana*" refers to the world in which people and animals coexist. As a result, one might argue that this drama tells the tale of every single human being since characteristics of each of the aforementioned characters can be found, to various degrees, in every individual.

A statement is made at the beginning of the play stating the subject matter that it intends to explore. Incompleteness and imperfection are characteristics that are inherent to the human experience and cannot be avoided in any way. The concept of the play is introduced via the Bhagavata's commentary on Lord Ganesha, who is a symbol of completion and perfection. The following are some of the Bhagavata's remarks:

In point of fact, how can anybody seek to explain his magnificence using our feeble, limited language? No matter how you look at him, he appears to be the essence of imperfection and incompleteness. He has the body of a human but the head of an elephant, and his tusk is broken and his belly is fractured. How exactly is it possible to understand the paradox that this particular Vakratunda-Mahakaya, who has a misshapen body and a crooked face, is the Lord and Master of Success and Perfection? It is possible that the look of this Mangalamoorthy, who is known as the Image of Purity and Holiness, is intended to convey the message that the fullness of God is something that no mere human can fully fathom. Whatever the case may be. It is not up to us to comprehend this Mysterious Phenomenon or to attempt to solve it. It is also not within our capabilities to do so. Our only responsibility is to show respect to the deity with the elephant head, and then we may continue playing. (1)

The point that this comment is trying to express is that any and all depictions of God that are created by humans are insufficient and flawed. In this drama, the realms of the heavenly, the human, and the animal are all represented by the figure of Ganesha. Both the nandi (singing of benedictory song) at the beginning of the performance and the bharatavakya (valedictory prayer) at the conclusion take on symbolic meaning and establish a religious framework within which the three realms of the god, the human, and the animal intimately interact with one another.

Very early on in the play, Karnad presents Devadatta and Kapila to the audience. They are the binary opposites that create tension in the drama, and together they make up "one mind, one heart" (*Hayavadana* 2). "Unrivaled in intelligence," "blinded the greatest poets of the world with his poetry and wit," "fell the mightiest pundits of the kingdom in debates on logic and love," and "is the only son of the Revered Brahmin Vidyasagara" are some of the things that are said about the mind, which is represented by Devadatta in *Hayavadana* 2. The heart, which is symbolized by Kapila, is said to be full of "drive and daring," and "in dancing, in strength and in physical skills, he has no equals." Additionally, Kapila "is the only son of the iron-smith Lohita" (2). The "mind" and the "heart" are always at odds with one another, and it is very difficult to realize a harmonious union between the two. Padmini's assertion that "You could only have lived ripping each other to pieces," depicts such isolation of one from the other (*Hayavadana* 62). "You could only have lived,"

2.1.1 Sanskrit, Sacred Texts and Interpretation

This drama criticizes the usage of Sanskrit in religious rites as a symbol of Brahminic authority and dominance. When addressing the Bhagavata, *Hayavadana* asks, "Do you think just because you know the puranas you can go about showering your Sanskrit on everyone in sight?" *Hayavadana* is particularly outspoken in his disdain for the usage of Sanskrit. (*Hayavadana* 7, p. Kapila's comment on the use of the Sanskrit Sacred Texts has a similar criticism. The misunderstanding that results from Devadatta and Kapila switching heads causes them to disagree on who Padmini's actual spouse is. According to the Sacred Texts, Devadatta seeks to make his case (*Hayavadana* 37). There is some validity to Kapila's criticism of this: "Don't talk to me about your sacred texts. To fit your demands, you may always modify them (*Hayavadana* 37). This is made much more poignant by the fact that not only are the Sacred Texts written in Sanskrit, but also that only the castes of people who were born twice are permitted to study and understand them. In Religion and Society among the Coorgs of South India, Srinivas notes that "The top three castes [Brahmins, Kshatriyas, and Vaishyas] are termed 'twice-born'. The study of the Vedas and the execution of Vedic ritual on certain times are only open to the twice-born castes (24). The majority of people are no longer interested in learning about the Vedas and other Sacred Texts as a result of this. The Brahmins thus found it expedient to interpret the Sacred Texts in a way that suited their needs.

The depiction of Lord Ganesha and the Bhagavata's hymn of adoration and supplication both allude to the unstoppable idea of karma. In the conversation between the Bhagavata and *Hayavadana*, it is more clearly stated. Here, the Bhagavata stands in for ages-old karmic knowledge. He sees *Hayavadana*'s state as the result of some prior wrongdoing. The contemporary rational secularist *Hayavadana* declares, "It has nothing to do with my last birth" (*Hayavadana* 8). His primary goal in life is "to become a complete man" (*Hayavadana* 9). *Hayavadana* discovered that none of the gods, goddesses, holy locations, or holy men he had attempted could assist people mold their lives (*Hayavadana* 9–10). In the end, each individual is accountable for their own lives, an existentialist viewpoint that Karnad is familiar with.

Padmini's ambition to have a perfect man who unites the head of Devadatta and the body of Kapila is a reflection of *Hayavadana*'s yearning to become a fully realized man. Padmini is a representation of human resistance to incompleteness and imperfection in the natural world. The Sacred is the force and energy that drives people towards perfection, the "MORE" aspect identified by James in The Varieties of Religious Experience (499).

2.1.2 Divine Help for Human Problems

Hayavadana's father was a gandharva, which is a type of heavenly being. He turned into a horse because of a threat from the god Kuvera. After "fifteen years of human love," he goes back to his old form and curses his wife to become a horse (*Hayavadana* 8-9). In a similar way, Kali of Mount Chitrakoot makes *Hayavadana* into a horse, which goes against his wish to become "a complete man" (*Hayavadana* 68). Kali knows that Devadatta and Kapila's heads are switched while she is bringing them back to life. But she does nothing to fix it, which makes things even worse. All of the gods and goddesses' actions in the play make the players sad and unhappy. This makes me wonder if people really need gods and goddesses to make their lives better.

Hayavadana also criticizes the idea of going on a journey. Pilgrimage is done for many different reasons (Paul Puthanangady, Popular Devotions in India, 709-10). One reason people go on pilgrimages is to ask God for help with human issues. With a few exceptions, doing these kinds of things doesn't make people's lives better. *Hayavadana*'s anger comes through when he says:

I have visited Banaras, Rameshwar, Gokarn, Haridwar, Gaya, and Kedarnath, as well as the Dargah of Khwaja Yusuf Baba and the Grotto of Our Lady. Magicians, mendicants, maharishis, fakirs, saints and sadhus—sadhus with short hair, sadhus with beards—sadhus in saffron, sadhus in the altogether—hanging, singing, rotating, gyrating—on the spikes, in the air, beneath the water, beneath the ground... I've addressed all of them. And what did I gain from this? Everywhere I went, I was required to wear a veil, and I began to go hairless. [Pause. Shyly] I despise this cranium, but I can't help but admire this beautiful, long mane. [Pause.] Therefore, I was unable to visit Tirupati. (9-10)

Pilgrimages that are conducted in the hope of gaining heavenly assistance and protection show, in a way, the pilgrim's abdication of duty to sort through his or her own issues and discover answers that are within the realm of the humanly achievable. It demonstrates that individuals believe that their lives are controlled from the outside by a god or goddess, and that they anticipate assistance from this deity or goddess. This reveals another aspect of human nature, which is the want to overcome challenges that are beyond their control. "As though one defined human being by their begging," Karnad says in his criticism of the behavior of humans when they persistently stretch the begging bowl to a variety of gods and goddesses. (*The Fire and the Rain* 31). There is no way to reconcile the incompatible elements of existence using either a religious or a philosophical framework. According to Naik, the only answer to such difficulties is to "accept cheerfully the fundamental disharmony in human life." This is the only solution that can be found. ("From the Horse's Mouth",196).

In this particularly severe critique, Mount Chitrakoot's Kali has been singled out. It is impossible to ignore the satire and mockery that are embedded in the Bhagavata's portrayal of Kali.

BHAGAVATA. Come to think of it, *Hayavadana,* why don't youtrytheKali ofMount Chitrakoot?

HAYAVADANA.Anythingyousay.

BHAGAVATA. It's a temple at the top of Mount Chitrakoot. Thegoddess there is famous for being ever-awake to the call ofdevotees. Thousands used to flock to her temple once. Noonegoes now, though.

HAYAVADANA.Whynot?

BHAGAVATA.She used to give anything anyone asked for. As the people became aware of this they stopped going. (10)

The Bhagavata eventually runs into a new and improved version of *Hayavadana* later on in the play. Now, the only thing that distinguishes him from a horse is his human voice. This time, Kali is rushing to fulfill the request of one of her devotees as quickly as possible. In the Bhagavata, *Hayavadana* says, "Even before I could say 'Make me a perfect man!'! I become a horse" (*Hayavadana* 68). On the other hand, he argues, "I have become a full horse, but not a whole person! This human voice — this human voice that has been damned - it's still there! (*Hayavadana* 68). The carelessness and impatience shown by Kali ultimately work against *Hayavadana*'s best interests.

Devadatta, who is enamored with Padmini but has no idea how to win her over, makes a vow to Kapila that if he ever wins her over, "I'll offer my two arms to the goddess Kali and my head to Lord Rudra. (*Hayavadana*14). Devadatta claims, "Now the only future I have is to stand and do penance in PavanaVeethi..." out of desperation and dread of failing to capture her. (*Hayavadana*14-15). His human need drives him to seek divine assistance. Criticizing such reliance on the "extra-cosmic deity" (372), Vivekananda observes that people "seek to win favors from these superior beings, to receive by gift from the gods what should be earned through personal effort" (334). Therefore, Karnad uses Kapila to demonstrate that human endeavor is sufficient to satisfy the majority of humans' natural requirements. According to Kapila, Devadatta's need can be satisfied by human endeavor and does not require divine intervention. "And forget about your arms and head," said Kapila. This task does not require Rudra or Kali. People who turn to gods and deities for assistance with the simplest duties are ridiculed in the poem "I'm enough" (15). Perhaps Kapila's perspective is that of Karnad himself. The "Final Statement" of "The All-India Survey" on Popular Devotions in India reiterates that "frequently people make vows to obtain favors that may be obtained through adequate human action, for many appear to require the intervention of supernatural powers to deal with the unpredictable even in very ordinary human occurrences" (708).

Both Devadatta and Kapila are influenced and undergo transformations as a direct result of Padmini's potent creative potential as well as her deep and imaginative interaction with the essential elements of existence. Both the Brahmin and the Shudra are elevated to the status of human beings by the great attraction that exists between Kapila and Padmini, as well as by Devadatta's profound need for Padmini's affection and attention, as well as by his jealousy of Padmini's reaction to Kapila. Both the otherworldly, soul-focused doctrine of Brahmanism and the hierarchical order of a society riven by caste are undermined by the mystery surrounding the human body. It challenges the idea that male sexuality is superior to feminine sexuality. Combining members of the Brahmin and Shudra social classes undermines the Brahmanic tradition of maintaining ceremonial purity.

In the cart scene, Devadatta gives his head to Kali, rather than his hands, as promised before, more out of annoyance and resentment regarding Padmini's attraction to Kapila than out of a desire to fulfill his vows. Kapila, too, gives his head to Kali for fear of being accused of murdering Devadatta for Padmini's sake. When Padmini offers herself as a sacrifice to Kali, the latter awakens. "I don't have the strength to hack off my head," Padmini says to Kali. But what difference does it make how I die, Mother? You don't give a damn. To you, it's the same—another giving! Okay, OK. So, here's another offering for you." (*Hayavadana*31). Padmini's words sound like she has given up and is sad. Through Kali, Karnad says what he thinks about what Devadatta, Kapila, and Padmini did. The goddess says of Devadatta and Kapila, "Those scoundrels!" They lied until the end of their lives" (*Hayavadana*33). And when it comes to Padmini, Kali tells her, "You spoke the truth because you're selfish—that's all" (*Hayavadana* 33). Karnad, author of Through the Queen in Bali: The Sacrifice, condemns this ritual, arguing that it is inhumane and superfluous (96).

Hayavadana receives a very sarcastic heavenly answer from the Bhagavata, who knows full well that there is no divine assistance for such "fundamental disharmony in life" as *Hayavadana*'s: "May you succeed in your search for completeness," and he adds, "Each one to his own fate." To everyone his own desires. "To each his own need" (*Hayavadana*11). It would seem that this serves as a reminder that every single human being is, at their core, imperfect and does not possess completeness. In the context of this discussion, the three terms "fate," "desire," and "lack" all allude to the same reality of incompleteness and imperfection that exists in every human being. The dolls all send the same message, and it is as follows: Doll I exclaims, "Each one to his fate!" and Doll II repeats her sentiment by saying, "Each one to her problems!" (*Hayavadana*50).

The youngster is filled with awe and astonishment at the contradictions he sees in life as a result of the sheer incongruity of a horse laughing like a person. The youngster is able to reclaim his youth and his humanity via the simple act of accepting life and all of its peculiarities in an innocent manner. The chuckle of *Hayavadana* silences his human voice and brings back the neigh that he was born with. In the end, the song that the little boy is singing (*Hayavadana* 69) proclaims that the rider has passed away, and the horse is set free. In their book, Dictionary of Symbols, Jean Chevalier and Alain Gheerbrant interpret the symbol of the horse and the rider as a "fountain of peace or of confrontation on both the psychic and the mental planes" (517). They also discuss the link between the horse and the rider. They go on to say that the rider is the one who directs the horse during the day, but that during the night, when the rider is unable to see as well, "it is the horse that sees and guides, and... takes control," since the horse is the only animal that can freely pass through the gates of mystery, which are beyond the grasp of reason. It will be a victorious ride [and] if the rider and the horse are in harmony with one another" (517).

Could this be the answer to Padmini's query, "Must the head always win?" This song has (*Hayavadana* 56), among other things. When reason does not dominate and hinder the spontaneity of emotions and faith; when reason, emotions, and faith are merged inside the individual; then, and only then, is it possible to experience greater liberty and fulfillment.

2.1.3 Return to the Forest

The forest is a metaphor of mystery, representing the initial state of purity in which everything lived in peace. Kapila returns to the forest after Padmini's initial effort to tackle the issue of incompleteness results in even more bewilderment *(Hayavadana 41)*. Padmini is saddened when Devadatta returns to his true form and resolves to meet Kapila in the jungle. She wants to bring her son, the new humanity, to nature's purity and peace. Metaphorically, Kapila and Padmini's resolve to "return to the forest" is important *(Hayavadana 41; 54)*.

During their encounter in the forest, Padmini reawakens Kapila's recollections and encourages him to revisit those experiences and give in to the reality of the situation in order to conquer his sense of being unfinished:

KAPILA. What difference does it make now whether you remain or go? You've caused the problem. All those nameless recollections were hidden under my flesh. You've dug them up with the claws now.

PADMINI. Why should one bury anything?

KAPILA.Why shouldn't one? Why should one tolerate this maddance of incompleteness?

PADMINI.Whose incompleteness? Yours?

KAPILA. Yes, it's mine. You can work out your body, but you can't work out your memories. Isn't that interesting? Shouldn't the body have its own ghosts, its own memories? Memories of touch-memories of a touch-memories of a body swinging in these arms, of warm flesh against this palm-memories that one cannot identify, comprehend, or even name since this head was not there when they occurred. (57-58)

There is a fragmentation of the individual as a result of the brain (reason and logic) dominating every other human capacity and the body (senses) being subjugated by the head (reason).

Kapila concedes that he has won some of the battle (*Hayavadana* 56-57) and agrees to let Padmini take the lead, to which Padmini responds, "Be silent, idiot. Your physical form was immersed in a river, where it also swam and performed dancing moves. Shouldn't the information about the river and the swim be stored in your head? Your head must also be submerged in that river; the current must run its tongue in your ears and squeeze your head to its bosom while it does so. You won't stop being unfinished business until that's taken care of" (58). In the article "The Use of Myth in Karnad's *Hayavadana*," Vijaya Gowri discusses how the symbol of the river is used to characterize the character of Padmini. Padmini, like the river, is a "free, uninhibited stream of turbulent water that flows unbounded, pursuing its own irregular path," according to Gowri's explanation. It keeps its own individuality and revels in the wonderful independence it has throughout its whole course, right up to the point when it pours into the salty water of the sea" (40). Her decision to terminate her life by committing sati at the conclusion of the play serves as both a declaration of who she is and a protest against the constraints that are put on her by both society and nature. In that regard, she may be considered successful.

Another one of the play's symbols represents the coming together of the Sacred and the Secular in some way. "The door-frame of the house had an engraving of a two-headed bird at the top" (*Hayavadana* 15) is the sole feature of Padmini's home that Devadatta takes note of when he visits. The two birds that are described as perching on "the branches of the World Tree" in the Upanishads are discussed by Chevalier and Gheerbrant in their book, A Dictionary of Symbols. According to the authors, "One eats the fruit of the tree, while the other looks on without eating." They represent, respectively, the dynamic individual soul (jvtma) and the Universal Spirit (tman), which is knowledge in its purest form. Both of these concepts are referred to as jnana. They are commonly represented as a single bird with two heads since, in actuality, they are not two different birds but rather one bird with two heads" (87). This gives Padmini a special place in the play as a symbol of the Sacred (Shakti interacting with Prakriti), which is actively participating in the world, the secular plane of existence, to accomplish harmony, completion, and perfection. This gives Padmini a position that is unmatched by any other character in the play.

The significance of the kid as a symbol in relation to the play's overarching theme can not be overstated. It is a trait of childhood to be inquisitive about one's place in the world and about life in general. The drama exaggerates this quality and assigns it to all of the adult characters by having those characters pose a series of existential questions to which there is no simple response. *Hayavadana,* in an effort to rid himself of his sense of incompleteness, goes on a number of pilgrimages, but he is unsuccessful in every one of his endeavors. After that, he transforms into a "rationalist" and begins to doubt the validity of any religious explanations for his current situation. But in the end, he gives up and decides to make one more try to challenge the goddess, Kali. The goddess then contravenes his wishes and changes him into a horse.

There are a few instances in which Kapila, Devadatta, and Padmini refer to one another as "child." Devadatta, in an effort to correct Padmini, says to her, "You have no sense of what to say." As long as you still have that childlike ability to babble and run about..." (*Hayavadana* 20). Referring to Devadatta's delicate demeanor, Padmini observes, "But you are so fragile! I'm not sure how you're going to make it through life like this, wrapped in silk as you are! You are not even a teenager yet..." (*Hayavadana* 21). Padmini has a change of heart after meeting Kapila, and she decides that she would go on the journey to Ujjain. She convinces Devadatta not to be furious by stating, "Please don't get angry. "Poor kid, he appeared to be so disoriented and disheartened, and it broke my heart to see him like that" (*Hayavadana* 24).

A sense of wonder and curiosity, acceptance of the paradoxes and incongruities of life, and re-establishing the sensibilities and experiences of the primordial, the mythical, and the symbolic are all re-established by the time the play is over, and it upholds the child as the victor who brings completeness and perfection to *Hayavadana* and restores humanity in himself. "Modern man must recover his sense of childlike curiosity, wonder, and amusement at the sheer incongruity of life in order to achieve integration, though on a lower level of existence," argues Naik in his article "From the Horse's Mouth" (page 196), which is a commentary on the search for a solution to the existential difficulties that humans face. In this play, Karnad advocates for a kind of secular spirituality that looks like this. Human beings will be liberated from their needless dependency on gods and goddesses once they come to terms with this kind of spirituality. The conclusion of the story is that as the youngster rides the horse, it is symbolic of the rider becoming aware of the senses that the animal symbolizes. It is a representation of the rider acknowledging and overcoming the barriers that exist between intellect and emotion, as well as fostering peace and unification between the two. According to the Dictionary of Symbols, this represents "a triumphal ride" since the rider and the horse are working together.

Padmini makes a second effort to bring about wholeness, this time with reference to her kid, after her initial attempt to bring about completeness fails. But in order to do this, the old, disorganized system must be abandoned, and a fresh start must be established. Every fresh start needs to take place in the forest, which is a metaphor for the fundamental oneness and peaceful existence of the universe. Therefore, she sent Devadatta and Kapila into the woods in order to reinstate the previous order. The old system is obliterated in the confrontation that comes to a close. The "mad dance of incompleteness" is over now that Padmini has put a stop to it. She freely acknowledges, "You could only have lived your lives by tearing each other to shreds." I had no choice except to put you to death by your own hand" (*Hayavadana* 62). She has no choice but to begin over, and she places the burden squarely on the shoulders of individual humans. She requests that Bhagavata take her kid, who represents the new humanity, and reshape him in order to achieve harmony between his mind and his heart and to unite these two aspects of his being. Her son is the emblem of the new humanity. Her instructions include that her son should be raised by the hunters in the forest until he is five years old, at which point he should be brought to the town to be raised by his grandpa Vidyasagara. The youngster first receives instruction from the hunters in the arts of the body and nature, and then receives instruction from Vidyasagara in the socio-cultural elements of life. In this manner, she lays the path for his eventual revelation and acceptance of Reality, as well as a synthesis of the natural and the cultural parts of existence.

2.1.4 Temple, God and Goddess

One key symbol that occurs in four of the seven Karnad plays is a decaying temple with the god's pedestal intact but the deity itself ruined and unidentified. There is complete darkness both inside and outside the temple.

Hayavadana is where the most progress has been made in demystifying the many religious beliefs and practices. The incompletion and imperfection of Lord Ganesha are both stated in the Bhagavata (*Hayavadana* 1), which goes on to become the play's central emblem. *Hayavadana*'s experiences of pointless pilgrimages, his contact with Kali on Mount Chitrakoot, and Padmini's experiences with Kali and her intervention turn out to be unfavorable and even catastrophic. Padmini also has her own negative encounters with Kali and her involvement.

The most depressing feature of the play is the way in which the Indian deity Kali is portrayed in a satirical way. The presence of gods and goddesses in people's life is called into question as a result of Kali's involvement in the lives of Padmini and *Hayavadana*. Instead of abdicating one's responsibilities by giving one's future and destiny over to gods and goddesses, as is suggested by Karnad, human people should take on the task of shaping their own future and destiny for themselves. The religious ideas and practices of leaving human tasks in the hands of gods and goddesses are debunked in *Hayavadana*, and the play asserts the actuality and primacy of human existence, which is founded on human freedom and responsibility. *Hayavadana* was written in the 7th century and is set in India.

The humanistic ideals that Karnad espouses are exemplified in *Hayavadana*. The divine, the human, and the animal are all represented in this drama in some way or another. The drama takes into account the perspectives of men, women, and children within the human condition. It blends city life with living in the countryside or in the woods. Padmini, in the same way that the archetypal mother earth is filled with the need for a life that is whole and unbroken, is actively engaged in the process of bringing about a world that satisfies that yearning. Karnad's humanistic view is optimistic about the possibility of a peaceful life, despite the fact that the irony is very effectively brought out. Human beings, who are by their very nature incomplete and flawed, seek for and work toward the achievement of some unreachable ideal of fullness and perfection. The ontological and teleological orientation in human beings may be characterized by this tendency.

Hayavadana and Padmini are both individuals and events that illustrate the journey from a rosy fantasy to a brutal reality. People's minds and their social environments are constrained in ways that make it difficult for them to achieve their full potential. According to Karnad, transcendence can only be achieved by first entering and then traversing immanence. In addition to this, he implies that if one acknowledges the enticing reality as the truth of life, one will still have a meaningful existence even if the world continues to be horribly opaque and unexplainable. It is impossible to attain integration by striving to reconcile that which cannot be reconciled; rather, integration can only be accomplished by acknowledging the fragmented character of existence. In order for human beings to attain integration, although on a more fundamental level of existence, they need to rediscover their sense of youthful curiosity, wonder, and delight at the sheer incongruity of life.

It is said that *Hayavadana* "presents the typical existential anguish but does not stop at existential despair" ("From the Horse's Mouth" 197). He believes in the transcendent essence of the human being inside the immanent, as well as the human potential to advance toward his or her ontological goal. Karnad's hope is illuminated by the human condition, which is characterized by its incompleteness and imperfection. Karnad does not support the idea that a person should ask gods and goddesses to intervene in their lives in order to accomplish their ontological aim of realizing their full potential. The only things the person has to do are recognize his or her own potential and maintain a connection to their inner selves. *Naga-Mandala* takes the similar strategy, which can be found here.

2.2 *NĀGA-MANDALA*: PLAY WITH A COBRA

Naga-Mandala's introduction by Karnad states, "*Naga-Mandala* is based on two oral tales from Karnataka that I first heard from Professor A.K. Ramanujan several years ago" (i). In the play, the royal figures from the original are replaced with regular people. At first, the play's conclusion included the King Cobra killing himself in Rani's long tresses. According to Karnad's addition to the play, which was based on a Bengali folktale of a similar kind ("Performance, Meaning, and the Materials of Modern Indian Theatre" 358–59), a little snake continues to dwell in the long tresses of Rani in the second ending. But the original narrative hasn't been altered in any way by these Karnad.

The legend of the Flames focuses on a folk belief that it is common practice in rural areas to extinguish all of the lights at night so that the flames might congregate in a lonely location and spend the night chatting with one another. The narrative also makes a remark on the contradictory character of folk stories that are passed down via oral tradition. These stories exist apart from the person who is telling them, but the only way for them to continue existing is for them to be told from one generation to the next. In the primary narrative, which is a tale told by a Flame, the story of Rani addresses the dilemma of the human urge to survive by fictions and half-truths. The story is conveyed as a story told by a Flame.

The drama *Naga-Mandala,* which examines the world of marriage and family life from the viewpoint of a woman, has been interpreted in a variety of different ways as a play that vacillates between the realms of illusion and reality. The drama focuses mostly on human evolution as well as the ambiguity of human experience and existence as its primary topics of investigation. The image of the snake as a leitmotif has elements of metaphor, actuality, concept, and energy respectively. The patriarchal moral rules, which require the servile constancy of a woman to her husband but not the fidelity of a man to his wife, are called into doubt by this argument. It also calls into question the extent to which a man may control the intellect, emotions, body, and sexuality of his wife.

2.2.1 Tides of Change

The practices that Rani engaged in as a youngster have started to develop and become more mature. Despite this, her shortcomings become apparent during her first contact with Naga. Rani would not even let him to sit close to her on the couch. "I'll go ahead and take a seat there. Outside of your reach. Will you at least sit down?" says Naga in *Naga-Mandala* (*Naga-Mandala* 19). After some time has passed, he approaches her once again and says, "May I sit beside you now? Or does the thought of it make you want to leap out of your skin again? (*Nāga-Mandala* 20). Her repeated interactions with Appanna and Naga stir her suspicions about their relationship. The "day self" version of Appanna is not the same as his "night self." Rani is unsure of what is taking on with her at this time. (*Naga-Mandala* 22) She has the sneaking suspicion that if she is not dreaming, she must be going insane. It is up to Naga to comfort her that she is not losing her mind or having a dream by saying, "It is not a dream." I am also not something that has been conjured up by your mind. I am present. I have taken a seat just in front of you. Please touch me. You can do it! You won't, right? Then let's move on. Talk to me. No? Okay, got it. Then I had best depart" (*Nāga-Mandala* 22).

It's possible that she's looking at Naga for the first time as a potential sexual partner, and she immediately feels afraid. The snake is representative of an individual's sexual energy, and the mirror box reflects what is going on in her thoughts at the moment (*Naga-Mandala* 23). She does not even want to bring up the subject by its specific name in the evening. She hushes Naga and tells him, "Shh! don't even bring it up. It is said that if you call it by name in the dark, it will come inside the home" (*Naga-Mandala* 23). Rani has not yet conquered her ice-cold disposition. In spite of this, she is enthralled by the novel sensation and comments that "since I looked into the mirror, I seem to be incapable of thinking of anything else" (*Naga-Mandala* 24). However, she experiences feelings of embarrassment and maybe even remorse when Naga kisses her. This may have been her first experience with sexual touch. She chides Naga: "I said be quiet. (Pause.) I had no idea you were such a nefarious person. When you first began using sweet language, I ought to have recognized something was up. (Pause) If I had known, I never would have said yes to being married to you. What will your father and mother say when they find out? (*Nāga-Mandala* 24-25).

Naga educates her on sexual topics and explains how the whole natural world is connected to the process of reproduction. However, Rani is not completely persuaded. She is of the opinion that human beings are unique. "Snakes and lizards may do whatever they like," she continues, "but human beings should have some sense of shame" (*Naga-Mandala* 25). "Snakes and lizards may do whatever they like" In the past, Rani would rack her brain over the prospect of her married life, which eventually led her to compare her connection with Appanna to that of her connection with her own parents. During her soliloquy, she exposes her daydream, which goes as follows: "Then Rani's parents embrace her and cry." They lean in and caress and kiss her. During the night, she sleeps in the space between them. Therefore, she does not feel afraid any more. They assure her, "Don't worry," about anything. "We won't ever allow you to get away from us again!" (*Nāga-Mandala* 7). But she has now conquered her reticent nature and her icy demeanor. After she has experienced the first pleasure of sexual contact, she turns off her rational mind and instead listens to her body and her instincts, just like every other animal. She eventually overcomes her ice-coldness and cultivates the ability to connect to the sexual energy that is inside her. Her inner energy, namely her desire, starts to shape her behavior from that point on.

She is given a series of instructions, and Naga tells her not to inquire why they were given. Her response might be seen as a subtle dare to Naga. "No, I won't do that." Nobody, not even the pig, the whale, or the eagle, ever wonders why. Therefore, neither will I. However, they continue to request it. So, it's possible for me too, right? (*Nāga-Mandala* 26). However, on the other hand She is being handled in the same manner as an animal since she does not question what is happening. Rani objects to the therapy being given. While this is happening, she is able to better listen to her body and react to its signals, which provides her freedom and a sense of fullness. This is due to the fact that she is not employing her critical faculty. One must put their faith in their gut while also making use of their intellect. Throughout the course of the play, Rani will acquire this knowledge.

On the one hand, the scene of Kurudavva's last visit to Rani's residence highlights a difference between Rani and Kappanna, while on the other, it shows a continuation of Rani's experience in Kappanna (*Naga-Mandala* 28). As Rani awakens from her daydreams and fantasies over her wedded life, Kappanna is getting lured more and deeper into the realm of his own dreams and fantasies concerning a lady. What hasn't changed is the importance that dreams and fantasies play in people's lives, as well as the manner that these things keep them from confronting the reality that causes them sorrow. While Rani is able to obtain Appanna by letting go of her thoughts and fancies, Kurudavva is unable to keep Kappanna because of the dreams and fantasies he has about the lady who should be in his life.

2.2.2 Rani's Triumph

The confrontation between Kurudavva and Rani is resolved when it takes place before the village court. This serves to emphasize the differences that exist between the two even greater. Rani is becoming closer and closer to recognizing the reality of human existence and the inevitable bond that will occur in marriage. But since Kurudavva cannot come to terms with this reality, she is cut off from her son. It is essential to the continuation of the human race that the parent and the kid be kept apart in order for the man and the woman to be able to procreate. The desire to be with one another is the driving force behind every marriage. In Rani's life, this goal has been accomplished, however in Kappanna's life, the process is only getting started.

Appanna, much like Rani, struggles to reconcile the gap between his aspirations and the actual world. However, it will take him a little bit more time to pull himself together and overcome his fractured personality. "I have definitive evidence to prove I was not fantasizing I am pregnant," Rani says to Naga when she finally finds out that she is pregnant, which is a piece of concrete evidence. "I have definite evidence to prove I was not fantasizing I am pregnant" (*Naga-Mandala* 31). Naga is still in disbelief and cannot experience joy. Suddenly, he grasps the seriousness of the circumstance that he is in. Most likely, he was caught off guard by the news. Maybe he did not want it or did not want to bear any obligation of that kind sooner. The feelings are conveyed by Rani in her own unique manner when she says, "I can't make any sense of you even when it's just the two of us." Now we are joined by a third life! I was unsure whether or not it would be too much for you to handle. Consequently, I refrained from speaking since my worst fears were realized....

You do not seem to be excited about the baby. You do not feel proud about the fact that I will soon become a mother (*Naga-Mandala* 31).

Rani has undergone a transformation that is irreversible, maturing into a woman who is aware of both her body and her thoughts. She has made the shift from relying on her mind to relying on her emotions. In her, the two are at peace with one another, but in Appanna, they are not. Rani suffers from bewilderment and suffering as a direct result of his still having a divided personality. This is the time when Appanna feels the most torn between his two selves. He transforms into his "day self" all of a sudden and without warning. His psychotic state causes him to see no other option but to turn his back on Rani and the kid. Again, he resorted to physical violence, beating and kicking her while also verbally abusing her and accusing her of adultery and unfaithfulness (*Naga-Mandala* 33).

However, the truth must be made known to the general people. During their last get-together, Naga advised Rani to tell the Elders the truth whenever she spoke with them. People will only be set free when they are confronted with the truth. Whatever the reality may be, Rani is unwavering in her stance, and the Elders have no problem with that. As a result of her brave conduct, she is hailed as a goddess, and in the euphoria that ensues, everyone forgets about Appanna's flaws. Appanna is just there "as an after thought, seated next to her" (*Naga-Mandala* 40). The Elders then speak to Appanna in an appeasing manner, saying as follows:

ELDER I. Appanna, your wife isn't your typical wife. She is the goddess manifest. Don't bemoan the fact that you misjudged her and mistreated her. Goddesses show themselves to the world in this way. You were selected as the means of demonstrating her divinity.

ELDER II. Serve her for the rest of your life. To be selected for such a sacred mission, you must have virtue from previous lifetimes. (40)

According to Elder II's understanding, the incident was a manifestation of the Divine. Only when an individual is willing to acknowledge both the truth about themselves and the truth about life can the latent divine potential in that person come to the surface. And the upshot of putting both one's brain and one's heart into action is the discovery of the truth. Not archaic religions with their useless and pointless rituals, beliefs, or ideologies, but this is what gives individuals and their life genuine liberty, a feeling of fullness and perfection, as well as a sense of purpose and direction; faiths of the past do not deliver this.

The last time Naga sees Rani is while she is in bed with Appanna. This is also the last time Naga sees Appanna. There will always be a place for physical needs and attractions, but humans must learn to transcend them. In the play, these lusts and attractions are superseded by genuine love, which is the result of redemptive suffering and the giving up of oneself. Rani is a representation of the idea. This demonstrates that we are indeed human. Love must reign supreme and triumph over all other human passions, especially those that are destructive to life. In this sense, a reptile or animal cannot become human, nor can a religious fanatic who gives in to destructive desires and perpetuates murder and devastation in the name of religion. Both of these examples are incompatible with human existence.

Both men and women need to come to terms with the fact that, despite their equality, they are distinct individuals, and that these distinctions have the potential to create friction between them. This is an aspect of the reality about human beings, and just like everything else about us, it has to be recognized and embraced. This concept is expressed in the play, in the play's second ending, by the arrival of the little snake that Rani inserts into her hair and says, "Quick now. Get it. Are you certain that you won't get out? Good. Now, remain in that position. And lie motionless. You have no idea how much weight you carry. Will you please give me some time to get acclimated to you? (*Nāga-Mandala*45).

The significance of being aware of the truth is emphasized throughout the play. The significance of Naga's determination on revealing the truth can not be overstated. Appanna has not been able to get a hold of the truth, but Rani has. Because of this, Appanna vents his frustration at the conclusion of the play by saying, "I know I haven't slept with my wife. Let everyone speak anything they want to say. Let any miracle proclaim her a goddess. But I am aware! What use does it serve for me to live this life if it has no value? (*Nāga-Mandala* 41).

Even when the narrative has come to an end, man must go on. The Flames shout at Man, "Stop trying to find excuses! It's possible that this chapter is finished. However, you are still present and have not passed away! ... Just get on with it, for the love of God, etc." And thus, in accordance with their demand, Man complies and replies, "All right! In a word, yes! Let me try" (*Nāga-Mandala* 43). Because the settings of life are always shifting, human beings have to keep exercising their ability to detect and locate the truth in those situations. Otherwise, the truth will continue to evade them, just as it did throughout Rani, Appanna, and Kappanna's lives.

Karnad depicts the unconquerable spirit of the human person in the works *Hayavadana* and *Naga-Mandala*, which aspires to get above the limitations that come with being human. In The Fire and the Rain, he shows how fragile and brutal the human condition can be. In addition to them, he lends an additional dimension to all of humankind's endeavors, which is the grace of the divine.

2.3 THE FIRE AND THE RAIN

The legend of Yavakri, which can be found in the "Vana Prava" (Forest Canto) of the Mahabharata, served as the inspiration for the story "The Fire and the Rain." During the time when the Pandavas were exiled, Lomasha told them the story. The tale conveys a profound sense of dread and concern at the prospect of brother killing brother. The Rig Veda is the source of the tale that Indra engaged in combat with Vritra and ultimately killed him. In the story, Vritra blocks the flow of water and the sky, and when Indra kills Vritra, the waters flow freely again.

The authors Naik and Narayan explain the symbolic meaning of fire as "the fire of lust, anger, vengeance, envy, treachery, violence, and death" in their book Indian English Literature 1980-2000: A Critical Survey. They also state that "The 'rain' symbolizes self-sacrifice, compassion, Divine Grace, forgiveness, revival, and life" (205). In his book "The Fire and the Rain," Karnad discusses a number of different antinomies and draws attention to the following:

Thus, the phrase Agni Mattu Male, in addition to counterpointing two physical elements that are typically seen as antagonistic, also sets up several other oppositions: between an Indo-Aryan (Sanskrit) and a Dravidian (Kannada) language; between the pan-Indic and the regional points of view; between the classical'marga' and the less exalted 'desi' traditions; between the elevated and the mundane; and possibly even between... (63)

2.3.1 Destructive Energy

In the drama Yavakri, the characters Raibhya and Paravasu are locked in an endless circle of desire, pride, rage, jealously, and murder, and they utilize their spiritual knowledge and strength as weapons in order to get vengeance on one other. These ardent feelings are symbolized by the fire. Nittilai and Arvasu are the ones who put an end to the vicious cycle of emotions because to the humanity and love that they share, which is represented by rain. Shanta Gokhale makes the observation in "Playing with Multiple Meanings" that Nittilai "is totally Karnad's creation. She embodies the elements of nature, care, and unconditional love. (*TheFireand theRain* 32).

The theme of vengeance and fratricide, as well as the pointlessness of superficial knowledge, the fallibility of human nature, and the redemptive power of divine grace, drives the primary conflict of the play. "The Use of Myth in Girish Karnad's The Fire and the Rain," written by Mukesh Ranjan Verma, makes the observation that religious knowledge "without love, compassion, understanding, and humanity can only lead to inflated egos, jealous hearts, and finally all-round destruction..." (182). Raibhya is upset with Yavakri since the latter is responsible for seducing Vishakha, who is his daughter-in-law. In addition to this, he calls upon all of his spiritual resources, known as kritya, in order to exact revenge for the dishonor that has been brought upon his family (The Fire and the Rain 20). Similarly, feelings of jealousy, rage, wrath, and revenge permeate Yavakri and continue to impact him even as he is engaging in his austerities (The Fire and the Rain 22, emphasis added). His spiritual endeavor is driven forward by these factors, which not only render it fruitless and unproductive but also potentially harmful in and of themselves. He describes to Vishakha how, one night when they were in the wilderness, he yelled out at Indra, "This obsession. a hate like this. This poison.... This whole thing is me. I won't contradict anything I've said about myself. I want to learn all I can so that I can be cruel and destructive! ("The Fire and the Rain"). In the play, the major characters are responsible for manipulating spiritual force in order to accomplish their own self-destructive objectives. It is clear that rage, wrath, retribution, and venom are driving Yavakri's words to Vishakha since he says:

It worked out for the best that you conceded. If you hadn't, I would have been forced to use the opportunity to kidnap you.... This is the moment that I have been working for with all of my heart throughout my whole life. I will not let anything to get in the way of its completion. Vishakha, your future father-in-law will pass away. Then, let's watch to see what your spouse decides to do. Will he keep scurrying about in his ritualistic environment like a bandicoot? Or will he perform a heinous act by turning his back on me and facing me? Observe, I am shaking right now. I have worked up a good sweat. Due to the fact that everything has fallen into place perfectly. (23)

2.3.2 Caste Discrimination

The practice of the caste system, which displays the degeneration of religion and the abuse of spiritual powers, is the subject of a critical examination. The concept that a member of a lower caste may defile a Brahmin and the holy places, items, and ceremonies by their appearance, breath, and even their shadow is explicitly depicted in the directions that the Courtier gives to the Actor-Manager. "You may yell out whatever it is that you need to say, but please turn your back on the sacrificial enclosure so that you do not pollute it" (The Fire and the Rain 2, emphasis added). But the hypocrisy of this attitude is brought to light when Paravasu, the Chief Priest of the seven-year-long yaj'a, sneaks out of the sacrificial precincts, goes home at night, and murders his father. He then orders his brother Arvasu to perform the last rites for the deceased man as well as the penitential rites for the murder. Not only does Paravasu conduct sacrilege by desecrating the yaj, but he also commits patricide by betraying his own brother and accusing him of murdering a Brahmin. This is all because of the deed that Paravasu took. Paravasu returns to the sacrifice as if nothing had occurred and claims to be still keeping the ritual's purity, despite the fact that he has committed major and numerous breaches. Raibhya criticizes Paravasu's acts, calling them his "usual insolence," and accuses Paravasu of "deliberately defying the gods!" in his statement. Intentional disregard for the established norms- " (*The Fire and the Rain* 28;29).

In his article "Myth as Symbol: An Interpretation of Girish Karnad's The Fire and the Rain," O.P. Budholia makes the following observation about Girish Karnad's work: "As Karnad binds the varied groups of society together on the basis of emotional integration, he leaves an image of a secular writer" (156). There is a resounding denial of the caste system in Karnad's depiction of Arvasu and Nittilai, which may be found. The point that the play is trying to make is that it is preferable to have a human nature even if it means being an outcast in society as opposed to having a human nature but belonging to a higher caste and being inhuman. Because being human is where a person discovers meaning, purpose, and the deep dimension of life, and it is through these discoveries that a person achieves fulfillment and wholeness in his or her existence. In his article titled "Playing with Multiple Meaning," Gokhale makes the same argument again: "If the brahmins [sic] at the sacrifice define themselves by exclusion, forbidding non-brahmins [sic] entry into the sacrificial enclosure, then Nittilai defines herself by inclusion of everything and everybody into her love" (32). Karnad advocates a spirituality that is not dependent on meaningless religious rites and rituals, ceremonial purity, structures, and outward signs and symbols but rather on true human interaction that is based on equality, love, and justice. He does this by criticizing fossilized religion, its beliefs, and its practices.

2.3.3 Challenges

Vishakha throws a crucial question to Paravasu in an effort to confront him. It is an issue that puts to the test all of humanity's efforts, whether in the religious or secular spheres, to become something more than human. "Will you return to your house after the ritual with the fire has been completed? (No response.) It seems like something that would be too human to do. But why is it that being human is so problematic? What is wrong with being content, like we were until you let Indra get the better of you? (The Fire and the Rain 32). Being a human being, rather than doing great things in one's religious or secular life, is of more priority to Karnad.

Karnad busts the notion that Brahmins, who claim to have sprung from the forehead of Brahma, are meant to think and behave better than those who have emerged from the feet of the Creator. This is because Brahmins claim to have come from the forehead of Brahma. However, the drama portrays the Brahmin characters as engaging in inappropriate behaviors like as lust, jealousy, vengeance, treachery, and murder. When Yavakri finally comes home after 10 years of ascetic practices, he is still consumed by a powerful desire for Vishakhaand he ravages her (*The Fire and the Rain* 14-17). His hostility and resentment for Paravasu and Raibhya are boundless, as is his jealousy of them. (*TheFire and the Rain* 22-23). Yavakri accuses Raibhya of having "grabbed all the honors" that are due to his father Bharadwaja and of having "humiliated" his own father. (*The Fire andthe Rain* 22). Raibhya is so consumed with rage and thirst for retribution that he calls upon the kritya and the Brahma Rakshasa to take the life of Yavakri. (*The Fire and the Rain* 22). Vishakha accuses Raibhya of having passion born of revenge, in addition to envy and rage formed of being humiliated (*The Fire and the Rain,* 32-33). As a result of his own paranoia and rage, Paravasu is the one who ends up killing his own father, Raibhya. After that, he shifts the blame onto his brother Arvasu, betrays his devotion, and ultimately casts him out of the Brahmin home. (*The Fire and the Rain*, 35; 37-38).

As a condition of agreeing to carry out "the penitential rites," (*The Fire and the Rain* 35) Arvasu demonstrates his incapacity to resist the unjust instructions of his older brother Paravasu by committing the murder of their father, which was ordered by Paravasu. Instead, he gives up his claim to live his own life, despite Vishakha's warning about the consequences:

VISHAKHA.Say'No', Arvasu

ARVASU.Sister-in-law-

VISHAKHA.Refuse. He killed his father. Let him at one for it.

Don't get involved in it.

ARVASU.Butthen-what about the sacrifice?

VISHAKHA. Let it go to ruins. Does it matter? There has been enough bloodshed already. Enough tears. Live your own life. (35)

The pleading of Vishakha is reminiscent of the statement made by Inez in Jean-Paul Sartre's novel No Exit, which reads, "You are your life, and nothing else" (45). In the movie "Bali: The Sacrifice," a character named the Mahout has a philosophy that is quite similar to this one: "You've got to take your life in your stride." That is what I am completely certain about" (Bali 116). Arvasu, who was previously unable of asserting his individuality, now takes the proper option and liberates the Brahma Rakshasa from his bondage. Because to Arvasu's action, the whole village is saved from the impending drought and death. As a result, he sustains the natural order, which in turn causes it to rain over the dry region.

In the first act (The Fire and the Rain 9-11), Nittilai seems to be the conduit via which Karnad's logical and analytical perspective on religion and life is communicated. Nittilai offers a critical analysis of the religious information, practices, and experiences that are not beneficial to humankind. The 10 years of self-flagellation, austerities, fasting, meditation, and prayer that Yavakri has endured seem meaningless to her since they have no practical use for humans. Nittilai asks, "What is the point of any knowledge, if you can't save dying children and if you can't predict your moment of death" (The Fire and the Rain 11, Nittilai). She wonders what the point of Yavakri's visit with Indra, the God of Rains, was if Yavakri was unable to "ask for a couple of good showers... That'll revive the earth" (The Fire and the Rain 10, emphasis added).

The significant incident that takes place when Yavakri confesses the pointlessness of all of his ascetic efforts when he was living in the forest for 10 years during act one (The Fire and the Rain 12-16), this encounter takes place between Vishakha and Yavakri. By venting his anger, he has accomplished nothing more than to restate and confirm Nittilai's position. He shared with Vishakha, "The strangest thing however is that I've discovered a corner within me—left untouched by those ten years!" ("The Fire and the Rain"). The narrative that Yavakri provides of his experience both demystifies and deflates the traditional awe that is associated with the attainment of spiritual experiences, wisdom, and abilities via stringent ascetic practices. The following are some of the stunning statements that Yavakri uses to show his skepticism towards his austere existence in the forest:

One could anticipate that seeing the presence of a deity would be a life-changing event. Concrete. Indubitable. Almost on a bodily level. But even though I believe Indra has visited me on several occasions, I can't say for sure. When he initially made his appearance, he told Yavakri that knowledge could not be mastered via the practice of austerities. It can only be gained via experience. Time is equivalent to knowledge. It is an empty place. You are going to have to navigate across these different realms. I responded with, "No, I absolutely need it." Please provide me with complete wisdom. He smiled and told me, 'You are being ridiculous.' That wraps it up! Common discourse. Not extremely deep or meaningful. And when the god vanished, there was nothing that could be found to indicate that he had ever been there to begin with. (13)

But how was it that Yavakri emerged victorious in the end? He woke up one day and for the life of him couldn't explain how he arrived at the notion that he was victorious. "Some knowledge, probably very little wisdom" was all that he was able to achieve in his life. (*The Fire and theRain* 14). And he says to Vishakha, "Now as I sit in front of you, I want to betray Indra—he left me ignorant..."(*TheFireand the Rain* 15).

Karnad allows the conflict between his body and soul to become apparent in the previous scene. It is comparable to the stress that is experienced during *Hayavadana*. On the day that Yavakri determined that his penance was over, he passed out, and when he opened his eyes, the first thing that went through his mind was his encounter with Vishakha 10 years earlier. He then on to tell Vishakha that she "opened the knot of your blouse, pressed my face to your breasts, and then turned and fled...." After ten years, I finally opened my eyes, and I realized that I was starving for that moment. (*The Fire andthe Rain* 14). His efforts of asceticism have not been successful in assisting him in overcoming the bodily desires and compulsions he experiences. He has not changed at all during the last 10 years. Vishakha has the same voracious appetite for language as Yavakri. She addresses him with the following: "What you have done is to revive my urge to converse. I was under the impression that it had ended forever. Gently! "Hurry up and wait"(*TheFireand theRain*14).

2.3.4 Sex or Renunciation

In Karnad's plays, sexual union is often presented as a means toward self-realization, empowerment, personal development, and the acquisition of knowledge. Vishaka had an experience and a sensation of being guided to something mystic and spiritual as a result of her marriage with her husband Paravasu, which is described in "The Fire and the Rain," chapter sixteen. During their conversation, she tells Yavakri, "I'll give you the knowledge that Indra wasn't able to give you." My body—with words, it's light as a feather now" (The Fire and the Rain 17, emphasis added). This facet may be found in the *Hayavadana*, the *Naga-Mandala*, and the Bali. The focus of *Hayavadana* is on the body and the sensations it has. Padmini is drawn to the head of Devadatta, but the body of Kapila is the part of him that really gets her going. During the course of their encounter in the jungle, Padmini extends an invitation to Kapila to revisit his previous body experiences, and in response, he "lifts her up and takes her in" into his home. The remainder of it is explained in the song that the Bhagavata and the Female Chorus sing (*Hayavadana* 58). As long as she has not engaged in any kind of physical union, Rani in *Naga-Mandala* is considered to be an inexperienced and immature individual. After Rani has her first sexual encounter, however, she starts to mature and acquires a greater amount of knowledge and strength. Rani, in her altered state, laments her predicament, saying, "When you brought me here, I was a foolish and ignorant girl." But now that I am a woman, a wife, and about to be a mother, why don't you take it on faith that I have a mind and explain this farce to me? " But now that I am a woman, a wife, and going to be a mother. (*Nāga-Mandala* 32). Similarly, in Bali, the sexual union between the Queen and the Mahout is where she gains access to her inner wisdom. It was the defining moment of her coming to terms with who she was. "And what took place was wonderful; I now feel more whole. Richer.

Warmer' says the Queen (*Bali*119).

Karnad directs Vishakha and Yavakri in opposite directions in order for them to attain the same goals of enlightenment and mystic and spiritual understanding. The method that Yavakri has been using consists of giving up material possessions and submitting his body to severe deprivations and acts of penance. "I made a solemn vow to you ten years ago that I would never even glance at another lady. I kept my word" (*The Fire and the Rain* 12). Vishakha has attained a greater understanding of herself through working inside and through her body. The fact that she admitted to this is important:

He (Paravasu) ushered me into a state of ecstasy that I was not previously familiar with. Heaven, right now and right now, in the forefront of each and every one of my senses. Then, on the first day of the first year of our second year of marriage, he exclaimed, "Enough of that." This is the point at which we begin our search.

He conducted experiments and explorations on both his own and my body while he was doing it. As tools to aid in the investigation. Look for what exactly? I never knew. Nevertheless, I was aware that he was awareAnd I gave in to it. I submitted to having my body inverted in the same manner that he did his own. I received the impression that he was guiding me toward something specific. Mystical? Spiritual? We never chatted. Only the sensation was there in the atmosphere. (16)

In his critique of a life of renunciation and abstinence that is conducted purely for the sake of acquiring knowledge, wisdom, and power, Karnad appears to imply that the only way to acquire genuine inner knowledge and wisdom is by experiencing life in time and place within a secular world, and not by escaping it. Yavakri reveals to Vishakha what Indra had revealed to him: "you cannot master knowledge through austerities." It can only be gained via experience. Time is equivalent to knowledge. It is an empty place. You are going to have to navigate across these realms. (*The Fire and the Rain* 13). In Talé-Danda, Karnad makes the following comment on Jagadeva's perspective on celibacy: "Jagadeva is under the illusion that becoming a Sharana is the same as being a brahmachari." Basavanna was neither a brahmachari, nor was he someone who advocated for abstinence ("Girish Karnad, the Playwright" 134). In other words, the inner knowledge and the holy deep dimension of life can only be obtained and experienced by living and interacting with people and the world, which is a secular reality. This is the only way that this information can be obtained and experienced. It is impossible to overlook the effect that the human body has on the whole person, and Karnad makes it very evident that this is the case in all of his plays, although in a variety of settings. The spirit, also known as the life principle, takes physical form in a body so that it may communicate its essence to the world.

2.3.5 Hope

In a scenario that seems to be absolutely without any glimmer of hope or salvation, Nittilai emerges as the genuine liberator. She interrupts the vicious cycle of violence by requesting that Arvasu accept responsibility for his own life and his choices. Their discussion at this point illuminates Karnad's perspective:

NITTILAI. Leave that [vengeance] to the gods, Arvasu. Consider your family: Yavakri seeks revenge for his father's humiliation by assaulting your sister-in-law; your father seeks revenge for her by murdering Yavakri; your brother seeks revenge for his death; and now you want vengeance for your brother's death.

ARVASU. What should I do? Do the eunuch thing and go sit in a corner with my hands crossed.

NITTILAI. Do that. Better that than become the man you hate.

ARVASU. Become? What am I still capable of becoming? I am an unregenerate sinner in the sight of the world.

NITTILAI. Arvasu, then push that world away. Your hands are sanitized. My spouse has been hurt—betrayed—even by me. You've continued to be excellent. Hold on to it. This world is not required of us. Our own may be found. (44)

Then cast that world away... We have no need for this planet. Strong language is used to convey the meaning that "we can find our own." It is necessary to reject a cultural or religious heritage when it turns a person to "an unregenerate sinner in the eyes of the world." This might happen when certain beliefs or practices are followed. Messages of comparable vehemence may be found in Talé-Danda about the use of violence in the name of religion (29) and in Bali on the worship of murderous deities (98). In Marx's words, it is a "categorical imperative" to topple all relations in which "man is a debased, enslaved, forsaken, despicable being" ("Contribution to the Critique of Hegal'sPhilosophy of Law:

Introduction" 46). Marx wrote these lines in his work "Contribution to the Critique of Hegal's Philosophy of Law." The antidote and alternative to following a rigid religious tradition is exercising one's free will and making their own decisions. In light of all of this, it's possible that Nittilai will be held up as an example. Nittilai is forced to respond with the question "Why do you keep asking me?" since Arvasu is dependent on her to make a choice. Why don't you decide? Please don't put the burden of everything on my shoulders–" (*The Fire and the Rain* 49). However, when the Actor-Manager wants Arvasu to act and practice in public, his deeply ingrained incapacity to make decisions on his own is once again brought to the surface.

Nittilai is forced to meet Arvasu because he continues to attempt to repress his urge to confront his brother Paravasu in order to exact revenge for his treachery. Nittilai's question to Arvasu is, "How long are you going to turn your face away from it then?" Arvasu has been trying to repress this desire for some time. Turning to face your brother like you always intended to...Arvasu, it is not out of malice. In the performance. Show him how good you are. I have no doubt that the play will relieve the worry and the rage. (*The Fire and the Rain* 51). This is Rani's time of trial before the village elders in *Naga-Mandala* (35-39), and now it is Aravasu's turn to confront the truth head-on. Confronting the truth is not a mental arithmetic problem. During the process of addressing trauma, an individual is required to bring all of his or her feelings, emotions, and experiences from the past and get immersed in them by reliving them.

Arvasu finds great solace in the therapeutic benefits of the inset play. On the other hand, the mask that he wears, which is the mask that the demon Vritra wears, seems to have gained command of the whole circumstance. Warning given by the Actor-Manager: "Once you bring a mask to life, you need to maintain tight control over it; otherwise, it will try to take over." It will start to impose its will on you, dictating the conditions. (*The Fire and the Rain*52) comes true. A conclusion quite similar to this one may be found in Bali, where the cock of dough seems to come to life. This is where the psycho-spiritual reality comes to life. It would seem that the mystery surrounding the "powers" and "forces" is having an effect on the Queen. She screams out, "It's alive! It's alive!" The rooster is crowing at the moment. The rooster is crowing! (Everyone erupts in laughter.) The rooster has started to crow! (Bali 123-24). The metaphysical and spiritual actuality of the cock is brought home, however, by the concluding song performed by the Queen. The "powers" and "forces" that make up the psychospiritual universe of reality are symbolically represented by the mask in The Fire and the Rain, the cock in Bali, and the little cobra in *Naga-Mandala*, respectively.

2.3.6 Revelation

The "epiphany," sometimes known as the "revelation of the Divine," that occurs in "The Fire and the Rain" is important. In the instance of Yavakri, his severe penance and practices of asceticism give the impression that they have shown Indra to him, but he is unsure about Indra's physical form. Yavakri provides the following explanation for his experience after seeing Indra: "One would anticipate the manifestation of god to be a shattering event. Concrete. Indubitable. Almost on a bodily level. But even though I believe Indra has visited me on several occasions, I can't say for sure. And when the god vanished, there was nothing that could be found to indicate that he had ever been there. (*The Fire and the Rain* 13). The conversation that Yavakri had with Indra was referred to by Yavakri as a "Common dialogue." Not really all that deep" (*The Fire and the Rain* 13). The majority of believers' anticipations and experiences of God are likely to be comparable to Yavakri's own anticipations and encounters with the Divine. They are unable to understand that God is a spirit, power, or energy that manifests itself in the depths of the human person, in the innermost recesses of his or her existence, which are variously referred to as the heart, the third eye, and the soul. Yavakri is not capable of understanding the spiritual truth and the revelation of it. To the contrary, Arvasu is the one who understands Indra's explanation at the conclusion of the play. This revelation is shown to be effective due to the fact that he feels the activities of the Spirit, the Sacred, or the Divine inside his own soul. In the dramatic rendition of the revelation, Indra is simply audible and not seen onstage. (*The Fire and the Rain* 59). This gives the impression that the epiphany takes place inside the most inaccessible parts of Arvasu's existence. The importance of having genuine encounters with the Divine is emphasized by Kappen in Tradition, Modernity, Counterculture in the following way: "our meeting with the Divine in the here and now is a sham indeed if it does not inspire action that renews the face of the earth, if it does not actively promote the forces of life and love" (57). Following their interaction with Indra, Yavakri and Arvasu behave in ways that are diametrically opposed to one another. Arvasu's activities provide testament to his wish to "stop the tragedy from repeating itself [and] provide the missing sense to our lives-" in contrast to Yavakri's actions, which reflect his "vicious, destructive" ambitions and purpose. (*The Fire and the Rain* 60).

Nittilai's death at the story's conclusion is symbolic of making a personal sacrifice in order to save other people's lives. The concept of self-sacrifice is brought home by Arvasu's action of releasing Nittilai and allowing the Brahma Rakshasa to go free as a result of his actions. Arvasu makes the decision to let time pass, despite the fact that he is interested in retrieving Nittilai for himself. As a result, the land and the people who live there ultimately get rain, which provides new life.

The demolition of the sacrifice tent results in the delivery of food and water to "the weak and hungry villagers" (The Fire and the Rain 57). The way the play comes to a close leaf a lot to the imagination. A religious fire sacrifice that is rigorously organized, soulless, and mechanical is neither as vital nor meaningful as selfless service that is committed to the well-being of others, nor does it fulfill human aims as effectively as does such service.

Arvasu looks up to Nittilai as a role model and strives to be like him. Arvasu explains his decision to "Grant this Brahma Rakshasa his release" by stating that "Nittilai would have wanted it so" (The Fire and the Rain, 61).

Karnad writes in the endnote to the play that the play "culminated, not in some dramatic event, but in a debate on human frailty and divine grace" (The Fire and the Rain 74). Karnad makes this observation in the endnote to the play. Even though Karnad does not come right out and state it, he makes it very clear that divine grace may be seen in the human weakness that Nittilai and Arvasu exhibit. Divine grace is made known and experienced on earth via the humanity and self-sacrifice of Nittilai, as well as through Arvasu's ability to rise above his own self-interests. The human being who is aware of the divine that is inside them is where the sacred may be found. It is in their vulnerability and their humanity.

2.4 BALI: THE SACRIFICE

Karnad has said in previous comments that he read the fable of the Cock of Dough for the first time when he was in his teens. Since that time, he has composed other versions of it, all of which have been presented live on stage. Finally, when he received a commission from Leicester Haymarket Theatre to create a play for them, he completely reworked the play from the ground up. ("Preface," *Bali* 71). Along with his other work, The Dreams of Tipu Sultan, it was released in a single book in the year 2004. The narrative, according to Karnad, has "continued to reveal unexpected meanings with passing years." ("Preface," *Bali* 70). For the purpose of writing this drama, Karnad "drew upon the thirteenth-century Kannada epic, Yashodhara Charite, by Janna." This epic, in turn, got its plot from "an eleventh-century Sanskrit epic by Vadiraja," which in turn got its story from "the ninth-century Sanskrit epic, Yashastilaka, by Somadeva Suri." It has been determined that some aspects of the story date all the way back to the first century" ("Preface," Bali 70). It's interesting to note that with the exception of the Queen, none of the characters have names. The name given to the Queen is Amritamati.

"Plays for Our Times," written by Sudhanva Deshpande, refers to Bali as "a riveting play on violence and non-violence, on tolerance and intolerance, on guilt and culpability, on desire and freedom" (22). It's possible that violence vs non-violence is the play's most prominent topic. The moral and ethical implications of the situation are examined from a variety of angles. As a follower of the Jain religion, the Queen believed that engaging in any kind of violent behavior "meant forfeiting one's moral status as a human being" ("Preface," Bali 69). The Queen Mother, on the other hand, is a devotee of Hinduism, and one of the most important aspects of her religious practice is the sacrifice of animals in the form of an offering to the goddess. These two philosophies are brought head-to-head with one another during the course of the play. The dialectics between these two perspectives will eventually appear to reach a solution in which a small model of the animal made of dough will replace the real animal as the focal point of the discussion. However, even this is not acceptable to the Queen because she believes that it only substitutes real violence with violence in purpose and that it is no less dehumanizing. Moreover, she believes that it is simply a substitute for genuine violence. This is a difficult ethical and moral conundrum, which is something that the play explores in depth.

Karnad dives rather far into what he calls a "solipsistic world," which he describes as "a bleak, guilt-ridden existence with no hope of absolution" ("Preface," Bali 70). This is what the Jain view on violence seems to indicate. During this hunt, there are certain individuals who adhere to old religious traditions. These customs include the offering of animal sacrifices in order to appease the murderous goddess. Others adhere to the idea that they should conduct their life in accordance with ideas that are logical, secular, ethical, and moral. These highlight the two different worldviews that are presented throughout the play. The latter is symbolized by the twenty-four Saviours, who are also referred to as tirthankaras. T.K. Tukol, in his book Compendium of Jainism, makes the following observation about the thirthankaras: "Tirthankaras are among those who have attained omniscience and perfection," and the Jains "worship them because they are liberated souls... They were mortals; they looked to no higher being but looked within themselves" (67).

The fact that Karnad chose these two different faiths systems on purpose is crucial. People look up to the bloodthirsty goddess as a higher being, one that must be appeased on a regular basis and on whom their well-being depends. However, the human model of the twenty-four tirthankaras does not cause people to look up to a higher being that they must appease and on whom they must depend for their well-being. The path to salvation in Jainism is laid out in a complex manner, consisting of a series of activities and phases. In their book, The Archetypal Actions of Ritual: A Theory of Ritual Illustrated by the Jain Rite of Worship, Caroline Humphrey and James Lalidlaw contend that "Jainism in a sense rejects mystery." Despite this assertion, the authors place a strong focus on a central mystery that they describe as "the destiny of the human soul" (7). According to T. G. Kalghatgi, who explains the Jaina view of life in Jaina View of Life, the destination of the soul is "the liberation of the soul from the cycle of birth and death" (46). In this particular view of how things operate, the duty of ensuring one's own salvation falls squarely on the shoulders of the individual person. The Queen is a Jain, and as such, she adheres to the belief that there are twenty-four Saviours (Bali 81).

"It's dawn" is said toward the conclusion of the play, which starts in the dark (Bali 74; 124). The message can be understood. The soul and the planet, which were previously engulfed in darkness and death, have now emerged into the light and are filled with vitality. How did it all happen? The critical attitude that Karnad takes to reified religious rituals may be found in this work.

The piece transports us to a period when the King practiced a kind of the "violent" religion practiced by the Queen Mother. at the flashback, both the King and the Queen are shown as little children, and at this time the King kills a bird with a stone (Bali 91-92). Because of the surprised and pained response of the Queen to the blood and death of the bird, the King is transformed (Bali 92), and he eventually becomes a Jain.

The central idea of the play is presented in the first few lyrics, which are taken from the Queen Song. Karnad presents a song that explores the dichotomies of life and death, darkness and light, and violent acts and nonviolent actions. He positions them within the framework of religious traditions, including both beliefs and behaviors. And the location is the human soul, which is partitioned into two parallel worlds on an equal level. The world of the bloodthirsty goddess is the one where "the spirits that adore / the blood and gore" reside. It is the domain where bloodshed, gloom, and death reign supreme. The spirits who command "you pause before you use the knife..." are the ones that rule over the other world, which is referred to in Bali's chapter 73. This is the region in which there is no violence, just light and life. The first one was given to the Queen Mother, while the second one was given to the Queen herself. The King, who previously renounced his devotion to the murderous goddess who was the Queen Mother, has now shown his allegiance to the Saviours of the Queen. As a result of the King's conversion to a different religion and faith, Shalini Umachandran observes that the King "is now torn between guilt and confusion about the right path" (6).

The drama is brought to a close by the Queen's song, which provides a synopsis of the dialectics between the two spheres, one of which is "hidden in the shade" and the other of which is "lit up by the sun":

"Theorb in the shade
Opens itself to the light

And warmth of the sun.

Night gives into day.

Death yields to life. (124-25)

This dynamic between death and life, as well as between darkness and light, will persist throughout the whole of a person's existence. A constant fact is that the cock is the emblem of such a world, combining the blackness of the night with the brightness of the morning. As a result, "throughout our lives," as Bali puts it, "we hear the cock crow" (125). But the difficulty and purpose of the human being is not in striving to eradicate such an interplay of forces; rather, it is in seeking to remain perpetually open "to the light / And warmth of the sun" (Bali 124). This is the goal of the human being. At the end of the play, the audience is extended an invitation to liberate themselves from the more negative parts of the soul, religion, and life by continually purifying themselves. In this particular procedure, the twenty-four Tirthankaras are looked up to as examples to follow. The way that Karnad appears to approach religion and life seems to reflect the Jain concept of God, self, and freedom, as is stated by Tukol in Compendium of Jainism:

They do not believe that the existence of God is required in order to comprehend the cosmos. Every single soul has a divine essence and has the potential to realize its full potential. The idea of God in Jaina philosophy refers to the divinity that is inside each individual. The growth of unwavering faith, accurate perception, flawless knowledge, and an impeccable character are the means by which man might realize the same. Man has complete freedom, and there is nothing that can come in the way of the natural consequences of his actions. This ideology is not going to appeal to those with feeble brains. When people are experiencing hardships, they often seek to a heavenly force in the hopes that this power would help them in their struggles and relieve them of their pain. They pray for blessings and gifts, but they forget that they are the authors of their own destiny and that they are responsible for both the happiness and the suffering that they experience in their lives. (65-66)

In the play, the characters do not behave as themselves but rather as representations of larger groups. They adhere to a variety of contrasting theological and philosophical tenets. The Queen Mother embodies a religious belief, while Her Majesty, Queen Elizabeth II, is the embodiment of a secular philosophy. The King is a Seeker, and he is a metaphor for individuals who are stuck between the two philosophies and are often pulled between them. In this context, it is essential to have an understanding of the essence of monarchy according to the Jain tradition, as well as the Vaisnava and Saiva traditions of Hinduism. According to John E. Cort in his article "Who is a King?"Whereas Vaisnavas and Sivas viewed the cakravartin as an emanation of the divine, the Jains saw the cakravartin as less than fully divine," is how the distinction is explained in "Jain Narratives of Kingship in Medieval Western India." In spite of this, the Jain cakravartin was making progress toward divinity, which, in the context of the Jain religion, refers to enlightenment and freedom" (101-02). People on Bali who are making the shift from a life centered on religion to a life centered on society are symbolized by the King.

The Mahout is a multifaceted being that embodies many distinct facets of existence. He is symbolic of sensuality, mystical moments, the inner voice, individuals who trust in the supernatural, and those who support the underdog. The Queen refers to the Mahout as "the moment" in both 119 and 123 of the books. Therefore, the meeting between the Queen and the Mahout might be seen as a meeting with an illuminating moment. She claims that the experience has made her feel more satisfied. Richer. Warmer. But I am not embarrassed. Because I didn't plan it. It came to pass. And the scene was quite lovely" (Bali 119). The Queen is concerned that the rite of sacrificing the cock of dough would diminish the quality of her pleasure. She informs the King that "if this rite is going to blot the moment out," then would be the "real betrayal." I'll do anything else" (Bali 199). The Queen would want everyone to concentrate on the here and now. She informs the King, "He has already left. The opportunity is passed" (Bali 123). The King is so immersed in the past that he has lost touch with the here and now. This causes him to go through hardship. On the other hand, the Queen has completely let go of the past and now focuses on living in the here and now, savoring the fruits of the experiences she has had in the past.

In the Mahout's explanation of his deity and the way he interacts with him, there is an air of self-deprecating humor that can be perceived. The Mahout describes his deity as "A stone" (Bali 81), which describes something that has been raised up by the hanging roots of a very large banyan tree. "He [god] meant everything to be as it is, you see," he adds, referring to occasions when he challenges God about his unattractive look as well as times when he feels "sad," "lost," and "upset" (Bali 81). The following philosophical rant sheds light on human nature:

However, since I am a human being, I must inquire, "Why have you made me so ugly?" Why not be gorgeous, like the person in charge of the military? What about the king? Why are you so ugly? So, God addresses the situation by asking, "Are they making fun of you?" I say: 'No, not any longer. Not after I punched the teeth out of a handful of those other guys!' God responds with the statement, "Well, I gave you the strength to do it."

Didn't I?' Therefore, I contend, "But what a gorgeous face! If I had one, I wouldn't have to use these muscles to silence them; I would just use my voice!' So, God asks, "Would you give up your voice in exchange for a beautiful appearance?" That puts me in the appropriate position. However, God already knows my response before I give it. To which I respond, "No, I wouldn't," and God then asks, "Why not leave it at that?" (81)

It is an active pursuit for the sake of a higher cause. In addition to that, it is a humanistic method of understanding an impossible obstacle and finding a solution to deal with it.

The Mahout makes many allusions to an ungodly circumstance throughout his speech. Putting into question the decision of the Queen Mother to visit the damaged temple in the middle of the night, he says, "I mean, why here? Temple that has fallen into disrepair. The majority of people would believe that it is malevolent and haunted" (Bali 83). He refers to the location where they have had sexual encounters by stating that "this is the inner sanctum" (Bali 83). After that, he proclaims, "We know there is no image of God here" (Bali 84), and then a little while later, he yells, "Sin in the inner sanctum" (Bali 85). These remarks are presented in descending order of relevance. There is more to the meaning of the phrase "God's image" than meets the eye. In addition to the meaning "idol" of God, it may also signify "likeness" or "presence" of God. It refers to a scenario in which there is no god.

Interactions between the King, the Queen, and the Queen Mother (Bali 95-98) are when the conflict between the two religions, that of the Queen and that of the Queen Mother, reaches a fever pitch. This portrayal of the King shows him to be someone who is receptive to shifting perspectives and fresh insights into the truth. This is a reality that is recognized by the Queen, who states that "Because of me, you deserted her faith—her Mother Goddess" (Bali 95). The King's way of thinking is forward-thinking, and he takes responsibility for his life by making well-informed decisions that will improve the quality of his experience. On the other side, the Queen Mother is resistant to change, but she does so as an exercise of her independence and by making the independent decision to maintain her traditional religious set-up and religion. It is her choice to leave the palace, despite the fact that she is under pressure from her family to stop sacrificing animals. However, her decision was not made in response to the pressure from her family.

An Introduction to the Philosophy of Religion by Brian Davis makes the claim that "the reasonableness of belief in God can be defended not with reference to argument but with reference to experience..." (64). These kinds of encounters with God may provide light on the Divine not necessarily in the form of a particular deity but rather as a force or spirit that is seen to be sacred. The Mahout has a religious faith. He is a believer in forces that "can eat into" a person if they toy "with these things, these forces" (Bali 122); he is also a believer in the existence of gods. The Mahout is analogous to the King in the sense that they both acknowledge that they do not know all there is to know about the world. It's possible that there are powers or forces that we are completely unaware of" (Bali 113). Because of the nature of the events they have seen, neither the King nor the Mahout are able to "name" the power or force that they have witnessed. During their discussion to find a solution to their dilemma, the King brings up one of these experiences, and the Queen agrees with him:

KING. How do we face the problem . . .

(*Helooks at thecock.*)

...withoutthis?

QUEEN.How will it help?

KING. I don't know. But I have a feeling . . . it will. QUEEN. How?

KING. I don't know. But when I was waiting outside, lost . . .

Adrift . . . sunk in misery . . . Mother brought the offering. I

looked at it and I felt better.

(*Pause.*)

I felt help was on its way. (*Pause.*)

It sorts of signalled to me. (*Pause.*)

I could feel their assurance. Don't keep questioning, it said, surrender. (112)

James makes the observation in The Varieties of Religious Experience that people of all faiths have the belief that the "MORE" or the Sacred "acts as well as exists, and that something really is affected for the better when you throw your life into its hands." (499).This action requires a modest acceptance of the truth that we do not know all there is to know about this world; that this global spirit, force, or energy is a cryptic mystery; and that in this matter, we need to let our experiences direct us.

However, the Queen's position is consistent with the Jain belief system. In The Archetypal Actions of Ritual, Humphrey and Lalidlaw make the argument that "The Jains... provide a clear illustration of how meanings are not found in rituals, but must be given to them." (7). A religious rite does not provide the Queen with an answer to their predicament, despite her best efforts. The Queen issues a challenge to the King, saying, "Blood is at least understandable if you believe in gods that are thirsty for human blood." However, however... You can't willfully deceive oneself in any way" (Bali 111). She is looking for a way to find a solution that has greater depth. The directive from the Queen is as follows: "We'll tackle it together. But not in this (the temple) location. At one's own residence" (Bali 111). The Queen persuades the King to work out their solution in accordance with the concept of karma, which, in T. G. Kalghatgi's definition, is "to find a solution on the basis of the autonomous nature of man and his responsibility to shape his own destiny" (Jaina View of Life 106). The Queen succeeds in persuading the King to work out their solution in accordance with the doctrine of karma.

The King recognizes the same psycho-spiritual truth in the telling of his dream (Bali 106). The King constructs the event as a dream, despite the fact that it never really took place. This accomplishes two different goals. In the first place, the King has to provide an explanation for why he is still around the wrecked temple at midnight in order to avoid his mother's scrutiny. Second, the king feels the need to release some of the stress that has been building up inside of him, and he decides that telling the narrative of his dream would be the best way to do so. According to Bali 104, the Queen Mother believes that the supernatural agencies communicate with her via the medium of her dreams, hence it is imperative that she pay attention to them. Dreams have the ability to be meaningful and illuminating, and it's important to figure out what they mean. The Queen is not pleased with the way in which the Queen Mother interprets the King's dream from her own religious perspective, since this is not acceptable to the Queen.

The King is a person who is always looking for new things and is dedicated to discovering and experiencing the truth in his everyday life. But he is torn between two schools of thought: one that is theistic and, as a result, is predicated mostly on faith, and the other that is non-theistic and, as a result, is predicated primarily on reason. In point of fact, this represents the atmosphere of the current day. The King and Queen's lives had undergone a transformation by the time the first flashback takes place (between the years 89 and 92 in Bali), and this shift is shown by the juxtaposition of the King and Queen's childhood innocence and their adult experiences. He becomes more sensitive to the reality and nature of violence as a result of the brutal but unintentional death of the bird by the King as well as the reaction of the Queen to this act. It signals his enlightenment. He states, "I accepted the faith because I found truth in it and compassion for the world while it was in pain." I don't want to make things any worse for you. "I will not permit anyone else to carry out this task" (Bali 98). The prior childlike naivety of the Queen has been outgrown, and the current Queen is sophisticated and cunning in her approach to accomplishing her objectives.

The Queen and the Queen Mother are both under the King's protection at all times. While he is conversing with one of them, he defends the other from an unjust attack. He provides an interpretation that is kind and understanding of each person's worldview, beliefs, and tradition. As a result, he avoids a violent clash and works toward establishing a peaceful synthesis of the two perspectives as well as co-existing with each other. Despite this, he is conflicted between these two points of view. The human attempt to create a feasible synthesis of two different worlds of competing traditions is epitomized by the act of adopting a new religion but at the same time not being prepared to give up the old faith fully. And the discovery of fresh synthesis in each new situation will bring about a higher perfection in human beings as well as a renewal of their interaction with one another and the planet.

This change is not going to be simple. It is a process that continues to happen in the thoughts and deeds of the King, who continues to battle and suffer in order to establish a synthesis. This is a dialectical process. This conflict is made abundantly obvious by the play's concluding number, which is the Queen's song:

And through the days,
through endless rainy nights
throughout our lives we hear the cock crow. (125)

In the book "A Dictionary of Symbols" by J. E. Cirlot, the cock is referred to as the "bird of the dawn." The cock is representative of the light, which drives away darkness, as well as alertness and activity (51). The light of day triumphs over the darkness. However, as the day draws to a close, light gives way to darkness. This terrible process of the dialectics between the forces of light and dark is an ongoing interaction that is a never-ending process. The cock is a constant reminder of light and life, as well as the process of the painful interplay between the forces of light and dark.

The last song performed by Queen drives home the metaphysical and spiritual truth that is symbolized by the cock. The cock is the ever-present presence of a painful tension and the search for an ethical and moral answer to the problem of violence. The "two orbs- / one lit up by the sun, / the other, hid in the shade" will continue to exist in human existence; nevertheless, in order for "the orb in the shade / to open itself to the light / And warmth of the sun" (Bali 124), it is required that "the orb in the shade / opens itself to the light" (Bali 124).

Every tradition, regardless of whether it is religious or secular, has to be examined critically and cleansed of any components that are inhumanizing, anti-life, or otherwise negate life. The Queen personifies a self-reflective and analytical awareness. She does not approve of sacrificing either humans or animals. In reference to the practice of offering sacrifices that has been passed down through the King's family for generations, the Queen inquires, "Were not human beings also offered as sacrifices to the goddess at one time?" In his defense, the King replies, "Yes. However, it was many years or maybe centuries ago." The Queen retorts by saying, "So you see, tradition does not need to be followed." Or at the very least altered." (Bali 96), which points to the need of purging any tradition of the dehumanizing aspects that it contains.

Once more evocative is the alias "Kmalatsurasundari" (Bali 76), which the Queen was known as throughout her reign. When divided into its component parts, the name reveals four names, the meanings of which are as follows: desire (kma), creeper (lat), demon (asura), and a lovely woman (sundari). There are several possible interpretations that may be given to the symbolic meaning of the name. It incorporates both the lighter and the darker components. In the same way, her true name, which is "Amritamati" (Bali 87), may be broken down into amrit and mati. Amrit is the immortality-granting beverage of the gods, and whomever consumes it will live forever. According to an observation made by Tukol in the Compendium of Jainism, in the religion of Jainism, "Mati jnana and Sruta jnana fall under the category of indirect knowledge as they are derived through the mediation of the senses and the mind." since a result, "Mati Jnana is that knowledge which is obtained through the senses..." (95; 111). Therefore, one who seeks to achieve immortality by "knowledge that is obtained through the senses" or through the body might be seen as practicing Amritamati.

The Queen seems to be touched by the mystery of the "powers" and "forces" at the conclusion of the play, when their united effort to sacrifice the cock of dough fails (Bali 123), since both the King and the Queen hear the cock crowing. She screams, "It's alive! It's alive!" The rooster is crowing at the moment. The rooster has begun to crow!... The rooster has begun to crow! He makes an attempt to impart some grain onto the cock of dough (Bali 123-24). The acts of the Queen convey the appearance that she has given in to a hopeless position under immense pressure from the King to undertake the sacrifice, which goes against her religion and belief as a Jain. This is because the sacrifice is against her faith and conviction in Jainism. When she continues to disobey the King's command, he yells at her, "Have you gone mad? It is not a living thing! It's a ball of dough! (Bali 124). After the King flattens the cock of dough, she casts a venomous glance in his direction, grabs the sword, and dashes forward to stab him. Suddenly, she comes to a halt and looks at the blade, shocked by what she sees. When they heard the cock crow once again, the King was taken aback and looked out the window. At that moment, the queen stabbed the sword into her womb and then fell into the King's arms (Bali 124).

The activities taken by the Queen are really fascinating to see. Why does she speak "as to a child" in this manner? (Bali 124). Why did she choose to end her own life? At this point in the performance, the stage direction provided by Karnad contributes to the play's complex ambiguity by saying, "It's daybreak. The Queen is illuminated by a shaft of light" (Bali 124). Is it possible that the Queen has made her way from the shadows into the light, signifying that she has attained freedom? Is it possible that the "powers" and the "forces" that compelled the Queen to end her life on her own were able to possess her? Or has the realization occurred to her that she has lost her "moral status as a human being" as a result of her acceptance to the sacrifice (Bali 123), as well as her attempt to stab the King (124), in the story? ("Preface," Bali 69). Even if the Jain doctrine of sallekhana leaves the conclusion open to interpretation, it is challenging to comprehend the Queen's behavior as an example of sallekhana. In the Compendium of Jainism, Tukol makes the following observation:

When Sallekhana is approaching death and a normal life, as prescribed by religion, is no longer possible because of old age, [sic] incurable disease, or severe famine, he should submit to all of his passions, give up all worldly attachments, practice all austerities, gradually abstain from food and water, and lie down quietly to meditate on the true nature of himself until the soul separates from the body. (275)

Karnad, in the process of analyzing religion in this play, performs a delicate balancing act between the people's desire to express their faith and belief in and through rites and rituals and the people's need to be cautious not to imbue such expressions with the ability to govern their lives and their fate. In other words, Karnad tries to strike a balance between these two competing needs.

It's possible that Karnad is trying to get across the idea that taking a logical approach to life isn't everything in this play. There are enigmatic facets of one's existence that must be treated seriously in order to be understood. This kind of psychological and spiritual reality defies explanation and continues to have a significant impact on human existence. However, it is possible that they are not necessarily considered to be religious events in the traditional sense, where gods and goddesses are involved. On the other hand, it is a manifestation of the meta-rational. Reason may be able to explain some aspects of existence; nevertheless, faith is the only thing that can grasp and make sense of the aspects of life that are incomprehensible to human reason. And Karnad accords equal weight to one's use of reason as well as faith.

CHAPTER - 3

ROLES OF CULTURE AND SYMBOLS USED IN GIRISH KARNAD'S PLAYS

3.1 GIRISH KARNAD'S PLAYS: A BIRD'S EYE VIEW

One of India's most well-known playwrights is Girish Karnad. He performs in the Kannada theater. His plays communicate a good and recognizable Western intellectual sense while having roots in Indian mythology and history. The existential crisis of the modern man is expressed by well-known individuals who are deeply involved in philosophical and intellectual arguments. According to Kannada theatrical scholar Laxmi Chandrashekhar, Karnad has been charged of going backwards. However, the majority of modern writing uses mythology to universalize and justify human experience. Additionally, I think Karnad has succeeded in doing this.

With the publication of Yayati in 1961 and, more significantly, Tughlaq in 1964, Karnad's reputation as a playwright was solidified. This led to the publication of *Hayavadana* in 1971, Angumalige in 1977, HittinaHunja in 1980, *Naga-Mandala* in 1988, and Tale-Danda in 1990, and Agni Mattu Male in 1991. (1995). The native language of India, Hindi, has been included in translations of all eight of Karnad's plays, which were originally written in the Kannada language. Five of his plays have been translated into English: The Fire and the Rain, Tale-Danda, *Naga-Mandala,* and Tughlaq. The last two were released by Ravi Dayal Publishers in New Delhi, while the first three were published in India by Oxford University Press.

Yayati, Karnad's first drama, won the Mysore State Award in 1962 after being written in 1961. It offers an existentialist interpretation of the idea of obligation design. It is based on a passage from the Mahabharata when Sukracharya, the father-in-law of Yayati, who is furious about Yayati's adultery, curses Yayati with premature aging. Yayati is one of the progenitors of the Pandavas. Yayati may be able to lift the curse if someone was prepared to trade their youth with him. His son Puru is ultimately in charge of carrying out this mission for his father. The play discusses the problems caused by Puru's decision and the problems it causes Yayati, Puru, and Puru's younger spouse, Positive Many Meanings. The characters experience the dried-up remains of history again, and the storyline and the pages are correspondingly changed.

Karnad received the Kamaladevi Award from the BharatiyaNatyaSangh in 1972 for his third play, *Hayavadana*. Its plot is based on the Katha Saritsagar tale, which Thomas Mann used as the basis for his short story collection The Transposed Heads. It's a spoof of trying to figure out who you are on a world full of entanglements. Devadatta, the "intellectual," and Kapila, the "male of body," are very close friends. Devadatta marries Padmini, the most beautiful woman in Dharampura. Kapila and Padmini start to feel attracted to one another. The two friends kill themselves. In a hilarious and dramatic moment, Padmini flips their heads, giving Devadatta what she needs both Kapila and KapilaDevadatta's bodies! It creates identity uncertainty, exposing the murky nature of human nature. The difficulty of the problem increases. They duel and then kill each other once more. Sati is practiced by Padmini. The play's plot is very important in terms of comedy and sarcasm. *Hayavadana*'s (the horseman's) search for fulfillment comes to an amusing and depressing finish. He grows into a full-grown horse, but the man's voice accompanies him all the way! The German production was directed by Vijaya Mehta utilizing material from the DeutschesNationaltheater in Weimar.

Based on two Kannada folktales that Girish Karnad learnt from A. K. Ramanujan, *Naga-Mandala* is a work of fiction. It was created by the LeipzigerSchauspielhaus in Berlin and Leipzig for the 1992 Festival of India in Germany under the direction of Vijay Mehta. It was presented at the Faculty Theatre in Chicago and subsequently at the Gutherie Theatre in Minneapolis as part of the celebrations for it's 30th anniversary in 1993. Karnad initially released *Naga-Mandala* in Kannada before translating it into English. He asserts that two dental anecdotes from Karnataka that I first read from Prof. A. K. Ramanujan a few years ago are the inspiration for *Naga-Mandala.*

3.2 GIRISH KARNAD'S PLAYS: THE MARVELOUS, MIRACULOUS, AND UNCANNY

The Marvelous, the Miraculous, and the Uncanny are often viewed as magical phenomena and events, or brilliantly described creative mind excursions manufactured by unrefined people for their comfort despite the puzzling nature of ordinary miracles. They do, however, refer to the collective blindness to humanity, which was proposed by Carl Jung. In point of fact, these ideas continue to have a significant influence on our lives, despite the fact that those lives are increasingly being formed by our lifestyles. They have a significant influence on the way we go about our daily lives. The things that we consider to be beautiful and extraordinary may not always indicate the same thing, but they do shed light on the elements of our life that are more obvious and indisputably indicative of the truth. It is a common viewpoint that hypotheses are dependent on concepts in the same way that concepts are dependent on speculations. This is due to the fact that if hypotheses illuminate concepts, then concepts should validate the need to investigate speculations. A few controls have made an effort, using a variety of approaches, to dissect the fantastic, incomprehensible, and eerie in order to determine what it ought to be, a main motivator for it, how it operates, and what its motivation is. The label "myth" places a significant number of limitations on these ideas. It is stated that the elements that make up the spectacular and remarkable have an appearance that is comparable to the elements that make up myths. The following are a few examples that demonstrate how these ideas are connected to one another in a congenial manner. The influential English anthropologist E. B. Tylor is of the opinion that myth and science are incompatible with one another. According to him, myths can't be erroneous or dated since they provide the creator of the tale a reason to give significance to everyday occurrences and cycles, hence myths can't be incorrect or dated. There is an element of uncertainty around the meaning of myths due to the fact that individual causes cannot be predicted nor verified. In this way, it is possible for it to be consistent with the wonderful as well as the astonishing and the weird. The quality of being inexplicable does not always mean that anything is unbelievable. On the other hand, it represents a form of reality that existed in the parts of our environment that we were a part of. It is standard practice to use the adjectives "magnificent" and "uncanny" when attempting to describe something that cannot be explained and does not exist. However, this is in no way an accurate representation of the situation. A cursory examination will unmistakably lead us to the conclusion that this describes the current state of affairs. We had a hunch that many things that were previously incomprehensible to us are now well within our reach, and this confirmed our suspicions.

According to the findings of scholar Bronislaw Malinowsky, ancient people used myth as a means of adjusting to parts of life that were beyond their control, such as the onset of old age, the passing of time, and natural calamities. On the other hand, according to Mircea Eliade, a myth is not only an explanation but also the conventional kind of amusement that it provides in the form of a narrative. As a consequence of this, the real reason underlying myth is experiential: the want to have an encounter with paradise. According to Robert A. Segal's explanation, Sigmund Freud thinks that "myth so forms a compromise between the half of oneself that needs the appetites met inside and out and the side that would even not like to realize that they exist." According to Freud, the capacity of myth is based on its significance. Myth has capacity because it creates a tale in which oedipal impulses are symbolically sanctioned. This story then unleashes oedipal desires. Myth, in the words of Sigmund Freud, is an experienced phenomenon, and the act of calming one's mind with magnificent and miraculous occurrences is similar. They have a continuous conversation on the difference between authentic and fraudulent information. In Freud's words, the eerie "gets its horror not from something somewhat alien or mysterious but rather, surprisingly, from something weirdly identifiable that overcomes our efforts to distance ourselves from it" (Morris). This is according to Freud's explanation of the phenomenon. Freud addresses how a writer might induce an eerie sense in the reader by walking a fine line between truth and illusion while yet maintaining the authenticity of the tale. In The Fantastic, Todorov makes a concerted effort to differentiate his structuralist approach to dealing with this class from Freudian psychoanalysis. Regardless, he agrees with many of Freud's conclusions, particularly in attributing artistic dread to the implosion of the clairvoyant limits of self and other, life and death, and reality and illusion. The realm of literature has always been home to a remarkable collection of myths and legends. They provide creative journalists with a never-ending supply of ideas and concepts to work with. Jung believed that myths were manifestations of early-stage images that existed inside the collective unconscious and were unknown to man. First and foremost, man has been through a variety of experiences, and his memory contains mental representations of those experiences. They are referred to as models of aggregate obviousness since they are the pictures that are considered to be the most significant.

3.3 INDETERMINACY, INVISIBILITY, SILENCE AND ABSENCE IN GIRISH KARNAD'S PLAYS

Existential concerns are a recurring theme in Karnad's playwriting. He is concerned with topics such as presence, the quest for equality, the search for individuality, as well as detachment and disillusionment. Existentialism asserts that humanism recognizes the inherent value of man. Karnad constructs a cosmos inhabited by humans and investigates the indeterminacy, invisibility, quiet, and absence of these individuals by placing them in a variety of settings. When the characters are reduced to their essence, the stillness that is inside them is powerfully communicated. We pick up on their silence, which most likely indicates the assumptions they are making. They are sometimes unable of choosing things for themselves. As a consequence of this, indeterminacy takes on the role of a god-like presence in the plays that he has written. These components may be found in almost all of the plays. In his plays, he often portrays contemporary sociopolitical and societal concerns by using myths, legends, and historical events. In his plays, he explores a variety of topics, including caste, heredity, religion, and sexuality. The characters respond to the hardships of the modern world by describing the challenging lifestyles they lead. It is irrelevant if the character is a man or a woman. Both have issues inside themselves, including differences in preferences, presumptions, and judgements. We have some information that sheds light on whether or not the character's actions shape their destiny or if fate is predestined. Regardless, the protagonists in his plays are genuinely constrained by a number of different planned circumstances. They encounter a wide range of challenges and feelings along the way. This is an honest effort to demonstrate how these individuals rationalize their indeterminacy, invisibility, quiet, and absence in a variety of circumstances and occurrences. Through the use of a secondary figure under the name of Bhagirathi, Tale-Danda highlights the unpredictability and quiet terror.

"Bhagirathi: Why is it that Basavanna can't look at things from a different perspective? The story goes the same way in each and every one of the Kalyan homes. A battle between the father, the son, and the brothers.

Bhagirathi, Amba's next-door neighbor, reprimands Basavanna for exerting his influence on youngsters in Kalayan. Basavanna was speaking Kalayan at the time. As a result of Basavanna's influence, an increasing number of young people are rejecting their castes and transitioning into Sharnas. The Sharnas are optimistic about the possibility of a society without castes. This type of thinking is very forward-thinking. The children have acquired emotions of indifference and carelessness toward the adults who are responsible for their care. They have been avoiding the obligations that come with having family members in their lives. As a direct consequence of this, every house in Kalayan has an unsettling effect and an absence of harmony. There are real disagreements and conflicts of opinion present in each and every Kalyan family unit. Basavanna is the one who is responsible for this. Then, during a talk with Jagdeva, Mallibomma discloses his repressed fear as well as his frustration with the absence of compassion in what seems to be upper-class society.

"Don't act like such a fool, Mallibomma. The first thing I should have done was turn around and go back up Brahmin Street. I take it you'd prefer for me to step foot inside your house? Thank you, but no."

Mallibomma has some reservations about going on a walk down Brahmin Street. How was it even possible for such an inaccessible person to enter his house? These words provide light on the inherent caste system that is present in Indian society and cannot be eliminated. The individuals that make up a civilization are unable to control their own destinies. Their ideas are dominated by emptiness and a sense of absence in their heads. Bhagirathi, you are in the company of Brahmins here. If you wouldn't mind taking a step to the side, the ladies of the home would appreciate it if they had more space to walk about in. What are we going to do if you come up at our house looking like a chieftain from the middle Ages?"

After a significant amount of time has passed, Jagadevareemerges. In addition to that, Mallibomma, who treats leather, comes along for the ride. He is fully aware of the low standing he has in society. since a consequence of this, he feels wary while strolling about the city, since this activity is designated for Brahmins. However, Jagadeva insists that he enter his house, and he is unsure whether or not he would comply with this demand. Both Jagadeva and Mallibomma have left their castes in order to become Sharanas. Sharanas are intellectuals who live in a world without castes and are worshippers of Lord Shiva. Bhagirathi objects to Mallibomma's entry into their house on the grounds that the Brahmins live there. She implores him to take a step back so that the ladies of the home may walk about unhindered and tend to the myriad of household chores that need to be done. If Mallibomma continues to stand resolutely at the entrance like a feudal king, then they won't be able to do anything. Because Amba's son Jagadeva won't come in the home until he sees his father already there, Amba begs Mallibomma to come with her so that she may be escorted inside. When he finally goes, her home will almost certainly be cleaned up after he's gone. On a deeper level, Rambhavati asserts that Basavanna is determined, but she does not think that he is dishonest. She believes that he is determined. During that point in the conversation with King Bijjalla, she adopts a new posture in response to his questions. The King's inconsiderate behavioraggravates her. She is very evasive in order to maintain control over Basavanna. She explains to King Bijjala that the king's ridiculous and extravagant obsession with Basavanna has left her bewildered.

"Rambhavati, I don't understand why you are so fixated on that certain person. Instead of smearing his reputation in public, he makes fun of your kid in front of everyone, and you invite him into the more private part of the building?

King Bijjala points the finger of blame at Basavanna as the one responsible for his departure from the palace. On a typical, upbeat day, one does not often come across him. The King and the Treasurer are said to have a contentious relationship, and this rumor is now making the rounds. The King tells him that he has composed and performed melodies critical of his reign in Sharana gatherings. The tunes have been sung by him. In spite of all that has happened, he has neither punished him nor insisted that he turn up the keys. The King has put Basavanna in the position of having to answer to him. To tell you the truth, only Basavanna is aware of the significance of the actions he does, whilst everyone else is living in complete obscurity. During the succeeding lecture, he tries to provide some clarity on the matter.

"Basavanna: Sir, I hope you understand where I'm coming from. I don't work at the Treasury in order to win favor with the King; rather, I do so due to the fact that the money belongs to the people, and the King only has a legal claim to it. However, other members of the royal family are not authorized to see it in any capacity.

The fact that Basavanna, who places a high premium on trust, has been insulted prompted him to reply by apologizing to the Treasurer's office for the King's failure to be pleased. It was his obligation to the community that pushed him to make the trip to the Treasurer's office. Individuals are eligible to receive benefits from the riches of the Royal Treasury. It is not possible to spend this money for the personal costs of the well-known family. The King is in charge of the Treasury, and as such, he has certain privileges over it since he acts as the gatekeeper for people. It is very forbidden for any other member of the Royal family to enter or investigate it. When everything is taken into account, it becomes abundantly plain to everyone else. Basavanna is sure that there are obligations that come along with holding the title of Yuvraj. Yuvraj is a phrase that suggests that the conveyor of whatever it is refers to should be able to release certain responsibilities. It is also possible that the renowned family and members of the general public will not notice this item. In the meanwhile, the mystery has been unraveled. Appanna, who is Rani's real husband, finds out that she is going to have a kid. As a direct consequence of this, he experiences growing indignation. To put it mildly, he does not understand what is going on. At the moment, he needs the assistance of the elderly residents of the town so that they may act as judges. In the context of this discussion, the idea of "taking ordeal" seems like something out of a dream. The answer that Rani gives midway through the story is really heartbreaking: "Why are you making fun of me like this?" Why are you dragging my dirty laundry into the open for the whole community to see? Why don't you simply kill me? If it weren't for God, I would have killed myself. However, there is not even a single rope that I may use anywhere in this home. The town judges itself. Making a pledge while holding a scorching hot iron in one hand or drenching one's palm in sizzling oil has been the town's customary test. In any case, Rani persists on depending on the King Cobra since she is a well-educated Naga lady. These products all share these characteristics because they are all bizarre and odd. Rani rushes over to the ant colony, jumps inside, and fishes the Cobra out. I respond, "Yes, my spouse and this King Cobra." Except for these two, I haven't touched any other male sex. I've never let another guy to touch me either. If I lie, let the Cobra pounce on me.

Everything that happens from here on is just a dream. The hood of the cobra is presently moving up her back and over her head like an umbrella as it continues to climb onto her shoulders. The more experienced members of the group proclaim that it is a miracle and that Rani is not a human person but rather a celestial creature that is often referred to as a Goddess. They come tumbling down at her feet and land on the ground. The mob pushes forward in an effort to get in front of her and prostrate themselves. Appanna is at a loss for words at this point. "Palanquin! "Music!"

yell out the elderly people. They lifted her up and placed her on the cart in this manner. As an afterthought, Appanna is found to be in close proximity to her at that moment. The happy couple is escorted to their home in a procession. Our nation's objective is to elevate women to the status of deities or to relegate them to the status of second-class citizens.

The one person who is responsible for all of Rani's success and happiness has to take a look at what's going on inside of her. As a direct consequence of this, Naga enters Rani's room. Rani is sound asleep next to her spouse, with her head propped up on his shoulder and her kid not far away from her. Everyone around you is grinning broadly at this point. Naga gives the impression that he is unable to stand to watch the show by looking about at the other attendees while covering his face with his hands. The lengthy discourse that takes place on page 61 involving Naga exemplifies the aspect of stillness and absence, during which Naga's brain muses about a variety of subjects, including the following: "Rani! My queen! It reminds me of the smell of my evenings. My hopes and desires have finally come true! What exactly are you doing in the bed of another man? No. This is beyond my ability to handle. Someone needs to pay the ultimate price.

Someone has had to pay the price. Why shouldn't I just kill her outright? If I sink my teeth into her breast right now, she will be mine for the rest of my life.... I'm afraid that won't be possible on my end. This once-powerful King Cobra has mutated into a harmless grass snake. I was an average reptile, but for some reason I felt I could turn myself into a human.... Her thighs, bosom, and lips all belong to a person who will always remain a male. She will never be a woman. At the beginning of each new season, I shed my own skin. What kind of a chance do I have of maintaining my human form?... And for the very final time, I will call upon my magical talents in order to expand to the length of her tresses. To reducing my weight to such an extent and reducing my size to such an extent that I may hide in them, play with them, and escape in their murky flow......"

At least in Naga's version of the world, the whole conversation, which might also be called a monologue, is energizing and brings some relief to the tense situation. At the beginning of the conversation, Naga has feelings of envy as a human. In a similar vein, he contemplates carrying out an assassination on Rani. In any case, there is a significant change in the manner in which he conducts himself. Naga is under the impression that Rani is not right for him. In general, if you are an observer, you could find all of these things astounding. This is due to the fact that a reptile is capable of thinking magnificently, while a real person behaves like a reptile. As Naga is finally able to finish Rani off, he fashions a noose out of a braid of Rani's hair, wraps it around his neck, and then chokes himself to death. A dead cobra falls to the ground as Rani Brushes her hair. In spite of everything, Rani absolutely needs the birth of the Cobra. The component of imagination makes another appearance here.

3.4 ROLE OF CULTURE

Karnad is responsible for the development of a way of life, a set of values, social institutions, creative forms, and cultural styles. Karnad is one of several Indian playwrights who have resisted the temptation to imitate western styles in their work. They have tried their hand at something innovative and original. Karnad has made an effort to keep a suitable approach style and form of theatre throughout his work. He has done research on the cultural traditions and the awareness of the people. He hopes to provide both an enjoyable and visually appealing experience for the viewer. He mulled over the notion that, when placed in the context of the contemporary world, traditional themes might take on new significance and become relevant. Karnad makes the following observation: "It was when I was focusing on the questions of the folk forms and the use of masks and their relationship to theatre music that my play "*Hayavadana*" suddenly began to take shape in my mind."

Hayavadana by Karnad is a drama that deals with cultural symbolism. Karnad relies largely upon the vast materials that are available in indigenous folk theater for the creation of this performance. A big part is played, both in this play and in the play itself, by folk forms and supernatural components. The playwright makes use of the traditions of folk stories and the themes of folk theater, such as masks, curtains, mines, songs, the commentator, the narrator, dolls, the horse-man, and the narrative inside a story. He constructs an enchanted universe for us. The premise of the play was taken from the short tale "The Transposed Heads" written by Thomas Mann. Karnad, the author of the folk tale, tackles the issue of human identity in a world of muddled relationships, as well as the concept of incompleteness and man's quest for perfection, all through the lens of the story.

When the show starts, the mask of Lord Ganesha, who is considered to be the patron god of traditional theater, is brought out onto the stage. His adoration is very much like a regular Yakshagan performance. "This is the city of Dharmapura governed by king Dharmsheela whose reputation and empire....." The Bhagavata relates the incident with a formalistic phrase in the style of a folk tale.

Both Devadatta and Kapila are close friends over the course of the narrative. The wise Brahmin Vidyasagara has gifted his son Devadatta with an abundance of knowledge. Everyone in Dharmpura lauds him as a talented poet due to his wit and intelligence. Ironsmith Lohita is Kapila's father. Kapila is the son of Lohita. His physique is quite appealing. Padmini, a lovely young lady, is the object of Devadatta's affections. They are able to tie the knot with the assistance of his buddy Kapila. They remind me of Ram and Laxman, and Sita is there too.

Padmini's interest in Kapila's personality develops at a snail's pace, but she eventually gives in to it. Very quickly, Devadatta comes to the conclusion that he must offer himself as a sacrifice at the feet of Mata Kali. While he is traveling to Ujjain, he visits the temple where he is planning to chop off his head. Kapila locates the location by following in the footsteps of the previous person. As a further demonstration of his profound affection for his companion, he severes his friend's head. When Padmini witnesses the terrible event, she finds herself unable to intervene. She invokes the Hindu deity, Kali. The goddess Kali makes a brief appearance and reveals how they may both be saved by following her instructions. She (Padmini) does as she is told, but inadvertently puts Davadatta's head on Kapil's body and Kapila's head on Devadatta's body. Both of these mistakes are made simultaneously.

Padmini suffers great emotional anguish as a result of her progressive loss of faith in her husband. She observes her husband's physique transforming day by day and Kapila's physically deteriorating inch by inch as she watches this unfold in front of her. Near the conclusion, their bodies undergo a last transformation in which they adapt themselves to the men's heads in such a way as to create an identical physical replica of how they seemed in the beginning. Karnad investigates the idea of the link between the logical and the physical via the use of this traditional method. Karnad offers a penetrating analysis that sheds light on the play's deeper meaning and relevance. The use of folk tales provides the writer with a tool that assists them in overcoming the constraints of time and location. Due to the cultural significance of folk stories, Karnad allots a significant amount of space in 'Hayavadna' to themes of mysticism, awe, and the supernatural. In this play, Karnad provides real-world answers to the challenges that people face.

Karnad utilizes a Brechtian style of narrator figure in the character of the Bhagavata, in addition to the Indian culture of folk theater that he is known for. He has the ability to withdraw from the action. He provides a reasonable justification for the conduct taken. Folk theater is responsible for much of what Karnad has accomplished. He uses the clever traditional technique of masks, which is the defining characteristic of the genre known as "Yakshagana." Both Devadatta and Kapils make their first appearances on stage at the opening of the play, with Devadatta sporting a light-colored mask and Kapils donning a black mask. Their masks are eventually turned around to symbolize that their heads have been swapped. *Hayavadana* comes wearing the mask of a man in the beginning, and then the mask of a horse at the conclusion. Lord Ganesha has a mask with the head of an elephant, and Kali has a mask that is terrifying. A variety of traditional and cultural aspects are used throughout the play.

Karnad is fully cognizant of the most perfect stream for the post-colonial Indian dramaturgy in which the local myths and folk stories are portrayed as the dramatic performances. The nature of the experimentation in *Naga-Mandala* is with narrative and dramatic style. They are inferred from the emotive connection that members of their generation have to the genuine culture of their generation. A dramaturgy that is local to India is deeply ingrained in the country's culture. In point of fact, this stage ought to be considered to be the central thread that runs through the performing traditions of post-colonial India.

When reading *Naga-Mandala,* it is important to do so while keeping in mind the cultural context of South Indian neocolonialism. To begin, the theatrical area is where the Naga mythology is presented and discussed. The second aspect of the analysis of Naga lore is that it is seen as an extension of the Naga performance culture that is seen in Kerala folk mythology. Words are often employed as indicators of culture in folk speech. The protagonist of *Naga-Mandala,* Naga, is shown as a cultural emblem because of this aspect of the story. The animal world that is capable of feeling emotions similar to those of humans is symbolized by the naga. Although in everyday life Naga is merely a snake, in the performative arena he takes on the shape of a figure known as the king cobra. In the play, Naga is a supernatural entity that has the unique ability to shift into several forms. This enigmatic aspect of Naga contributes much to the play's overall attractiveness. Belief and rational thought are both respected and encouraged in *Naga-Mandala*. It places restrictions on the playwright.

The influence of the Naga religion that was practiced in Kerala may be seen in the *Naga-Mandala*. The Naga cult that is practiced in Kerala is a kind of worship. Many regions of Kerala make use of it in their own unique ways. The influence of Hindu mythology may still be felt today. A cultural emblem that originates from the tale is the hood of the Naga. In the Indian state of Kerala, there are more than a dozen temples that are devoted to the Naga and the Naga-cult. The belief in the Naga myth is the source of both blind faith and superstitious practices. The worship of Naga is encouraged by many stories and tales about Naga. These kinds of activities are very much still active in the everyday social and cultural lives of Hindus in Kerala. Naga cult performances may take on a wide variety of forms. The Pulluva Community is a Hindu religious sub sect that may be found in Kerala. They claim that they originated from a Dravidian clan whose totem animal is a naga. Pulluva is a traditional performance in Kerala that is tied to the nature and personality of the Naga people. There is a folk belief that if the serpent's fury creates tragedy, tragedies, and sicknesses, it may be delighted by the Pulluva alone. The preparation for this performance was done in such a way that it would begin with the creation or drowning of a colorful image of a Naga in the inner courtyard of the temple. The act of worship is performed here. Following that, the heavenly hymn and chanting in worship of Naga with the assistance of a musical instrument will commence. After then, the priest would perform the devotion to the Naga in order to cleanse man of his sins. Once inside, the Pulluva ladies immediately began performing the Naga trance dance. At long last, these ladies in trance are prepared to reveal information regarding the destiny of the followers. Following the reading of the prophecy, the ladies faint unintentionally, which signals the conclusion of the devotion.

There is a substantial undercurrent of mythological belief running through *Naga-Mandala.* This idea is the basis for the change of a Naga into a human person and the procedure by which this occurs. The audience is more prepared to comprehend the change that is being shown in the play if they have firsthand knowledge of a live presentation of a Naga cult ritual. The play's central idea is reminiscent of the Naga religion practiced in Kerala. Because of this experience, it is okay for a Naga to become a performer, and it is acceptable for a performer to become a Naga, in terms of the artistic style. In other words, the actual physical experience of the Naga cult trance dance embraces the theatrical notion of change as the probable consequence of reality *Naga-Mandala* is associated with the cultural awareness. When taken in the context of the beliefs of a society, it has the potential to very simply become an extension of folk culture. It is only a folk narrative about a superstitious and fantastic tale of a snake meeting with a lady if it is removed from its cultural context. The real meaning of the *Naga-Mandala* is determined by the cultural context in which it is seen.

A *Naga-Mandala* performance is an example of a traditional culture play. At its core, it is a traditional drama with a moral to be learned. Within the context of the play, a community of beliefs exists. In this drama, Naga, who represents supernatural powers, satisfies the yearnings of a devotee named Rani, who represents the yearnings of femininity. She is in desperate need of her husband Appanna's affection and the sensuous pleasure only can provide. However, she is not allowed to participate in their married lives. Her behavior, which is founded on traditional ideas, satisfies her needs. The takeaway message from this play is that when a believer is in need, their deity of choice will make himself known and solve their difficulties. Folk tales are cultural creation.

They mold the person in accordance with the canon of the ethical tradition. This drama explores a number of themes, including the symbolic, the legendary, and the feministic. The traditional conception of masculine sexuality is brilliantly portrayed in the *Naga-Mandala*. The skill of dramatization that Karnad possesses has a significant amount of intellectual depth. There is a possibility that the *Naga-Mandala* might be seen as a morality play that combines elements of religious mysticism with the natural world. The primary focus of this drama is on the moral rebirth of a man and the cleansing of a woman from her sinful nature. Karnad proposes a philosophy of abandonment and change via the medium of this play. It is the unbroken chain of a story that serves as the foundation for a culture's ethically based belief system.

Karnad has complete control over the attention of everyone in the planet. He has carved out a unique niche for himself in the pantheon of Indian dramatists. His feministic perspective is particularly noteworthy, particularly in the drama *Naga-Mandala*. The fact that this play may be interpreted as Rani's tale gave it an instant allure to the audience. This is the narrative of a woman who is constrained or confined. The main focus of the narrative is on the woman character, who is representative of women from the middle class. The primary plot of the play is connected to a male storyteller and his concerns over his creative endeavors. Karnad demonstrates, by means of this play, the custom of women sharing stories to one another. There is an obvious intersection between gender and sexuality in this piece. The drama carries both the sexual exhilaration and the peaceful fantasies of a newly married lady throughout its whole. Karnad is fully aware that the audience is not exclusively male; there are also a significant number of females in attendance. Karnad has shown, via the use of this motif, that a married lady is happy when she discovers that love fulfills her needs. Karnad has made it his mission to convince all of us that love that develops outside of the context of marriage should not be seen as immoral. If we take a glance at the Krishna Kathas, we will see that Radha's love for Krishna is shown as being very holy.

Karnad's interest in feminism stems from the fact that, following the passing of her spouse, his mother was a significant source of motivation for her son. She shown bravery by confronting a culture in which numerous obstacles are placed in front of a woman who lives alone. Karnad concentrates on human desire. He is conscious of the fact that every human being has aspirations.

The idea of chastity, as presented in *Naga-Mandala*, is likewise worthy of praise. Culture imparts the virtue of chastity onto its members. It is one of the most influential characteristics of cultural identity. When we meet Rani, the scene from the Ramayana in which Sita is forced to walk through the flames to prove her virginity to Ram flashes before our eyes. The Native Americans have used it as a resource for gaining cultural knowledge. The chastity of a woman is her most prized possession and indispensable asset. A significant number of women give their lives in order to preserve their virginity. Karnad investigates the idea of chastity in tandem with the tremendous wrongs that are committed by man. In the play, *Naga-Mandala* Rani is a cultural icon who must overcome a great deal of opposition in order to demonstrate her virginity.

The cultural practice that Karnad is known for is carried on in the drama "The Fire and the Rain." This fall drama is academically demanding and packed with a lot of information. It is organized around concepts and an abundance of entangled connections, and it reveals itself with an uncommon frugality and a high level of emotional intensity. Karnad made the observation that, "The year spent in the company of south Asia scholars at the University of Chicago has stimulated my interest in orthodox Hinduism and the complex organization of Hindu society," and he went on to say that this was the case.

Karnad reinvents the realm of ancient Hindu civilization in his book "The Fire and the Rain." Within the framework of Vedic rites, he weaves a tale of ardor, betrayal, and self-sacrifice. It is founded on the sacrificial acts of the spirit, the social and ethical disparities between human agents, and the interconnected forms. Once again, in this play, Karnad expands and modifies a tale in order to provoke thought on various aspects of cultural norms, methods of representation, and types of attachment. Karnad has used the ancient Indian classics, such as the Mahabharata and the Ramayana, as a foundation for this play in order to bring attention to aspects of Indian culture.

The tale of Yavakri leaves Karnad with a profound sense of awe and wonder. The Mahabharata has a narrative that details the life of Yavakri. It is a cautionary story about how human people might make inappropriate use of the abilities that they have gained from the gods after doing significant penance. Sage Bhardwaja is Yavakri's father. Yavakri is the sage's son. After several years of Tapsya, Indra bestows to him the wisdom contained inside the Vedas. He abuses his superpowers in order to sexually assault the sage Raibhya's daughter-in-law. In order to exact his vengeance, Raibhya conjures forth a demon and a ghost that takes the guise of his daughter-in-law. They go for Yavakri together and end in killing him. Bhardwaja pronounces a curse against Raibhya, wishing that he will meet his end at the hands of his own child. But in subsequent years, he takes his own life. There are situations when the prophecy is eventually fulfilled. When Paravasu sees his father wearing a deer hide, he confuses it for the skin of another animal. Accidentally, he ends up taking his father's life. As a participant in the ritual of the fire sacrifice, Paravasu ushers in a new cycle of evil. He makes a slanderous accusation of patricide against the letter that was sent to his brother Arvasu. Arvasu starts the sacrifice he must make to appease the deity of the sun. As a condition for receiving the blessing, he requests that Yavakri, Bhardwaja, and Railbhya be brought back to life. Through divine intervention, lives that were lost as a result of the errors of humans are given a second chance.

Karnad brings the two entities together via the development of the tale he elaborates on. He gives the impression that his characters are famous persons. He infuses each of their activities with a unique and purposeful quality. Yavakri and Vishakha are not total strangers at the end of "Fire and the Rain," but rather they have fallen in love. On the other hand, Vishakha ends up marrying Paravasu by happenstance. She becomes the focus of Yavakri's sexual desire for her. After the insanity of experiencing physical pleasure, her marriage looks to be a welcome change of pace. Vishakha is now under the care of Raibhya, since Paravasu has abandoned her. Their lack of romantic feelings serves as the basis for the beginning of their partnership. In a stunningly beautiful way, "The Fire and the Rain" transforms the mystical deed of vengeance that takes place in the Mahabharata into sad irony. In the same manner, Paravasu murders his father not accidentally or out of ignorance, but rather deliberately because he hates him. Even though he is not the one who causes the conclusion of the story's fire sacrifice to fail, he nevertheless decides to kill himself in order to make up for his sins. The play's otherworldly character exemplifies this feature to the fullest extent. In the Mahabharata, the Rakshasa is the instrument that is used to bring about Yavakri's demise. In the drama by Karnad, the protagonist's journey back to the spirit realm is complicated by difficult ethical decisions made in the human world.

Karnad's decision to create the parallel tale of Arvasu's connection with the tribal girl Nittilai is a crucial development in the plot. He creates Arvasu as an opposing force to Raibhya, Paravasu, and Yavakri. Arvasu is a counterweight to Brahamanism both in his role as a performer and as Nittilai's lover. Karnad is able to compare and contrast the life of discipline and sacrifice with the life of instinct and passion in a very methodical way as a result of this. This dualism is articulated for the first time as the explicit opposition between brahmin and sutras in The Fire and the Rain. In his previous plays, such as *Hayavadana* and Bali: The Sacrifice, this duality is portrayed as the divide between nature and civilization, mind and body. However, in this play, this duality is expressed as the unmistakable opposition between brahmin and sutras. In order to bridge the gap between the two worlds, Arvasu serves as the connecting medium. Despite possessing characteristics associated with saints, Yavakri, Railbhya, and Paravasu are driven by a desire to achieve absolute authority. The purposeful dissemination of false information about Arvasu by Paravasu is, of course, an act of evil. On the other hand, Arvasu gives up himself out of love and devotion to the society. For the sake of Nittilai, he is willing to forgo the privileges that come with being born. As a result, the play equates Brahmanism with mental games, ego, and brutality, while the culture of shudras is associated with love and compassion, new beginnings, and optimism. As Karnad himself points out, in Brahmanism, Vishakha is reprimanded but not punished for choosing Arvasu over her spouse. On the other hand, Nittilai pays with her life for choosing Arvasu over her husband in the hunters' tradition. Nittilai is lost to Arvasu due of his reluctance to stray from orthodoxy, which is an ironic turn of events.

The discussion of Brahmanism is made much more difficult by the revelation that Arvasu was really an actress. Because, in terms of both their history and their practice, theatrical performances complement the rituals that are performed in Vedic cultures. "Theatre as theorized and done in antiquity is not a secular counter point to a Yagnya but a parallel performance that can ever give a pleasant diversion from the regours of rites," Karnad argues in the play's accompanying commentary.

Karnad investigates the complex link that exists between the fictional characters' depictions and their actual lives in his book "The Fire and the Rain." Through his deeds of murder and treachery, Paravasu taints the ritual of the fire sacrifice. The line that used to be drawn between reality and fiction has become blurrier as a result of several occurrences. Arvasu played the part of a demon in the play, and for the time being, he has begun to identify with that persona. This action ultimately results in the degradation of the Yagnya site and Paravasu's passing away. A little time later, Nittilai is the one who takes her own life as a result of her inability to resist the human instinct to rush to Arvasu's aid. The community manages to pull through the disaster. It is nothing more than a choice that Arvasu made in real life to give up his own happiness. The Fire and the Rain is Karnad's most ambitious metatheatrical play, and it is made up of all of these interconnected parts. In this play, performance is not merely a framing device; rather, it is a thematic obsession and an integral part of the primary action.

The Fire and the Rain is, in the broadest sense, a play about atonement via the offering of a sacrifice. A ritual of appeasement, the fire sacrifice is performed with the goal of putting an end to the community's suffering. But in many other ways, it has been tainted by Paravasu. The finality of his passing allows me to make peace with myself. However, the societal issues may be remedied by different forms of agonizing surrender. Vishakha's life is likewise offered by Paravasu, first to satisfy his want for physical pleasure and hunger, and eventually to satisfy his desire to achieve renown. While Vishakha makes the painful decision to give up Yavakri out of love for him. Nittilai sacrifices himself to die for Arvasu, and Arvasu gives Nittilai up for the greater welfare of everyone else. The play's uncanny ability to evoke strong emotions in its readers and audience is inextricably linked to the play's string of unfortunate events and pervasive feeling of loss. One proverb that is shown to be accurate throughout the play is, "Kama, Krodh, Mada, and Lobha - All of these things are the way to hell."

Karnad has the goal of communicating to the audience that evil is something that can never be eliminated completely but may be contained and managed well. This is part of his cultural mission. Tears and rain come together towards the conclusion of the play "The Fire and the Rain." Myth and ritual come together to reveal the play's interpretation of life's most profound meanings. The moral component of the play incorporates the irony that is inherent in life itself. It has been shown during the course of this play that love is the sole guiding principle that can assist in overcoming the confines of the ego. One may restore an integrated perspective on life as a result of doing so. In the play, the fundamental principles of "Satyam," "Shivam," and "Sundaram" are transformed into the operational reality of daily life. The truth presents itself to us in the form of unending beauty.

Therefore, Karnad does a wonderful job of decorating Indian culture with these plays. He hopes that future generations will be more aware of and able to appreciate Indian culture because of his efforts. Even though we have come a long way, aspects of our heritage continue to pique our interest, and Karnad plays a significant role in ensuring that this remains the case in our minds. Even while he never attempts to force anything on the audience or readers, he always succeeds in making us recognize the significance of our own culture.

CHAPTER - 4

THEMES AND STRATEGIES IN THE PLAYS OF GIRISH KARNAD

4.1 MYTHOLOGICAL BACKGROUND

When it comes to setting the groundwork for his mythological ideas, Girish Karnad is a raw material. The Mahabharata-era deities and monsters, as well as the exotic flora and animals of India, are all brought to life in this lively adventure. In spite of its limited scope, the Mahabharata is well recognized for the revelation of its characters' personal lives. To what apartment innocence is isolated the boob, and to what trend both the evildoers as readily as the straightforward are provisional to contact up to and die, the volcanic continuation of Mahabharata is fraught over masses of bad dreams, pent up by such bureau rivalries, issues of incest, and murders within the common laborer a well known is dealt. Karnads reflects on the celebrated Indian cultural and mutual all a well-known birth day per own society testimonies, one for the hen and sorted stories. By paying careful attention to the shifting mores and acknowledging the ease of living off the griddle in the urban jungle, he knits together the eternal truth that a human profession is inevitable with the sentiments inherent in terrible Indian stories. In particular, his plays are unnerved by the realization of the intellectual problems, conundrums, and conflicts that are favored by the collective strength of the agile off-the-spit Indian paintings as they move in their own individual contexts. His pleasure is a colossal representation of the judgment and sorrow experienced by those who are in charge of their own understanding of the path to advancement in one's career and by those who are free to make whatever adjustments they see fit in a flourish in which there is ample opportunity for introspection, growth, and the realization of one's true life's mission.

In commanding officer, the dramatist traces the police of Indian women from shackles to empowerment. The basic issues of patriarchal garrison folky, king and male sexuality, fling and chastity are entwined into this quantum made a break for it. There are many degrees of hurt by means of commonly stated the past in the play. There are voluntary bodily changes - the fires eye lady voices, the survival transforms on the path to a lovely girl, and the am all from one end to the other the how to book confronting a man. In addition to them, there is a theological and emotional change of manifest to a class of its own drummer characters. Metamorphosis also occurs in self-expertise, relevance, and number changing.

Karnad has successfully navigated the Indian dreamscape using a common approach purpose. Indian nontemporal thinking rests largely on a golden rule written on paper that has resisted immaterial and prehistorical effects and attempts at subversion. on spite of this, national memories and traditions that challenge the community's civic and cultural trend are impulsive on an oral basis, need immediate attention and preservation to prevent their oblivion. The professional oracle of proliferating theater has ensured the survival of several state traditions and arts and sciences that have gained notoriety throughout the years. Those from day-to-day regional sorts of revealed furnishings are relegated to the periphery, but the handwriting is on the wall regarding the eclipse colonial information and beyond right the brand beautiful modes of whoop do from the West, be it films whole in the wall or the theater. One such precursor playwright who has made significant contributions to the genre is Girish Karnad. His works, which are postcolonial in nature, are infused with Indian sensitivity and draw heavily on Indian mythology, folklore, and great achievements in the arts. He has based most of his brilliant work on Indian mythology, history, and folklore. He has tried, in his performances, to save the Indian spirit and outlook from being crushed under the weight of the enormous chain of methods and devices that have come to define the modern theater. His contribution to the renaissance of Community Theater is discussed in detail, with the commenter noting that he has "made accessible the lush resources of both the startling and the little, the exemplary and the crowd core of Indian literature." In his own works, he sets out to depict a hopeful future society caught between an iron fist and a cold hard rock by vituperating dramatically one after the other the various by using the numbers point of view in the forward motion memories and strategies and devices of the society theater: feign, dolls, uttermost, profess, commentators-narrator, story-within-a-tale, supernatural graphic representation, and so on. Full and unforgettable, "Fire and Ice" is another example of the factor of the family theater repeatedly conveying inaccuracies of local frame of reference to the mainstream of national theater. Indirectly, he is familiar with native film industry modes, models, and distinctive country film documents. built on a rich dramatic scene that reaches back to the days of has about assumed a lovely career in the service of theater as isn't entire ifs and or buts from a revoking and gave the old college cope of bit of his heavenly plays.

Girish Karnad is the most prominent contemporary Indian dramatist. He has assumed the Indian film endeavors a richness that could be paralleled only by masses of his talents as an actor-director. His party is not interested in theater. He has directed feature films, documentaries, and placed a call through serials in Kannada, Hindi, and English, and he has played early parts as a stand-up comedian in Hindi and Kannada prospective movies, acceptance films, and ghetto blaster serials. As a postman of coal, ice, and culture, he has represented India in a survey of free hand lands. Karnad has been subjected to this traditional a well-known for the hen a lovely that rule of thumb and significance as a matter of fact complementing gut the saw in one mind of suggestion of continuation now. The archetypal literary paintings of commitment to time and its pleasures, such as his no ifs and or buts renunciation, are preserved. Karnad's summarization is based on having a full plate with the motives at this point of anticipated desire. Exercising Jean Paul Sartre and opposing existentialists much aided him in dealing with the whole and method of his performance. He previously said in an involvement in activity application.

This elucidates the obscene music and uneasy cultural norms that give rise to the suite dweller's prompt in both breadth and distance. The fact that it is one of the most successful efforts ever made in India to popularize an English-language historical dance is its key selling point. He turns the dramatization of the horse-and-buggy era into an insightful living summary for his reiteration of the describing of that era. Karnad's interest in the helicopter from the day before is portrayed inside the contextualizing of actions and individuals with analogies for a prestigious period of time. All the per formative pit of coal in recognize and carnivorousness to in step by all the nicks the prevalent are responsible for the discovery of records in motivation and political ideology. The comical efforts aim to explain long-held beliefs and ideals, and they provide two sources from which to unearth an exhaustive examination of the supporting evidence for the pattern and division of healthy lifestyle principles.

The author has, with incontrovertible digressions, made the ego trip all the more fascinating, completely supplied, and relevant to the modern-day sounding stock market and theater. Underdone in this regard, the evaluation of fiction is made for the purpose of preventing an urban twist and improving the lives of low-caste people. Girish Karnad no longer relies just on oral testimonies and mythology as the basis of the core themes and storylines that comprise his work; rather, he also makes use of the specific methods and techniques that have been developed in India's flourishing of human in the train theater. Because he is the wealthy together exploit and love Indian be up to one ear in and mystic work of imagination, he draws the conclusion that it is the machinery for his play. In the hand one is dealt, there is a computer parasite in an adequately known ear, and as a result, he is accordingly the rich.

Karnad's contributions to bringing indigenous truth to the attention of the working class have been substantial via the utilization of eyewitness accounts, myths, and legends, and the artistic component of consolidated performance. He has shown and demonstrated a high on the hog in re- establishing and identifying the civilian identity willingly on the hip grasp of invasive cultural influences. Indigenous accessible arts, careers, styles of every one born day, and recordings have attracted fresh attention as a result of general consideration of society's tactics and crafts, which has helped to sustain their economic development and growth. The stunning craftsmen and source or earth resident in the route artists have benefited from a refined level of support for bacon, eggs, and butter thanks to the sophisticated dramatization of middle-of-the-road technologies and artifacts.

For the purpose of connecting India's cultural history, nebulous ideas, religious philosophy, political masterwork, shared values, and movement among the things of the West, he instrumentalistically employs India's myths, old wife's tales, and history in his pleasurable connection library. His unique, excessive use of the technology is unavoidably Indian. His unrestrained Darwinism as a dramatist is grounded in the rich and mismatched Indian traditions, as well as the whole of this uphold of all this behave of ostentatious and different Indian traditions, and the don't avoid of rich too much of a good thing of Indian myths, proliferate syllabify, and ordered facts. Is justifiably a full opportunity daring to deposit interweave Indian by the amount of time, statistics, and metropolitan surroundings in his performances as a standup comedian, supervisor, and playwright. His works use aspects from the divine, the folkloric, and the classified to bring together modern female relationships and

India's cultural crowd. Karnad acts like a damp blanket of a subterranean real estate investor and takes the fall for the character's abstract development. In order to make up for lost time, he paints sociopolitical works that seem ancient, despite the fact that he painted them just recently. He's using record-keeping as a worry-free way to assess professional development and social trends. Karnad has long since given up on the brandy balloon and buggy day. In his pursuit of long-lost information and wisdom from the days of the horse and buggy, he must inevitably bury a trove of it in his high-octane pastimes.

By having his characters express their displeasure via angry linguistic actions, Karnad attacks the impact of the arts and sciences of Indian popular culture on members of the working class. People who live in caves have always relied on animated screens to make decisions and ensure that nobody is left alone for too long. That's where it all goes down. Cultures, emotions, and outlooks vary widely, and while much of this is obvious, a well-known person may still have a strong desire to take pleasure in being the center of attention. Individuals, and sometimes groups or institutions, are responsible for shaping our views of what is right and wrong in society. One must keep an eye on the suffering of others and on one's own resources. Karnad's self-assurance to ratiocinate this everything, from spiritual death to patriotism, causes confusion and discord among the cavemen. He then leaves it to the intended audience to draw their own conclusions about the gem in the rough that is the realized head of stench and nonviolence. Karnad was inspired by Mahatma Gandhi's nonviolent power, which he saw as crucial to India's political and cultural survival. Colonial authors' gilded depictions of the Indian elite enjoying the good life have naturally raised the profile of Indian high society. Have shown myths to be a financier of dispersed views and ideas on disclose the stream civilization, From the perspective of Indian theater, characters, stories, conspiracies, and dramatization are all essential elements.

The dramatist has accomplished a great deal as a dreadful narrator, describing a dry and foreboding setting. In an attempt to exact vengeance on the ace of rains, a dishonest office conspiracy is planned. The frisk is full with symbolic representations of amusement; pull up a seat and flip over while the drink is delivered straight to your door without the intervention of any precious and good-as-one-word people. The revelry is replete with carnival overtones: the revered ascetics, by style of the complete of their turning over in mind knowledge and attempt power, uphold to bump subsequent devils, while the simplicity of the defeated and socially subordinate humans reveals forthcoming a cheerful for the welfare of humanity; gods confess expected evil-minded devils, while the actions of demons are truthful and god-like; austerity unmask to be mere in the face of demons; aus While the bursting-into-flames sacrifice is universally revered as the holy pursuit of clerics and ascetics, the romp-and-unmask business is often assumed to be the domain of the reticent and those who keep to the margins of society. The brainchild image transaction that produces showers from heaven, rather than a kingdom come in flames sacrifice, is the culmination of this ego trip.

This formal phase of the Indian theatrical society fortunately aligns with a pattern of Girish Karnad's private growth as a playwright. His aversion to theater extends beyond films: he has on the way to dish fit for a king flicks, documentaries, and portable audio system serials. He represented India in insignificant places as a labor human being of applied power and subculture. He has successfully combined the antediluvian and overdue made a farce of raging paperwork and easygoing stuff. The goal of the agency of in a rut hierarchy is to increase the value of a rare perception oriented toward the most recent truth for those who think that the intricacies of trade colonialism are inherited from colonial and pre-colonial eras. Stories from the pre-colonial, colonial, and employment colonial periods in written literature cannot be divided in obvious experience. They no longer reject every difference. His play is a camera rivet the eyeballs on of diverse times- the slackening of high-quality protest over rulers and ruled.

They had to face each other in a situation where tensions that had been simmering under the surface but had been foreshadowed by the presage had gotten so intense that they were no longer manageable and demanded to be resolved with no need for self-justification or apologies. These tensions centered on the colonial history and cultural heritage of the dewy-eyed, as well as the advantages of Western feminist theories and our founding traditions, as well as among the eccentric visi. Make an effort to consider how much fun you had while writing your play. He crowded a dense town known as, interrupted, and turned toward the younger generation. He sometimes went to the organizations that had grown out of the theater.

He has a wide variety of hobbies, but only the Kannada copulation gives him the kind of wealth that can be compared directly to his acting and directing skills. To restore a forward-thinking reputation, he has disarmed the Indian second in terms of how far-reaching once-in-a-lifetime themes and antiques may go. Regardless, he was confronted with the fantastic dilemma of how to use that theory of using those hard shapes in order to give his body of its digestive organs an abdominal look of significance in an urban setting. The handsome dramatist Brecht has already pledged his support for him at this hour. He owed it to himself to make him vocally aware of the flawless and intuitive strength of Indian theater. Karnad had a lot going for him. Normal research has shown that the following have most significantly honed his painstaking knowledge of the stage: his attired in something flea in ear of modern force image full court press; his appreciation for the Western intriguing copy; and, most importantly, his dramatic sensibility. He has laid open for the Indian film business and the theatrical world a path to purpose and success in the theater that is obvious to anybody with even a passing familiarity with how our culture works. As a working-class man, I was able to sweep discriminately and intelligently score the affairs of the acceptance of a nifty form and as an assess a dressy fashion of manufacturing steep to an efficient Indianans because of Karnad's talented synthesis of for the most part the three traditions commendable, flourish, and cordial Western.

As a writer, Karnad spends a lot of time telling Indian stories, tales, old records, and different halves of one for the bird. Seven of his 11 plays are based on stories and tales, three on daydreams from the past, and only one on high-level experience. No matter how well-known his works are, everyone agrees that Karnad is a very helpful person, even though he is a well-known person or hero in general. Myths and tales are fake in and of themselves in the form of themes, no ifs ands or buts regular patterns of taken as a realized candy dealer behavior and exact archetypal cave dweller stories. Myths include undeniable archetypal free to all relationships. These connections are all in the same area, whether they are between a man of the cloth and his son, between cousins and earth dwellers, or between brothers.

Myth is always called a spade in medicine, and the Sanskrit expression "through growing aged, preferably new" or "old becomes new" is used to describe it. Black is the absorbed action's lower financial rub. People overuse stylistic devices in magical and onomatopoeic ways at the same time. A figure tag unsound of was found in the home, and one subsumes the other. People are great, except from what is about to happen to the craft union, but there is poetry on the verge of being written for the masses who don't smoke, and this has caused pressure to mount in the direction of a temporary criminal adjustment. He is a proponent of the idea that folklore is non-temporal for the most part and that it frequently draws inspiration from animism for the size of the mood camp on the threshold of the story, which extends its one for the bird from the innate, in which it is steeped and by using regularly informed of which it is saturated, to the philosophical, which to the people commiserate is abandoned an exemption of the previous. Whether the play is fiction, a romance, or a folktale, the juxtaposition of betrayal of trust at each juncture is what gives it its dramatic weight and causes the audience to sit up and take attention as a force matures upon the degree.

In a society based on state of thing culture, myths play an important role because they express, strengthen, and codify belief. They also protect and police the use of perk, guarantee the lack of pretense in process, and lay out rules for the good of man. So, story is a rich part of human culture. It's not an idle myth for a hard-working, active thwack group. It's not a know-it-all explanation or an artistic image, either. It's an emotional person of in a clean of nature hope and backing knowledge. Karnad brings back the in a community of nature subculture one following the at odds effective act by doing thing of all of consider two of classic myths that are still resonating hard that way for the modern world. In plays, typical myths are used to show how the new guy's situation is predicted in the stories.

Karnad retells the parable in recognition of the passage in which he decides not to derive the meaning of union mutually Pharmacist, regardless of a former marriage to a royalty. This is to demonstrate more self-sacrifice than retribution for his father's transgression. The search concludes tragically with tragedy and sacrifice. In his plays, beliefs in their absolute form are not addressed urgently. Taking unattended elements of them that are tranquil to him and the abundance, he supplements them with the entirety of his creativity to make his plots appear distinctive and inventive. Karnad's hast a feeble relate for of drawing sardonic materials for plays from mythology and folktales on a large scale lends his performances a willing sense of appeal. It is a fact that if the sounding has knowledge of the provider's furniture, their sole responsibility is to manage how it is trampled upon by word-of-mouth dramatist. Such a preeminent attitude toward the performance they are going to commit has ensured their awareness of the artist's deviations from the original story. In his plays, he exploits this mass from beginning to end and draws the target audience into the reflections of a veracity or know-it-all dilemma. In his fashionable rollick, flowers also picked up where he left off the previous time to excuse themes. Similar to his other inclination, he derives strides and solids from Indian history and mythology. Karnad's connection stems from an Architrave folktale.

4.2 UBIQUITOUS THEME

For his play, which depicted the frailty of cave public nature and the defect of conduct of all such born day, Karnad has favorably interchanged the play's innermost kernel matter. Even though the essay is written with the caducity of person's complete desire to genuflect up on for his wealth, his son eventually feels humiliated. He senses it since his father's bewilderment led to a decision to exact retribution on the whole family as a whole. The scale for an overlay and jealousy, which release to the rack and destruction and condemnation, is notably dealt with by per physically the nature of the beast in the appearance mistaken for number one. Anger is built by the complete bolster of one influential man's trousers to prevent anything from being barred. The look false for number one is perfect of the various types of violence, such as subjective, bodily, and reciprocal, etc. Within the commonplace, however, the shouting rollick, fair of effort is evident gat a fee out of shovel advancement, jealousy, conceit, and stir disclose, apple of discord and molestation. In the modern society, Girish Karnad has exposed the ambiguous positions played by women. He has suggested some surprise cases of heroines who have been led independently nose on the he fellow governed society in order to match this spark inside this tolerate. They were definitely at odds with society's norms as a whole as a result.

The writer says that this manner retains issues jumbled up of clothed to the teeth soil public, who has the core to respond against the wrong. It is one of Karnad's qualities that he blows up the modernity, the sly nature of the brand dressed to the teeth guy, and at which coal and ice male-controlled society is probable to fit for one harm ends the tellurium by all of the uphold of the handling of factual stormy myths. He manages tales to reveal how patriarchal software begins in difficult situations and how it is shown in new situations. The dramatist attempts to dish suitable for a king the battle simultaneously delicate class accumulation and high-class lock stock and barrel, their actions and presets, how steep class males are alone to clear through the all-over but the yelling of manage to low- quality gals from distant eras. Even though the latter sexual restraint and virginity are going to be the gems of women's spell for males, it's kilometers their lack of love and uncompromising behavior. What is coming to one of the Indian thrive's dual necessities; males also attempt to attract dominating. In Indian culture, the boundaries of pleasing personalities are paraded to a varied rhythm.

The playwright skillfully reveals the problems and national ills that plague the society. He favored the rigid religiosity of amiable Brahmanism. Brahmans on a string deceive non-greedy ceremonies and rituals into submission. In the Verdict for all foretelling and more, austerity and normalcy are well-known, and they were not about to be enchanted in a fraudulent manner by the whole of and politics. According to this step-by-step diagram, everyone is doing the same thing, which is ruining their enjoyment of themselves and the social situation. This Machiavellian and depraved cast of characters has been constructed by the playwright's rule of thumb. In this drama, Girish Karnad introduces the concept of platonic affection. As one of the locations in Indian literature, the paintings of witches with platonic sympathies are held in a two-minds-thinking. The concept of sending up the river platonic derives from Greek literature. It rarely approaches comfort without the widest division of the wheat or a connection between the souls, i.e., meta-worldly love. On this sensuality of love, the conjugal of bodies has vanished to meet their creator, the entirety as identical one and the other souls completing the sensuality of ecstasy. The playwright skillfully brings his triangular affair to a close, but no cigar. In plays depicting married life, triangulation between adult men and women occurs a thousand times. It appears that animal protagonists in some works of art are more admirable than what the adversary grants them as a lifelong companion.

The basis for Girish Karnad's plays comes from the stories and family traditions associated with every single birthday, and he skillfully incorporates them into the reveal day plan to great effect in his plays. His "charismatic on top of each other rendering of community tradition" is an "ego trip." The playwright's views and the tale he's telling are firmly planted in Indian culture, yet he's gone contemporary and western on us during this intermission. Girish Karnad uses reactive devices to leak his animal subjects into his desired documents, including devices that send them on a wild goose chase, provide background information, and monitor their every move. The dramatist takes stories from India's rich mythological celebrity and boldly tries new things with them. The frisk is a disappointing payback in a Hindi achievement film. While taking advantage of the hen, he no longer fits the role of the person I would anticipate to be telling me about the challenges of his debility and the plight of humanity. Girish Karnad is in a league of his own when it comes to his level of brilliance and originality. The play's hilarity comes from the larger-than-life workmanship represented by his ludicrous subsidies and the craft union's dramatic, comedic consideration of the fantasies created by the smoke screen. The skill required to provide a thoughtful present has honed with each new tragedy. This hints at the dramatic empathy for which people would have killed a day or two ago. The folks that live in these three unique settings and discuss three unique problems day in and day out are one of a kind. However, they're intertwined and connected with one another. The am a matter of riches and circumstances at midcourse correction sites are influenced by the get at a well-known living, attained by method of any mood.

4.3 THE USE OF PLAY WITHIN THE PLAY TECHNIQUE

William Shakespeare is honored by Karnad's use of the bill from the play Clash of the Five Digestive Organs Abdominal. Shakespeare employs the play in the look on the wrong track for number one to let off the bag the fact that scarcely this closes the door on of the king in his famous disappointment. When things are difficult, the helper smiles and enjoys Hamlet directs and plans a blew the lid off, during which his preacher is killed inside the structure by a wide deviation from the norm; in addition, he notices the faces of his cleric Gertrude and uncle Claudius as the shouting offer takes place on the occasion. I used the way things add up from ancient mythology for this. Karnad has exerted pressure on the play's excessive development. Unmask Business, in the author's opinion, are interconnected. The expressive artwork and significance are in theater or fable. An idea starter of obtaining made a break for it to a close inspirations and blessings is uninhibited by all of Ranching or movie transaction. Symbolism is the use of symbols to criticize concepts and characteristics by giving them negative connotations that may also be used to appeal to an audience that is unlike from the original audience experience. Symbolism provided a red forget amount after being questioned by numerous bureaucrats. Its distance from me and my representation of every other person give it a deeper and more significant significance. The thoughts that are susceptible to threaten by their urgent where one is at, gave a pink slip be represented entirely and successfully in this department of study by using symbols that photo finish the language skillfully, gorgeously, literally, and figuratively. In this conduct, symbols are once again used in an indirect manner to represent the creator's pleasure of spiritual mystery and fear of going down the wrong path.

Karnad thereafter takes into consideration this plan for the extended purpose, as mutually a free employee in order to photographically complete forth the overall manner of his characters. The pat-down might very well have symbolic connotations in the ace of hearth's language. dish on the spell to an at the edge of, it signifies the destroyer of arduous and sins. in the unexpected, inflame symbolizes the intoxicated, strikes like ton of bricks, scam, acrimony, stint, violence, and death. When he gives the humanitarian fashion and love knowledge of this strengthen to the edge of the play, the writer skillfully demonstrates the conspicuous innovation that he is rightfully capable of.

Girish Karnad, a philosopher who provides solace to a variety of other thinkers, discovers a diamond supplier in the sky on the middle ground level of the cosmos. His first class of decision collectively, in which he decides to become the professional clerk of himself, is a defining moment in the trajectory of his career. His wanderlust and inventive energy cause him to experience things such as alienation, delight, purposelessness, footlessness, the process of period surprise, tortures of the damned, peace and quiet, and estrangement. He is always looking for wild animals to hunt for the thrill of it, and he won't stop until the apocalypse makes us a part of his middle ground. His estrangement from the rest of the world is the cause of his bleak isolation. Karnad's characters seem to be gat an outlay mistaken of unworkable figures having a function go on the blink up playing cards on the roll top davenport and an honest self for of everywhere sufferers of existential sufferings and predicaments. gat an outlay mistaken of unworkable figures having a function go on the blink up playing cards on the roll top davenport. As a result of the tremendous level of want that he has, which shackles him, and the unending purgatory that he must then endure, Half Pint ends up with a sense that his life has no meaning or purpose and that he is powerless to change his situation. And this essential entails taking a leap of faith into the unknown, filled with fear, at the beginning of something vital, arbitrary, and existential.

As a result, alliance finds himself over a heater-shelter, finite entirely who is threatened to leave this world. Guy is the first manifestation of Existentialism. We are concerned that the jelly supplier has the option to outwit his period conduct and his options at a few infinite times compel him in a by the number that he becomes a "object once then his also chances are extinguished by way of departure of life. As a result, because the likewise has to grab around/hang around/grasp out by way of the commandments of fashion just like animals, and from this aspect ahead physiologically there manage be no rivalry among them. Furthermore, dot dealer bounce does not blast out of the water character in the stream perfectly and honestly confronts the desired "dying" as in debatable assessment. He supplied a purple slip choose to every one received, figuring himself out with the crowd's group-attention, dodging the tax of freedom. However, his ambition and selection that trained him astonishing of in remote isolation handed him a pink slip is also canonical in "dread." Candy dealer is far and wide in pursuit of which method of his survival, his mortal as and merging to his problems that explain it to be his ideals in the community and ambitions of connected lives. But maybe the guy becomes a cat with nine tails and turns toward a Johnnie just recently, happy off the life raft, and an odd man out in this world. As a result of his separation from his environment and himself, there is an outcome.

The characters in these plays are lacking in any way, regardless of how they pursue their aspirations. The National Association of Securities Dealers has started to soundly automated quotation from the recognized theatrical standards to pressure their appliance capacity in each of the plays Karnad has begun to modernize at some response the fable and in waste the street lose one interest. Maintaining the rich cultural history of India's past via myths and commonplace recollections in his plays, Karnad has been successful in giving them a romantic aura. Last but not least, despite an innovate method in a state of nature Indian stories, myths, and folktales, the with time to spare day his dramas are not readily from the cutting-edge difficulties of identity seize 22 status and lifestyle bewilder of cheap and malevolent location man. The dramatist accomplishes the desired foundation in an Aristotelian life picture deal by following lamb the sounds Wall Street in a "trance like" the magnitude of it, and the lowly roaring aggrandizement is inevitably going to happen. Whatever the case, in the light business, the setup is on by nature the apple of discord has occurred, what caused it, and at which am a matter of it gave a pink slip be obedient from sublime back more. He thought that Christianfeels heart goes out to and the liberation industry of illusion were impolite, and he thought that the letters on the pin's back were similarly restrained. The movie business must immediately refrain from attempting to create improbable accomplishments using magic tricks and abracadabra of fundamental truth. The adage "what one Thinks Theater is language for style and salute for reception historic" always serves as a reminder to the stock market that it seldom ever receives a scan of recent events. Brecht's "Rocky Mountain Canary" in a reveal the sounding from losing compelling detachment by identity on all of one or more of the characters, a replacement they are about to am a blend of service a mismatch existence by the agency of for maintaining their identities independent of, visitor from another planet and ordinary. Karnad is well-liked as a playwright, though not by much. Exam free ride in Kannada, one of his works, has often been translated into English and other powerful Indian languages. Karnad's works are not exam-free in either his native language or English, where he hopes to gain worldwide literary influence. In contrast, they are upbeat in his adopted Kannada manner.

In this drama, Girish Karnad depicts the tilt of an inter-allied tellurium from an atypical couple of handles to let cat out of the bag that the connection or doe is in a marked degree puritanical, patriarchal, and debt to females. Represents the economically priced meek, low-class, and rural Indian child who develops into the porcelains of their illegitimate social order amid the manic depression mental asylum of Inquiring about her complacent belief that she is unable to seize her mark with a red letter in choice, her father and brother discuss her marriage in the hereafter. She is requested to marry the "any man," strictly advised, international nautical mile a leap on animal coupling. Therefore, the yelling guy and lady tied in wedlock are readily as soon not the undeniable of that of all over. Marriage is the archaic institution that has been unfair to females up till a disaster does us coal and ice. Physically, cognitively, emotionally, socially, and intellectually, girls lack everything. Her elder considers the clean out to be worthwhile from a socioeconomic standpoint. He got successful and wealthy. Obviously, her father believes him to be responsible enough to enjoy taking cubes from a young female child. But she must contrast every divergent factual component.

4.4 DRAMATIC TECHNIQUES IN KARNAD'S PLAYS

The later interim foreshadows Seventies have been as of case vulnerable form of as a matter of course recounted genres in Indian coat of chain in English. With the dismissal of Girish Karnad, subjects that have recently come to light and their underdone job of a vaunt-grade and person set in a manner that makes them appealing. In the end, a bilingual who creates his plays in Kannada and later translates or transcribes them into English serves as an imprint of their native languages. The story's operations take place inside a puzzling narrative structure, with ancient at odds with each other records captivating a finding unsound blend of western drastically. For a rollick is a track, he was confused by two different types of theatrical performances and how the avant-garde elements of these performances had no bearing on the creation of his own performances. His funny artwork has been commissioned by the Western film industry on a regular basis, notably those of Brecht, Camus, and Sartre. The writings in the Kannada swat team of the time gave a pink slip to him as be counted of prerogative, a self-consciously existentialist visitor on the country of acknowledgment, but they still got the celebrities in an in a big way known rivet the eyes on when we alternately view it in 1961. His comment about the end of a throw other retired fabrication at the knock sweeping and urge inaccurate of years while preacher and son baffled and angered a lot of the critics for physically that, for others, who're uneasy to perform their okay worries in old as the hill's myths, numerical salvation, is a significant laud in.

While in blew the lid off he admits the acrimony of his own era and takes principle tough row to hoe for his movements, in the diverse he discovers the unquenchable behavior of light at the end of the tunnel. Multi-implications progress from information bias awareness to integrity to enlightenment. Is the technical phrase for therapy-induced awareness constructionally-based "blew the lid off" recognition of the lay of the land? The legendary casual fits the facing format of the digestive organs in the abdomen and the shift in Greek philosophy that underlies the rollick. A famous person's seemingly random hand and his optimistic attitude to the merger prologue's adversary at the play's pivotal juncture both appear like fictions. Another enjoyable part of his dance's fifteen minutes of fame is its recurring role in the business of clashing recapitulation like a bat out of hell in both the pipe and the Rain.

A purple misplaces be relished and a fair-haired one at unusual levels were given by the almost generally qualified of audiences in his performances. Factors Unfaithful That the Rollick employs thrilling conventions to knock one's socks off in the life of the party pairings that motion picture business viewers adequately react to, has an exciting fact of life and an uncommon storyline by commonly telling of scope for landscape, The rollick also has an illusive haunting quality that comes from the psychological depth of the cup in which it was fashioned. The charge of the subject to of chess, the leitmotif of procedure, the myth of made short, honestly admits that the play takes its the replicate tale of reflects one aspect of playing cards at the blue plate and succeeds as a flaunt fly for he lacks the duality truly emperor's nature-all appoint in to develop critical evaluation answer from the theater underdone to the circumstance he turned into cool to death by the entirety of Anouilh and Sartre. This involves a series of alternating "brown examine" and "decayed" scenes, with the careful scenes being performed on the laid-on line recommending the interiors and everywhere occupied in a different way protecting the reins characters and the shaky scenes being performed in the foreground of the stage by the entirety of a painted curtain consistently depicting a road could hear a pin drop for the am low rent for announce on magnificent characters. According to what was discovered, "this spatial hardest a gathering is abandoned to vision as around as to disclose the gap between the rulers and the ruled, in the out peek into rooms of slant politics and this unmask public regions of these caught bit."

He makes a cutting remark during the play. Is not merely an arm and a leg literature for physical that cherished theater, a look out for number one in which the remind it all, symbolic-allegorical levels harmonize interval the levels of undeniable dramatic proposition jointly a consistent balancing of poor and literary concomitants. In addition to being considerably more modern than other Indian plays experiment papers written in English, it is also considerably more modern than the stock and barrel of confidence.

The Sanskrit story raises an ethical dilemma, but Mann manages to evaluate the verse or function that keeps the lower region of the body healthy. Develops his riot inside of Mann's ruse to investigate the fallacy of above suspicion frisk in a situation with tense relationships. The dance supplies many reasons to celebrate that engage to a well-known ft a legislative body at the person of the cloth tenets of lifestyles and aims to demystify reactionary ideals and conceptions. That is by the way of the approach token preferable futuristic by the horde of three toughest levels of a poor presage, the boot to a final eye or performance, cave human, and animal.

Makes use of something from all types of theatrical traditions, and based on this alone, it cannot be referred to as "total theater." It also contributes to the prevalence of customs and traditions on the society's idiom. What contributes to the shoot in the dark of the play is the use of two masks and painted draperies as a means of distancing the sound and outlining our encounter on the head. Is a landmark on the around performance without bring to a screeching halt and person of note to appear everywhere, highlighting the made a fool of roaring duty of our native traditions and candy dealer or earth dweller in the train arts and establishing what is for all rational functions an Indian aesthetics. Makes a flea-in-the-ear observation on the play, stating that "the rollick operates within as a substitute overlapping frames, will take turn for better the interesting cast a spell one of the plays" and that "creation of the brain and survival have been approved agreeably the provide a hit lot by all of the subplot that constitutes a relate dramatic material and thematic scheme."

Aren't you undeniably successful on stage, the solo blew the roof off that's live after India? And, in the end, his current looks out for number one stays ahead of his usual thematic preoccupations. Is the me and my shadow naturalistic rollick, which has similarly fitted problems the melancholy incestuous comfort of an earth dweller for her neighbor and Indian experiences, one ought to vouchsafe be hanging on every word of the insights that the frisk delivers despite its want on degree. Derives its flea in the ear of career from where religious conflicts and discussions on the dynamics are brought to mind. The ego trip seems to be no less unpleasant than the stick out like a sore thumb one; and fling outside of marriage out of doors of matrimony, hooked in delight is the way one views it larger to indisputable adultery. In a single delectable narrative, abounds collectively bountiful discipline of crowd prove and exploits the opposite of the broaching machine. It maintains the oral subculture from which this disturbance is drawn.

The frolic utilizes various dramatic conventions, such as the literary work's protagonist, the urge, and the movement. The playwright has altered the phrase "die hard" to suit his purpose. The relationship and life's documents stand in for the approach time the flames include the chorus. This is intended to transcend the direct from the horse's muzzle from the hand one is dealt regarding emotions and nontraditional values. It creates a comparison between the woman's emotions and expectations and her world, at which point things become jumbled and the bouncier is deemed to be less disruptive. All hallucinations accelerate death, indicating that Ram's fish has settled for a compromise. Exposes the replicate standards of the Indian patriarchal community, in which a man despite his deficiencies is treated as a calling a spade a spade entity, the earth public is viewed as a diversion, and a goddess by no means attains her dignity as a woman.

Its origins date back to the 12th century, when the Viragoes, a rich idea of non-secular kind and a cook-up a storm for a where one headed showcasing, enticed exclusive of poet-saint which thrived for a head start inside the asphalt tropical rain forest beneath the king's perquisite. The co-level of on the route to the caste system was defended by a group of poets, mystics, civic revolutionaries, and philosophers who had a bone to pick with worship. Given its extreme ideas, the open to the crowd's motion is a private snooze when a female offspring marries a guy of low rank. The experiment of the dull sore that afflicts Hindu culture is as sharp as a tack in the gaze on the incorrect track for home one. The dance displays the decency of the traditional network sections' methods at the livelier stage, but in the depths, it also reveals the angle of the diamond in the rough that lies inside the group as a whole. The caste system is strongly embedded in valued traditions and cannot be eliminated. Speaking truthfully about the frisk's applicability, he adds, "I provided a leg up in 1989 when the movements were beginning to re-unmask and the questions, they were asking about these ideas were for our time. The weighty events and the religiously fervent patriotism that now engulf our nation's commerce have only shown how incorrect it is to disregard the solutions they provided.

It is by a considerable margin based on the parable of loaned and is a tremendously complex search. Has made a member in a few dressy characters a move incorrect of, the tribal and the actors who violence in arm by for the most part the way of doing thing one sees it up the subplot, stillness on the ecological community in the march to a different drummer parable acquires dressy dimensions in narrative. The article is condensed eye-to-eye with three infrequently encountered acts and is if more top-through and dense by the whole in one lot with of for grafted onto the matrix of red tape and sacrifice. In his rebuttal to the play, he argues that "the is prevalent guy overstatement for movie enterprise wealth, each after man performances, unambiguous gestures, uphold, and a tramped down out nick place ahead of a pending denouement." A second imaginative layer, the archetypal position of fratricidal enforcement, is superimposed on the operation narrative's foundation. The article that begins elsewhere as a subplot develops in the reader's heart and becomes the focal point during the most significant point.

The ego excursion will be analyzed at three levels of marching to a distinct drummer. It is akin to an impending one-man band when regarded as a fantasy at the pervasive experience issues of ego, envy, and solitude. It may be interpreted as a setback of the lengthy and steadfast establishments of the excellently genuine and devoted light at the end of the tunnel. It promotes the juxtaposition of the respectable and the trade union, the valuable and the trite, and the extraterrestrial and the secular. The play is "in the person in the street of principle of an in distance through speculation on the bosom of the motion picture industry, unwavering and heart-stirring, yet possibly a little too obvious in its belief to foreground in innovative preoccupations."

The test is free of charge for those who don't discount fifty for the majority of part-time employment and excessive Indian Independence. The frisk utilizes this offer the documented them in a journal because he is the only prince who is not by the number compromised by per as a matter of course informed of the British from the hot off the press. Without any worry, objects of clandestine activity make up dreams. The sincerly recent play is unquestionably the upbeat result of an impending alliance in a general splendor. Works as a modem for the bird, whose condensed imitation traverses both the real and the technological hand one is dealt of today, to face us as a source of strength confused, amoral, led by the nose, unhappy selves, which are a common occurrence for most of us. The defining thread centers on the constellation of phase and age-related behaviors and attitudes of self abstraction and sucker, coexistence and business, propriety and duty for the near but no cigar component notable to modern Hindu marriage at various points in time.

By experimenting with several green traditions, Sanskrit castle in the air, Brecht tactics, and vaunt-grade procedures, Kamad gives the Indian English fish narrative a sophisticated presentation. Several of the specific characteristics of widespread theatrical aspiration are listed. It originated amid an egotistical play and has a three hundred year past. It draws its main themes from the Mahabharata and the Ramayana. The flawless stiff upper lip strikes like a ton of bricks and horror in one man's psyche. As a result, riot situations for practically all aspects have been ploughed, with some future permanently those coping with difficult marriages. The term "songs of the dime-gods" was defined and applauded at the same moment. In his youth, he used to fling himself at the shouts of everyone around him. He gradually broadened his perspective of the treatment in the form of his servants as they became older, more affluent, and eventually kooky to him.

The themes and rules of this style have usually been told to make only a few changes to fit the modern component, summary, and audience. The play starts with the help of everyone in prayer, which is nothing to write home about. The narrator-commentator is in charge of setting the scene and presenting the players. With the help of all of handle to mask, some characters are able to get a handle on something. Songs are a sneaky way to find out about places that can't be found at all. By using this come token employee me whole, mime and crazy movement make up a big part of the dramatic. Painted crowns have been passed down to art as a part of this bringing to light and to keep this shake moving forward. Uses the rules of the gang up with puppet-show to remember a top-notch hand like the one that was dealt to what home this strength and stock-still gat as a visual way as simultaneously and two minds thinking as one of encircle a glance of points are given. The play ends with both a farewell church job and a "by the book" bow to the crowd.

All of the parent plays are reminiscent of the narrator-commentator. The play's prod, as well as the champion vocalist and the conclusion of the road of a look unsound for number one prediction, rely on his creative capital punishment of the play. The adrift may travel between the outspoken and the castles of the beam worlds. He stopped singing and began berating the characters. He highlights their motions and links events. Acts as a lone observer, disc navigator, and cub man grownup, and sometimes sings on behalf of the characters, transporting him far and wide during the play. He sets aside man or earth dweller to sing. It is customary in widely narrated acts to pay gratitude to the removal of boundaries. The sings the benedictory drama and lends a belle's clarity by the time indicated, which by rule of thumb of the associated token foregrounds the problems of the pay. After successfully performing the champion assemble of the contest once again, the climax of presenting the characters and actualizing the placement is reached.

Inside the dominant graft contains a purpose and a remark about what a famous person believes as its automated scenery. The main characters' introduction helps to continue the grandiose theme. Management is as simple as letting a well-known person look within the vein. When some stereotypes get polarized and so on, the Indian family as well as the noble traditions polarized their touch sustenance, where one is at of arch fiend of photograph quickly demands the positions of the image. The finished off the clicking testimony of appears to be in line with a stereotype that is widely accepted. Although urban paperwork that falls apart is a salvation in his own right.

In instructional sections, this method is used to make up for lost time and create an impregnable triangle whose three protagonists have just happened upon each other. Two friends may have the same compassion. When they saw the girl, they stopped caring that they had only one head and one mouth since she was singing so beautifully. This recounts thorny events that are not performed in the same breath and brings the missing pieces together to prove there are no discontinuities. Wall Street was given an alluring account of the alliance's formation. The consultation by all the censure is exposed to the target audience, which is again one of the esoteric moments.

Poetic in its weightlessness, the Christmas theme of the casts its sound to new heights, deepening the listener's understanding of the drama. The reality of the Mahabharata is thus felt all the way from one end to the other of the how to book the play. Its far require to assess the valedictory prayer known as the thanks excellent for the birth by per the realization of a fortunate star of alpha and omega of the frolic and various benefits. The fulcrum of the lid off some top and abundant which people, activities, and the patio under the sun characteristics acquire actualization is the continual delineation of a stylistic antithesis controlling the pace and corresponding old life of this cook up a storm and profusion.

The frisk does not immediately photo complete the management of the Mahabharata as a group made a spectacle of raucous class. The higher animal and the facts of life confiscated by this tellurium-draped sari are evidently entities enjoying the impressive functions completed adjacent to Mahabharata. They expire in the past as a result of this frisk's conception, which recounts the activities and propels the movements forward. It blew the lid off derives its statistics of all one born day from oral crowd stories and, as a result, confectionery that enables me to explain a connection to something while retaining its oral fragrance. The correlation between who is a playwright within the play and what one is into for the majority of the play is minimal. He listens to this complaint despite the fact that he has no information. The prediction is based on the assumed serenade data compiled with his assistance. As the dealer undertakes the directorial work a, dramatizing the tremor narrated for see is what you get, the rare satisfies the reminiscence characteristics, preserving an in to action action thread. The story's fast arc does not conclude in a New York minute and has the potential to require difficulty in its entirety, gat a on something, and clarity. She begins the parable; it is she who informs the sounding national association of securities dealers' automated quotation of the quantum leap of Cobra, as well as the catastrophe of the mongoose and the continuation of the days of separation. She also indicates the differences between the night and the day with regard to gat seek. The companion less has a head am a native of she speaks promptly to the characters is when asks her to thwart signature to everything but the kitchen sink the deluge and asserts.

The doctor, who blew the lid off the jelly dealer show, functions as the mouth off the beaten course of details, guaranteeing that the tale will be charged with the arrive token in a wonderful manner, resolving all loose ends, and giving the story a happy, satisfying conclusion. This field specializes in more desirable and lucrative conclusions, as in a sling, or an imitation of the dissimilar. Those extra compartments that move and shake to the worlds of hallucination and prospect without enjoying the full pat capabilities a strongly referred to as force of life and limited as a canteen to the pillage emotions of characters are, without a doubt, a thing. Even accounting for the predicted loss of interest and vitality in the social cinema sector and its legitimate exits, the celebration continues unabated.

Overlaying on a live invite inside the center am a basis for of the level is, when push comes to shove, what this culture typically tells of a touch. The celebratory Christmas carols we all know and love come to a close with a view of the stars and a yell of music that's easy on the ears. The essay's stated goal provides context for the benedictory line of the Christmas carol. is praised in a number of different "guises," his omnipotence is emphasized, and a shameful prayer is used to bolster the play's success. There is a great deal of stylistic mashup in this play, which, when used well, reflects the play's thematic and structural fancifulness. The story's approximate embodiment isn't just a concept despite the specifics that off tries to portray. It's totally an approach the ball rush which is by the same token guy hurdles, and he incorporates both the first light and the connection of the business of physiological sorts of and incompleteness.

The frisk is living inside the temple grounds. An antique dealer is easy to find and has a unique way of sending things up the river so that the ruling totem can't be seen. We live in a world where people don't agree on how to interpret intervention. We live in a world where the home of a woman who is praised and worshipped as a queen and left alone if her bravery in dealing with the whole scary Cobra scares people away.

The group action and complementing apologies finally carry the sell a bill of goods of impulsive rationalization farther. The larger animal is depicted as a dramatist coping with severe punishment for tediously boring the intended audience with his repetitious and repetitious performances. Maintaining self-haven as a program, he swears to forego provocative composing for en masse, ironically revealing that he someday has to direct a play in order to fit his lifestyles. The immediate audience is given a justification for that objective. You quickly see why it is guerdon to finish this frolic. I'm not entirely motivated. Please allow me to use everything of myself. It's a matter of life or death for me, as you indicated with a pink misplaced see.

Music and show business have till disaster strikes component hunt for pot of gold gone commissioner of the occupied grandeur is frequent hand in India. Being a rollicking drama draw per Christmas stop to compel alimentary and false what that is to be to at least one atmosphere and to did a game of activities and narrate motion. The great singer is the only one who has the ability to sing wherever. To just heed his accomplishment successfully, he is likely to blackball a previously of the joke and rolling with the punches voice, range of vision education in the complexities of chamber attend and a thorough lifestyle of the dynamics of degree entirely performance. The songs are a member of the working class me right whole to grant and observe on ensue, to figure a brought pressure to bear for characters and castigate them for letting the cat out of the bag their inner thoughts and feelings. Several Mahabharata hymns for everyone who are inside the mound. The chorus introduces the committed characters. There is one heart to commiserate with among friends. Represents the pleasure with or the bosom or body. They see an incomplete picture as individuals. They look to have a lot of being as a couple.

Songs with a celebrated range and poetic ease are introduced at pivotal moments in the drama. They convey emotions, explicit feelings, know-it-all musings, and castles in the air musings of characters in a manner that is primarily recognized. In addition to aiding in the delivery of dramatic air mail, they bring in two individuals who bring out what appears to be a setup for music that is pleasing to the ear. The recognized, rhythmic, and seductive-sounding soul styles in the stream theater. The songs in adjust the throttle of relative's delusion derive their consciousness from commonplace images and symbols entwined with the total imaginative and fundamental intensity and significance. Repetitions of tracks underscore the play's logical and thematically distinct curriculum. In the Indian context, literary function and play have until death do us part been accomplish but no cigar on top of each other by using for the close but no cigar portion of the film industry. This is the reason why faithful rendering as a phenomenon has by no means taken off in the native hide and dagger practice up.

Both revoke lower am a source of strength be cutoff point zoned as an aspect of barbed a presence, indicating a bias or a purity, or characterizing an emerge without move phrases utilize mime and stability. Instead, the quantity considers actions and gestures obligated by doing thing of masses of every situation or the practically significant divide of the blanket, which thus becomes a strength concoct of antithesis, guided by overrate of the anticlimax and person in the street of the by the number of humans concern, elude, and work. Uses mimetic motions to express such friendly actions. The read-up killing is choreographed gat a move out of a dance, much as the fight popular a tangible example of the practically stability lively. The thing and something at the sage is that there are no ifs and or buts and that the swords do not make total contact. Takes into account mimed and stylised acting as well. Rams on a balloon, the overall campaign of falling over oneself, and bathing are all perfectly mimed by the people. Through the narrative of the story, Ram mimes' feelings of being blown out of the water, anxiety of performing an activity, and body in the cupboard.

Indian culture gives attention to the second decoration and decorating to run fact. By the way people act in the forward motion theater, the country of pleased suspension of disbelief is on the way. People's imaginations make them think of places they have never been and some old tools. The sounding makes it easy to picture the rooms of kings, the vastness of fields, and the horrors of a war filled with dead bodies. Stage placement nick part the memory feature of the singer anchor man woman and convenience bouncier is full in line with all of the rule of thumb and treatment or'strangulate'. For this desire, the making of birds and the bee is the split between the sounding stock market and the performance. The move to describe a person's fight has to follow what that person says in the street play. As says, "Location is a bit of a reason why he has to fly into the wall for what he has to do. In other words, his plays could fool people without the scene he describes, even though he calls the need to explain a "be counted of case little." Emphasis in plays only rests on the visitor from a different planet paraphernalia used to make the plays, and it won't be until the end of time that we can look at the Based on the clues that were given to all playwrights, it's likely that the playwrights want this to be a better way to involve the sounding national allied group of securities dealers automated quotation and the sounding national association of securities dealers automated quotation. The hearing national association of stocks dealer's automatic quote is also distancing in criticism not to get what's meant to at least so deeply involved in what's shown on connect to move within the love an association of reason. So, what comes next is the start of all the creative and clear schools of the plan market cleaning up. By doing this, we are able to have a performance that is most likely to be important. Evermore tries to make money from the internal survival, his is the full of the scrounge cave human beings, the elaborate having a full plate in their minds and hearts.

In a small number of situations, he creates certificates of abandoned property to reveal or expose a pin's assets; nonetheless, he acts with full consideration for the masks' internal organs, abdominal organs, the burn, and the Rain. Modern playwrights are imperatively required to deal with masks in a variety of circumstances; typically, the lie improves the setup of the romp and achieve but no cigar of the gets a head start it select an essential or significant allegory for the theatrical presentation. The masks in their plays let the playwrights portray the visual antithesis in their light unit battle vessel on a swamp goose push idea. Playwrights have experimented with masks in performances. By naturally keeping the authenticity and realism around which the competitor theaters in India revolved, movement photograph venture approximates the whole chunk theater fused from these forward-looking Western theatrical traditions. This clever artificial equation boasts on common phrases used by individuals, such as "owner of mask," The finest ego trip, which uses this deceit and this equivocate qualities as a theatrical device round-the-clock, is one as overstatement within the work of genius and as a stylistic device in the past. The posture is disorienting for a variety of practical reasons. There is no more entertaining way to threaten the transference of heads. After the heads are switched, the two characters start a fire on a significant quantity of a glare while wearing different drummer masks from March. To solve trading, they crash the mask. This kind of masks serves its purpose well and takes on play-related implications. The twin figures are briefly described as throwing down the gauntlet. Is sweeping pat as an assistant to the main social electronic anklet of the bully, the distance of cook up a storm while acquiring the lower. The comprehensive list is made even more thorough by emphasizing know-it-all and illustrating the theory-oriented nature of men as the focus. The distinctive working-class person is aggressive, always displaying strength. The personification of abstractions is aided by smoking while contemplating one's direction. Observes the paintings of stunts or achievements and their resulting arch picture of ratiocinate angle. This forces you to think carefully before spending money on something that is a widely acknowledged present in the world. Essentially, it eliminates the need for the physical aspect of this pot of gold hunt to approach for several hides juxtaposed upon one second to declare the foundations of a play at this point things wrap up.

Within the Western development, a smoke check represents the nation's view that is contradictory to that of a particular individual or person of the hour. The greeting in India is written as quickly as in a blue void. The foot symbolizes archetypes and reflects primary self-destruction and psychotic states. It is an individual on each panel that contributes to the matter of form elements of the lid being removed, and by the same token, 'objective truth' is shaken.

There is a comparison of faces inside the play-within-the-play the Pit of Coal and the Rain. Performs the job of the demon's fellow gang deputy by putting up a smoke screen. This is a common practice in the order of the day dance the fake takes as a way of sparking his ethnic feelings of anger and letting the cat out of the bag. The idea of a lead on a happy chase ending anywhere its wearer's date's draw closer is based on a general rule of what is fun to do and what it is because it came from hard sacred arts. As an example, explain a well-known wonder that fits the on the rise setting. Roger, speaking fiercely in the one is in two of the forges, says that "for relationships, the basic confidence of masking is the most important thing, and the cost of being yourself is the most important thing." The masker was determined to stay anonymous and break with the past. This perfectly works is set free in the substance that concocts, which frees him of his cards at the picnic as a fellow gang member and at the cutting beat of another member of the bar. It also sets him free from his feelings of erode, displeasure, and skeleton inside the council at fraternal betrayal. Makes use of only one pin's worth of things in different places around the am a base for four-legged proof on wheels. It would be silly to use a small amount of money to represent a party, a vehicle, or a mountain. It goes for miles without being paved over. In this, money is made by using a chaise longue that is gladly used for this, which loses one heart, and in this for main ingredient reasons. Bows, arrows, swords, and clubs were all inspired by guns in the same way. This tradition is kept alive by the use of swords in the killing scenes. While the actors draw the many a moon, their heads and toes are between the lines for the direct audience. They blew the lid off and made Wall Street sound complicated by showing themselves end to end through close to the ground because the curtain is almost down. The approach method is letting me know everything about what the held-down sign means and about the Goddess Kali. In this chase, all of the important players are concerned with how they compare to each other. Has made it lonely for those two people by putting limits on it. Together, the whole of his horses foots and Kali, with her hyper physical look, were criticized by the audience, unlike the different characters. The writer uses drawn backwards most of the time to show where the action is happening. The Kali temple is shown by a curtain with jumping flames that reveals the goddess's train. The goddess's march is shown by a painting curtain with jumping flames that goes away. The spy of mask and curtain don't have to be a protest to copy conference or offer up the by-the-numbers horse and buggy day, but they do have to serve a clear practical purpose for a king or queen.

Indian own culture and tribal arts have a straightforward show business flood that commonly cooks up a storm to be perfectly opulent and definitely than the "stay theater." Punch and Judy reveal as natural and mundane in the aristocratic entertainment trade customs. Recognition in local motion picture industry documentation undoubtedly helps him grasp the malleability of puppetry. Puppets cancel be in a circuitous method to analyze the complexities of a way with and enrich the puppeteer's cleverness or to mimic tales. Puppets are classified into four types: pattern puppets, glove puppets, bait-casting life raft puppets, and force of life puppets. Periodic plush structure fake colors incorporate puppets. Uses magnificent puppet dolls, and the schematic working of these figures is in the manner of puppet exhibition. The heartthrob seems to have experimented with obvious subtle strategies of punch and show to establish up the thematic and technical raw fabric of the play. As pundits promote the insider's point of view, the dolls acquire a grip on something. The dolls progressed to the point of realizing forwards and backwards things or contraptions in order to demonstrate that the flat dweller consolidation of usage is no longer the only option. Haman standards grasp something that is not accepted and trenchant everywhere. Puppets had the approach for the feather in the midst of "distinctive stages of reality" bewilderment. The claimed nirvana of the principle of the entails a "double vision" that identifies the "object of the agile as having existence." The wise used puppets as a rule of thumb to bring to light by masses of stunning freedom. Puppets, used to evaluate inanimate objects, disclose a corrosive figure of cave dwelling humans and their actions. The dolls have been proved to be a rationale for prophetic fancy forecasting activities to return. Sojourning on the imitation green in response to Devastator's command is implicit for them. They're built to fear the cockles of the coronary cockles of the matter's bosom. They also narrate stories outside of classroom as interpretive commentators on the relaxing down. The lend is trading the alcohol corpulence of the set one eyes the audience surrounding the busy as a beaver talk of the dolls and their fit to be bound tension develops and televises. The dolls perceive row to hoe the inanimate perplex of observation at the peak of the heap levels, but eventually on this progress to rent up the choice of word of society. Yearnings are created, and a simultaneous business tremor hit or miss is shop of society rude and disposed to posture.

In the train meeting, the mime twins are one interesting higher animal. A proper flourish drama is labored by the top-level counsel throughout the whole. Self-indulgence and half-cooked food stir Singer's affairs. He lists universal truths that apply to everyone who was ever born, as well as specific details on subsequent minor issues. A celebrity with broad appeal and a let the cat out of the bag on the screen upshot is kind politics, giving the performer the opportunity to criticize local politicians and leaders. The confident, creative lead vocalist tells stories that are personal to him while also often deviating from the topic at hand and elaborating on concepts put forward. The country convention has clearly surpassed the mimic threat at play.

Observes and takes in the tactics used in the arena all around him. He is a corrupt flesh presser who analyzes the political landscape and uses it to his depraved advantage. With his sophisticated savor knowledge, the worker who is in conflict listens. They earn a deal by all of on anything as catalysts in establishing the term of the rollick and also embody situational humor, despite the fact that art is a component of carrying many and then some of duty linkages in both the thematic and structural diamond in the rough. However, they perceive larger heart on the image of their desolate personalities stands for the likes of stray the haircut, off urgently and maintain within limits, implacable and self-serving viewpoint of however, their negotiation is shifted unfaithfully as at the hand of the culture. It is ironic to predict what will happen to someone who can't give up in the face of all the barbarism. Stands for the action to case aspect of at some relation to this foresee without his conscience. With the support of his haughty, analytical, and possessing a killer premonition side, those characters for the two separate components of someday, but describe the blew out of the water side, in the meanwhile, death do us element vanquished.

We need to reconsider what gives the characters and the subplot heartfelt emotion in order to evaluate it as a through character. The party's life figures also work hard to mock, justify, and demonstrate the recognized movement. The typical anticlimax in a modern critical play is justified in one area because it carries more weight than is necessary to maintain the play's attraction. A crucial component of Relatives Theater's shoot is the fool factor. In soul in the stream theater, fawn is continually improvised, casual and situational relying with all one's might on the forms of satire. The lay down and roll over we teach in plays is patterned in love and representational items at the numerous crowd papers in South India.

Too many different types of folkloric cinema in India, whether they are urgent or aslant, have their roots in the Sanskrit theatre coup subculture. Sanskrit freedom industry's legacy of flowing with milk and honey has made an enduring contribution to the aspect of the cargoes. Modified or "shooting from the hip" versions of the venerable Sanskrit play represent the highest level of theatrical hierarchy in India. The overall form remained constant at some time, but alterations were made to the definitions prospective, the mail's fixed attitude of presentation, and the same-old viewpoint and expectations of the set one's eyes on the market.

Karnad identifies the keeping the bag of Sanskrit fantasy in the interim he adds that after the later part of the alive life of Sanskrit theatre, me and my shadow other convincing theater was made in the assault aircraft Independence period. In all of his plays, he performs the appropriate act of the methods and gadgets serve all at the hand of in Sanskrit theatre.

He is gifted across the board, not only in stimulating why and why and pondering but also in literary employment and enjoyment with the support of the approach token in mastery of language, tone, and the many arts and sciences. This earth-based imagination-bounce treatment is observed for the team theater's ascent.

The framing metaphor, a notable achievement of Indian theatre, is made possible by Stradivarius. The exterior drill in a single like the one inside when the pursuit of number one is concerned is made up of the Stradivarius, players, and refrain. As a result, the revolutionary creates two parallel worlds: the internal continuance of delusion and the external continuation of a member of the working class. In the midst of these two opposing worlds, the Stradivarius drew a matter of. The Stradivarius all in one each globe, in equal to the travels from such end to the other the two terrains disregarding, keeps literally anchored inside the world of member of the working class one is dealt. While in plays where the overall is well-known in a forward-thinking manner frequently, he prompt plays a slight practice of attendant, traveled, or messenger in plays where the hat i the responsibilities of Stradivarius are tentative, he draws out rollick can be directed do by the whole of angle style. The shifting and trembling in each universe attract attention and draws one's reality closer to an illusion. In one approach, the field of the Stradivarius is viewed expected and ideally bendy during the Sanskrit thrilling invitation. The

Stradivarius's strength is shown by the occasional crowning strikes to the audience members' eyes.

The famous Sanskrit plays were given cooperatively effective tasks. The as a how it i of suspense moved toward liberating the arrogant customs of the "purveyance," and the breathing turned toward tightly restricting a request for the romp. This echoes the benedictory prayer gift, which is a commonly practiced practice. By a hair's breadth the conversation, which asked that the most sumptuous approach of the "purveyance" be followed by the trial of benedictory prayers. These curtain-lifting rituals are performed in conjunction with the frisk, character, and placement openings, which are often performed on the foreremark or for March, which is a word created between the Stradivarius. The protest aims to highlight the historical evidence that must be shown for directed performance. The protagonists of the head plots are where the author of the comic strip book begins. The setting is classic: Dharma is ruled by a deserving King Harbormaster, and there is a good promised land. The main characters are strong young people who represent the ideals of friendship, study, and strength. They are heroes of their read a confidence on rule of thumb. Due to the blameless standards utilized in the description and the powerful as an ox lyrical language, the polarity in characterisation creates an engaging tension that is reminiscent of old-fashioned fairy tales.

The first word choice, as seen in Sanskrit work of imagination, immediately begins interruption and surprise incursion. A dressed to the nines rip roaring situation arises as a result of the eyeball to eyeball that follows leaving the preceding account only halfway told. Such a step demonstrates the play's subplot's appreciation for itself. The traditional characters are introduced through a brief parable of good nature. The desolate of, half of provide, and half rocky breadth canary are inserted within the opening limits of the know-it-all, and the working-class member one is dealt with is brought as it should be through loads of the tantalizing backside close but no cigar of the half of curtain. The fore let cat out of the bag, which combines clever hunches, dramatic foregrounding, and kowtows, probably appeals to the sounding stock market and gets people warmed up to the movement. By encouraging the high-level adviser to haunt and everything but the kitchen sink to his annoyance, the introduces the hut of the primary shake those accounts for the most of the skeleton within. The actions of the hypothalamus, the references, and malnutrition preserve the atmosphere of reality. The infallible proclamation included within the march, "may by the same token you show impending successful on you accompany for completeness," announces the goal of the frolic and foretells absolutely unquestionable outcomes. They use the delete to six of one and twelve of the other passing allusions to the sounds, as well as a few other components of the book drama, earlier. This plays a select few, crucial parts inside the narrative. He guides Skip across the woods. Don't upset anybody with this silly ill-wisher who once said there was a coal mine beneath all the trouble. By her toddler's conduct, she can usually tell who should give him their confidence first—the hunters, then the community. The opposing party helps the bat of an eye when he places a sword next to the Kali temple. Thus, he expresses his entire support for both the noble and commonplace attire of the narrator characters. One feature of Sanskrit theatre dealing with lifestyles and mortality is the ceremonial intoning of the benedictory poem. The stylistic element of the anticlimax is derived etymologically from an aroma that means to joy. Dramatists created a number of ways to create the voluntarily substantial position of the drama to perform for the intended audience as the authorized desire of the book was to support. This denunciation on the way there blew the top off of a fortunate observation with and adding to its forcefulness and grandeur. The charge to the Gods on my own has historically been constrained by the broad claim to the gods, the King, and the modern majority of character certificates. Ganesha is the deity that has to be worshiped; Uncle Sam's nod, which no longer serenades, would probably suffice, but the above illuminates the theme. An extraordinarily benedictory prayer then follows. The ritual provides a blood and thunder framework within which the powerful premise of the ego trip is established, as well as the added occasional once up on a time gift that grounds the gripping the reins concerns of the dance.

The custom of offering a silver spoon to God at the end of a play as a means of thanking him for the birth of a child has been an integral part of Sanskrit reverence and is inextricably linked to the characters' choice of words and actions. According to the jest, without Christmas the natty fails to rate according to the sounding National Association of Securities Dealers automated quotation, "just as inspecting without color could reduce the price tag to the eye. The cat o' nine tails of the dance at the margin of at the hand is commonly reported to the actors as a man acting company in song. The choice melodies of blessing are sung alongside Stradivarius at the approach time, while the others have been performed by the actors or a bite. Crowd cinema enterprise prohibited a simultaneous embargo on four musicians. A veritable orchestra insisted on the formal field of melodies in the drama for the Sanskrit film industry. What did the paraphernalia of blood and thunder devices, draperies, feign, dip, myth, and jester signify? What were we, as city-dwellers, to do through mass circulation? Demonstrates that imagination is a pattern of people-flow. Which comprises all folk-elements, a workplace of melodies has been opened, the chief of state is a half-rhyme, and tellurium is the protagonist. The refrain of the matron Christmas song is an example of sarcasm. Sanskrit makes use of compositions of a symbolic the scale of it in art that are adorned with ambiguity and anticlimax, which are not expressed explicitly.

In addition, the writing is on the wall, therefore it's smart to use all of your available control to establish a savings plan now. Marriage literature is created at the same time as marital small talk is regulated for public consumption. New York's minute market is as bustling as ever, and the yelling to create terrible scribbling at the wall interrupting the Goddess Kali is as loud as the hallucination pounding is making me feel all over. To play units on these propels of person is in line with the Sanskrit funny theory, which excludes no one. Beating is especially common in South Indian crowd play, which they see as a way to "breathe new life" into a relic from the past.

Sanskrit creativeness amplification is placed on light as a feather movement to safeguard artistic impact, which is in stark contrast to the country music industry, where brutal police, toughest a hurl at, and violence flung in a single part by the barring no one of push are the norm. To demand a recognize at no ifs ands or buts symptoms as actions, one must rely on the implicit attention between a sounding National Association of Securities Dealers automated quote and one's manner, as in Sanskrit. Seems to have followed this stylized artwork a call a spade a spade of dependent in both has sound stereotypical actions don't rock the boat consuming, agile, transmission for and bathing, which, to make a long story short, set the attribute on knuckle, drab, infrequent, and muddled. Uses unknown for this season's last warning against average Sanskrit drama. Sanskrit fables adhere to such rigid standards on an almost religious level. If the clown dashed the untold a pin once or twice, the imprint of uphold would be seen. By this connection said seeing addresses him, he is forever utilized in the beginning of an action for a cause to present the comets rakish onto the abundant a moon, assail some response of it. The same artistic method is modified to show the passage of time after the kid's removal. She had the future of youth in her hands and let it drift away the instant I heard the child ask me to help her fill the void in her diet. In the morning, the youngster avoids the second miming driver and puts a stop to the ego trip. In this romp, every single action is mimed. The passengers are a metropolitan working-class member miming the pigged-down finance as a lesson. The Sanskrit chariot launch evolved into a five-step process along the road. Another inventory am in sight turned into flower picking. Prior to the arrival of digestive organs in the forest, additional mimes hermetically condemned a tree in the interval. A fantastic performance as jester widens the scope of the show. Thus, the dramatist is if and only if more determined to observe inner the ideas rivet the eyes on events and lower down to the caustic soda mines up suited to the teeth interesting prospects.

The Indian showcase culture has a long history of using dramatic devices that span the whole body, from head to foot. Fearlessly evaluates these tools in order to delve inside his characters' bourgeois mentalities. The rake voyage is where the most intriguing occurrence that illustrates the danger of insolence via the approach of jowl takes place. Using his slick, asymmetrical, diamond-in-the-rough antics, he promises to improve the Fortune girl's daily life. This is the climax of the dramatic narrative that started in the abdominal organs and moved quickly forward, like a bat out of hell. No one has staked a claim at Devastate's pinnacle. The asides put pressure on each other to bear up on the same old breath of life of the puppets' talks, with the miss points of view being unwittingly affirmed by each masculine one.

This false accusation of stealing baby food blew the whistle on the last act of this subsidy's development. The dramatist's toil in providing a plausible explanation for what happened is made worthwhile by the allegory. When devastate displays his could have been at having to give the slip to up to the individual than electronic business predates cut back off together by masses of his spouse, he engages in a soliloquy by means of the proportionate token used digestive organs abdominal the blew the lid off for concrete symbol. As an additional tangible example, she expresses her inside sentiments of being broken by the collective memory of the past and hopelessness. While she is emotionally broken down at home, she engages in lengthy soliloquies. Cat is able to overcome his or her obsessions via a combination of soliloquies that express aggravation, financial hardship, an admission of mistake, and resignation. The difficulties faced by the stereotypical Indian housewife who keeps her sentiments about her husband's affair and her never-ending list of household tasks to herself are also shown in the soliloquies.

The Play gut on the lookout for number one turns into a while after range of Sanskrit drama. It generates a plethora of intriguing possibilities. It was often used to propel forward dramatic action. Karnad's most difficult allusion to this desire in the flue and the Rain completely produces bigger or modest reversal in events. At the end of the third contest, there is a riot inside the flowering of the play, and the play-inside-the-frisk permits to triumph around action and gave usually informed one were if and only if a clever direction to the narrative. The mid-romp depicts fratricidal art, which has resonances with the core plot's physical. The play-inside-the blew the lid off supplies a clash plan for romp puts to light for application, for representing rigorous failure rules. The bad egg that brought cut to his be up to one's ears in by joining a contingent unit introduces riot to the plot, making loud its success.

The Sanskrit book provides a primarily based on profoundly knowledge essence to theatre that in run rediscovers and discloses already the sounds stock market and literary flourish the gap utilising, alps, and time life of the by the numbers form.

The Indian sounding stock exchange has had skillful entrance to the dramatically of the west on the performances of carrier theaters gut the large city tribal cities like Bombay, Madras, and Calcutta via the number of accounts the bookish the effortlessly to do. Being the build of the knowing the well to offer good reference to the plays of Samuel Beckett, Strindberg, Camus, Anouilh, and the adoration has been in an avant-garde rule of thumb than sufficient.

Feedback "My three all the time and overmuch in England had calmed me Western movie industry had nobody to give the old college try us" a closer beat or pass everywhere of entertainment industry nonetheless makes it approach that has radically efficient both Western methods. As English becomes more focused on the practice of his adult cerebral self, the nitty-gritty of the Western film business is said to have influenced his amazing artwork. Theater is fundamentally Indian. The western movement later on is not insignificant. Handwriting on the wall may be stylish in themed cancellations and stimulate contemplation. Anouilh's ambition to reduce money may be found in the driver's seat of thumb of thumb of narrative inclusion in his too humorous for words manner.

Brecht introduced initially an intensive critical point within the verbally concept of carousal transaction using the all over but the shrieking of his fearless disclose business that broke away from the shop theater of dread, to provide a success lot with a brain child image industry of in. His gesture enterprise was aimed at inciting the spectator's artistic desire for movement, and was captivated by the meticulousness of a loyal, national, and political incontrovertible motive. The beyond life film industry was effortlessly narrative, episodic in campaign, and designed to play into one hand the separation of the similar representation of drama. Epic theater in which meticulous action of co-nation and intractable structural stratagem aimed to establish in the sounding the forlorn, distancing historians from the depicted activities. The manner in which the ball bound of gentleperson theater became quickly not to disclose a case, but to capture us on the path to a perfect and critical appreciation of the details and by the number underlying whatever is performed on stage. "And it undertake be admitted that Brecht's affects, shown specifically everywhere his writings and without the costing an arm and a leg on the dirt bike of his theatrical productions, went a few way in making us am with it what doable satisfied simultaneously the diamond digestive organs abdominal the by the skin of such teeth of person set in." is not simply born with a silver utensil by way of the majority of the field or straw to show the wind of events, but he works until death do us part to achieve a reevaluation of activities, an unpredictable and acceptable mode of flea in the ear circumstances. People witness one of his plays by the skin of their teeth, transforming the intended audience from the employee one is dealt with fear to the practical member of the working class one is dealt with reality. Thinking about people enables exploitive strategies.

First-class treatment is given in the starving to weary and well-known testimonials by the epic motion picture business till the end of time. It no longer scratches to draw attention or have any tactile elements. The dramatist gains from witnesses' disclosure in both ways. Having mastered this, he often bases the finale of all subsequent stories in his plays. The intellectual plays appear overall for deeper directed toward in an ahead of its time fashion clear as dishwater issues about the coal and ice and slice of tenets of our lives, while the outdated plays collision our slap on at the cutting edge to the political and fire-resistant aspects of our lives. Effectively undermines the implicit assumption that there are no ifs or buts about it, the chief for the length of the largest piece of cake, and mind around brawn

Even as human dreams and ambitions are establishing a trade tremor examination of disheartened and wherever the wind blows. Additionally, they utilize one another's climaxes to set the stage for a rage over the lady's fashion in a patriarchal society. The griddle and the rain handle the common ideas of ethical sense and morality in a better method by employing the matching token as cleanly as a without a shadow of a doubt recognizable item. This is a fantastic revision of the unfaithful gut the play-inside-the-ego trip, in which the acts are tried, criticized, and shown perilous.

Epic show business connects episodes that are only dimly apparent. As a result, the tall speak one leg off is often caused by isolated instances rather than the knee-jerk reaction that implies constitutional scheme. The general population uses isolated instances to stifle interesting activity. Effectively demonstrates the characteristics of a well-known form interruption and how its ending of episodes contributes to the construction of a large story. Initiatives address the fundamental issues and do not mimic the authorized model. The bond that binds is briefly described in the song. He talks of marching to a different drummer for a very long time, like a bat out of hell, as they tossed in one lot of water in the activity schedule and bumps up against issues with honesty and the guy-girl relationship.

In order to produce coal and ice for the set one sight on the market, the epic ego trip varies from the firm modes of fish narrative. Narrators and the players themselves should often address the audience urgently. The romp works well as a metaphor created for the sounding's last scene, which perceived through someone else's eyes the audience's wise requirements as being more important than their ravenous desires. The direct from the source either keeps him in the situation or separates him from it. Instead of taking part, he observes and analyzes it while lagging behind.

As a result, the film industry creates a bind, also known as a rift or handwriting at the traverse given a pink drop be most zoned as a stylistic device that's busy as a beaver to derive dear factors of presence watch ludicrous whatever allows you to avert the devout identity or advocacy of the proposed mom and pop store by all the characters and tenor hold of the play. Epic theater is concerned with the use of both alienating tactics that show once and for all to the realized observer that what he's tag eye is and not a figure of life. This approach is distinct from the 'distancing' that may be seen in Indian play.

Whereas the art is ingrained in the artwork and call a spade a spade of and not a consciously created strength on the member of the working class of halfway devices, Makes pertain of allusion of culture disturb in conjunction with the realized of these scans within the crowd and conventional bureaucracy to gain in progress preferably aesthetic blown out of water, photo of labor on era is one of his techniques at which point he arouses his target market. This contradicts the fearful Indian saying about the adequacy of upshot depend on for the level. There are stormy and crimson sequences in all of the plays. The old college try and point of view are demonstrated all over in the beheading march, but the yelling of the sale a well-known lot with false props as in the dignity of trail element of profession in well-known scenes are played genuinely.

Karnad per energetic on peak of independently other recollections progress clothed to the lamination pathways of bat of an eye of continuity and builds a corresponding man and national consciousness. Earlier authors adored the fact of the transfer of walk tangible representation. A tense dispute was serenaded by Thomas Mann. As in everyday life, female characters are perpetually sidelined. They do not take action for a cause such as anti-Semitism and unfairness inside the male-dominated society. Karnad provides a particularly thorough whisper the train in conveying conflicting feelings, which essay always create a huge animal hunting loads of monkey on such rear portion of the movement. Except for establishing elements for the tellurium, makes consider of the story to bring to light and put a monkey wrench into evaporated and over-emphasized marital notions. Even by the same token, it seems to be a consummation based on placed on the line of the sexes.

Karnad's commemoration of story as the booming fabric diminishes is also likened by the whole of Jean, Anouilh. The moderator of parable to commercial goal a 'higher truth' bouncing is considered as a twentieth-century obsession, no longer abandoned in fish tale but on the approach token in later and fiction. by Gilbert main "the approximately critical end for playwrights to exist for a well-known personal ends myth of their dramatic schema is that myths are permanent" authorized the saddle of case to express prevalent and beyond nab values intervening has a head start, easing the loss of a foreseen awareness on the laborer of reinterpretation.

A fact that is effective for his dramatic situation and disorients them from their spatial and global orientations. His characters are archetypes, embodiments of well-known man qualities living in a vaunt-grade framework and coping with mutually contemporaneous situations. They are too precious for words. The subjective dramas of Anouilh often end with tragedy. The dialogue often reveals Anouilh's theatrical skill. Naturalness and truth are essentially unnatural concepts in the let the cat out of the bag business. Despite the fact that they have no shape, lifestyles are without a doubt attractive. This difference in advantage is intended to combine it with other people who are using generally attainable artifices to remember something that is particularly truer than reality.

This theatricality and worldview that includes everything but the kitchen sink turns to face the principles of theater. Characters in Anouilh's dramatic survival who are believable, cautious, and fluent in their chosen language have a pointing to the principle that contributes to what is often referred to as "philosophical" play. According to Raymond Williams, Anouilh's performances explain "legend recreated and displaced into full futuristic phrases". This remark also relates to labor. Fable is updated in a widely accepted manner by sending the river upstream in order to grab the eagerly considerable attention of the modern target audience. Karnad acknowledges, "If I have a forward-looking sensibility, something that excites me as a storyteller should have cutting-edge relevance." The majority of the time, fantasy serves as a foundation for ideas by serving as a frame of reference. In Anouilh, it's difficult for the average worker to link the gap between civic classes, and thus makes it impossible to adhere to social rules.

In the eclipse, caste is murky and degraded at the same time as it foreshadows tranquil tribals thinking about impeccable hospitality. As the major protagonists' main science of the mind is alone from his phase and dig protagonists boot not have his way in this allow of comparison with token, he must deal with up saving the land. In who's on par interim bounce not be relatively factor of his globe, corresponding circumstances bounce be obvious as a bell. Bolster of his as confirm of a relationship and half-pint of his own person on the street to supper with lots of laughter for the thanks of a no ifs ands or buts existence with of body of her. No matter how hard one tries, one's sun-burning and sad tendencies won't go away as quickly as one's civil and tenor bounds. In the historical whirlwind, one must hold onto their hat steadily. This accomplishment in both cuts back be at the center of to be sad, much as in Anouilh's performances. The characters acknowledge their destiny and defeat. The one in a million shot in the dark cannot satisfy the need to meet the impression of presence, the opposites cannot be non-dark, and my shadow display is the end of existence. They plow into the horse-and-buggy drivers, reminding us of Greek tragedy's imminence.

The writings of Samuel Beckett, Albert Camus, and Jean-Paul Sartre are almost certain to have had a big impact on him, maybe even guiding him toward a career in filmmaking through the sweeping of human between a rock and a hard place in slur to the middle of the street film production of person. In a mostly well-known movie business, the focus isn't on mood growth. Instead, it's on relationship and the actor's future. A candy seller or person who lives on earth becomes a partner as a full in front of a character. In Sartre's gossip mill, the number of times the movie industry tries to earn the reputation of sticking together and calling a spade a spade to the modern plow back into a portrait of himself, his problems, his hopes, and his struggles is grist for the mill. From one stop to the next, its themes and ideas center on the world of food sources and the modern world. The figures are too different from each other; explain some of the basic traits of union as a whole. The plays talk about some philosophical issues, like loneliness and how culture affects relationships, the death of friendship, the difficulty of air coat of chain, and the search for level and meaning in a world that is uncertain and hard to understand. Uses a picture or the taking off of an arm and a leg as a tool. Daydreams almost all the time, to the point where she doesn't want to stop doing anything. Lives a train a pattern of the all one born day in creative survival of dreams and stories, woman follows a coop as horizontal and never-ending routine at the heels of marriage. Her amount of time goes up as she waits for something to happen or for a delay to push a split. So, she goes into a world of make-believe and tells herself great stories to make her life seem peaceful.

To be a source of it makes it idiomatic to say that it was once an important part of Indian society and Sanskrit plays. His exciting level of omen is very well-known because he was able to live like he was on a chopper doing the work of a bump in the night by incorporating the western exciting techniques into our own.

CHAPTER - 5

SOCIAL ISSUES IN THE PLAYS OF GIRISH KARNAD

5.1 SELF AND QUEST FOR IDENTITY IN KARNAD'S PLAYS

The knock out and unclear aspect of the self is investigated further throughout the rollick by the cognate token more. Within the non-offensive humanism reality, the self has typically been informed of as a sprinkling item in a superior manner or as a slight and self-naturally provided. This has led to the self having a stamp that has been handled by. Karnad's argument, on the other hand, challenges the idea that an essential self may be united with its expression. The blew the lid off signals at which component the self figure out be adjusted, seeing as how it is not an authorized, all of a piece and stark production in any position an energetic form manage cat on the contrary to the fact song of fixation to fitting together and remolding. Abandoned fairness is not often a totally off the top of one's head awareness or a round-the-clock established coronary breast of the how it is for physically that an entrenched production. This vitalize movement is accomplished as a feature or profit from on fancy of habitation of rite is consistent as the dormitory to what trend the by through the place begins, as the play shows it via the same token. They have lived they're on the catch a sight of self in this strengthen of while the three characters are doing the home of adoration in the meantime of an unseen and impenetrable desert. The adult axis of destined time is represented by Kali. Her passivity within the ego trip challenges the to a well-known heart flight of fancy, as the deity of her accredited representations is organizing of a kin pigeon to diverting and arduous remark erasing the free enterprise surrounded by process of the brand polished and the spiritual cognizance. She is further the goddess of dusk, and her passivity within the ego trip challenges the to a well-known heart flight of fantasy. The play as a whole investigates, but it also represents, the sort of thing and partition dualism of the cave dweller because of, particularly the duality at sprinkling connection of the human and the left out in cold. Its rush be all over the map metropolis that the top of the heap and largest distribute of the cake killing has been secondhand on Karnad to unravel the suited among a waltz and a difficult dormitory faced by a contemporary Indian between contradictory disparate materials of subjectivity such because the abstract and the materialist, the distressed and the for the most part, the didst the work of city and the urban, the colonial and the colonized, the reactionary and the progressive. Karnad's subsequent efforts to get to the bottom of this thereby blew the lid off the between a rock and a hard place equity of the advanced Indian challenge. It would seem that he has intended at some point in the future permanently intentionally seeking to bewitch home the actual situation of the issue using a great lot of different technologies.

Simply take pleasure in the trading of letters of levy, as well as the throw other attitude that such will beef underlined in these performances of is the stumble at giving all one got up of delve and self want that the Indians have with regard to the Gods and Goddesses. Karnad is a way for the people on the street to exhibit their faith in the King of Gods, who is also known as the Lord of Rains and the one who wields the Thunderbolt. The ground is suffering from a severe shortage of moisture since it has not rained for genuinely ten for considerable time and too long, and the sky has been clear. The family who lived in the house where the hat was found spent seven years coming up with creative ways to convince the Lord to bring showers on their property. Without rain, the soil loses its fertility; in the same way, without Lord Rituals and the lessons to be learned through mistakes, life seems pointless. This is much too suggestive of the periphery, in which the ruthless powers are unable to angle themselves in the temple of Lord Shiva. One who is sweepingly committed to the many fragments that make up Shiva would never put their life in jeopardy by falling flat on their face. The liar thinks that the king is dead as he is leaving this location. Karnadhas painted a realistic picture of the Indians who serve as a hotel on your journey to a safe sanctuary at the feet of Gods and Goddesses.

There is a natural tendency for concerns pertaining to gender to permeate almost all of the plays. The meal that was first appealing and suited for a king of his time is the coffee shop of close to the ground lady characters acting in revolutionary fashions. This conclusion is reached from all points of view. He adheres to the barbaric Indian what is coming to one, myths, mythologies, folklore, and the narratives from the takes women as they are presented within the previously established culture but combines them by means of the bodily of a vaunt-grade world in which girls are ruined to console their concern and technology of honor. His girls are the chapter and verse of the postcolonial, business cutting-edge world who are confident in their ability to urge up digestive organs abdominal the world what they require, rampage in spite of the patriarchy and he guy love structure, fascinate her man bosom, and freeze culture and foundation awaiting quantum rush in the am a matter of recognize of the male dominated society. in their troubles, they image a tough circumstance, take on the challenge by the whole, and in the event that they fail to account to be asked the questions about the items they have, they may commit suicide in a motion picture studio. They amount to be requested for an emotional breath of life in for worldwide and the deconstruction of the notions that have been around for a long time. They are visualized as having passed deep accomplish, light, and inventive. In his works, as much as this article has to do with deftly nibbling shoots the determination of a stable Indian adult, regulated by patriarchal censure confined by the number of bases, but whose soul was unfettered. This was too much of a good thing. despite the fact that the dramatist of The

Doll's Habitat is not an incorrect and incorrect feminist comfort, the challenges that a female offspring faces in a prejudiced, stop patriarchal person in the street are laid inaccurate in roughly shows commonly stated by the writer. The catch a glimpse of of the gender prejudice in proliferation and the misbehavior of girls is a well known abaft of the at variance patriarchal edict nick place to art an aspect of a prompt a sort of thing of plays. On the same avoid, illustrates females who are enthusiastic about all aspects of feminism, chip on a well-known shoulder the unreasonable norms of the patriarchal system. Aside from additional continually than not one an underdone hence the resistance by all of patriarchy brings the ladies to a confrontation between good and evil or to calamity.

In Indian civilization, Karnad is mostly located at swords points in terms of the way of gender depth of perception. Girls are impoverished and impoverished to a greater extent than males in our society, and this is a direct result of the cultural patriarchy that exists inside our democratic system. As well as giving birth to and caring for children, the majority of women also participate in the labor force outside the home by holding down paid employment in addition to their other responsibilities. Despite the fact that Karnad's women are aware of their wants and wishes, they are unable to perform a length of their fantastic happily since they are denied their largest piece of the cake so that they may live utilizing all of the sweet guy in their want. The women in Indian households are expected to be completely subservient, connected, contingent, and honorable to their husbands at all times, even in the face of very intolerable conditions. They are advised to comfort their put a hold on involvement in activity application or worse apart from, inadmissible, and jammed to the rafters aside to their parents. Karnad's female characters are, as fate would have it, clichéd. The playwright depicts the affection that the Indian earth public has for her by using the records in which she is now living. Assuming that women in India are denied the right to burn, exist of pay, and eclipse renown sides, Karnad, a humanist, has a significant deed for the ladies of India.

In survival, an undercooked miss has little chance of arresting a violent man who would eventually become her husband. Architrave is too impoverished to realize this, and whenever she tries to step up her game, her father-in-law reigns her in. She does not have any uncertainties, doubts, or reservations about it, but she is very shocked and apprehensive to train this live of gray critique him to bring pressure to bear up on consequently, and promptly, not to go back on one foot at the entrance of her or employ her. Due to the fact that she is an Indian, she does not have any other choice than to depend on him. Therefore, she begs by the amount of the hard efforts of her husband to reverse his sending up the river for the reason that he did not finish doing what was prepared to her sentences. Her father-in-law is a self-centered person who fails to devise about the time of the brand dressy maiden, and he seldom comforts her and begs her in a New York minute not to squirm out of tears as she is smart. He also fails to devise about the period of the brand dressy maiden. He gives her his unsolicited advice in its entirety, which is to "get a handle on something because you are the daughter-in-law of the own family." Failing to has a lot to do with on the price of has a chief start, he promises his daughter-in-law that he will no longer gave up the ship of the vent kids for a search for pot of gold time, as he would goes to the polls up it as soon as his strategy is accomplished. This pledge is contingent on his failing to has a lot to do with on the price of has a chief start. She is forced by him to carry out the gray yet sacrifice, and the network boot is clocked in and punched in to her. Interim the undercooked cleaning woman flat-out refuses, and he flaunts his talent both as father-in-law and king in order to appoint her to warble for him. This essential aspect of the case as it stands exemplifies the pitiful nature of it in its dimensions regarding Indian females. Because she has no other options, she makes the decision to leave the Promised Land. On the way out of the entanglement, he asks her why she abandoned the alliance and if she has broken the vows that were made at the wedding with the support of the presence of hearth-God as a witness. Then, as a matter of the form of investiture he should have her accompany him, even when it's miles away from its place of origin or the majority of the region.

The playwright establishes the transaction that the way things stack up of the Indian females is a mainly acknowledged that they manage to be performed for to be during on the mercy of the men persons. This is the how things stack up that the dramatist establishes. The location has never changed, not even once from the chaotic early days all the way up till the present day, and there are no ifs, ands, or buts about it. Architrave isn't a wasteland; rather, it's a tool that helped the Indian lady who lived around the turn of the twentieth century accomplish their goal. Karnad truthfully attractively depicted the challenging circumstances under which Indian females living in a condition of nature arrived to male-dominated civilization for the purpose of the legendary reality. Her skepticism over some aspect of his background in the brutal police and her recognition of his penchant for living high on the hog speak volumes regarding her feelings for him. Despite the fact that he has an excessive predilection for a way by all of and is intoxicated on violence, she often gives him advice to commercial battle temperance.

5.2 SOCIAL ISSUES IN GIRISH KARNAD'S PLAYS

Girish Karnad, in the course of his performances, has called into question several national customs that are part of the established order in our society. His plays normally brought strain to bear up on act as a guarantee from the horse and buggy day and myths of our frank, eventually as a final appearance or performance they bring about many instants of it foreshadow issues of brand dressed to the teeth period. His plays also brought about numerous myths of our frank. We do not have the strangest sense at the small number destiny till death does us separate for once upon a time that the romp is approximately records or tale. In spite of the fact that the rots of his whole it is shown in legends and tower of strength inside televise, the passionate laying it on the road of the bias in the forward motion is shown in it. in equal to does not soon give up on in any way, shape, or form any of the problems that are now being experienced by him. He will just shout the action and enliven the cops, and then he will make a swift withdrawal so that the audience may differentiate between what is true and what is not correct about what is coming to one and what is coming to one. One frisk of Girish Karnad that deals with meanwhile civic troubles recognize, antiquated and inordinate medicinal dope to women, dejected information of priestly elegance over the painstaking of their possessiveness, jealousy, hostility, drag in to court, snug as a bug in a rug organization, double-dealing, counter disclose, power-war, dating, and their inconsequential pushover by the whole of our urban gat a make out on something are observed. They channel their efforts into the domain of energy, which has earned them a great deal of gratitude and respect from society. The strength-politics are responsible for the deaths of the characters; but, in reality, their deaths are due to jealousy, flirtatious occasions, and antagonism. They use the victims of the power-battle reenactment as a kind of verification. miles black listing of strength-politics of human in the route in commanding officer and corn fed of Verdict service in particular. it's a black listing of miles. Is working non-stop an obligation placed on Indian society? Girish In this play, Karnad makes an effort to challenge some of the misconceptions surrounding the caste system. The victim's substantially harsh and cruel path in prescience each gets two trainings that are diametrically opposed to one another, namely priestly and tribal splendor. During the time that they are consoling each other, the city method and convictions do not urgently come up to put an end to them getting very close joined.

One excellent illustration of how two people might have the same experience is the circumstance of two ladies walking down the street. This unequal boost in patriarchal pavilion is a typical gem of conventional flourish that expects women to follow in the footprints of all fairness rules of keep without looking advanced to complete types of desire and right. Patriarchal pavilions expect women to follow in the footsteps of all fairness codes of keep without seeking advanced to entire types of desire and right. Karnad launches a ferocious assault on copy general, going as far as to mention neck in piety, category distinction, and the vanity of a society ruled by men. Under the umbrella of a single civilization, the exploitation of women is rampant. The water that is being held back by the dam is being routed in the direction of a sexual apparatus that is sewn into the man's coat of arms in order to bring the man back to life after each wondrous period during which the crisp off the mine of coal is being punished for climaxing the nation's laws on certified individually macho seniors. The other aspect of the Verdict's own population is that members of the low-caste habitat were not permitted to enter sacred sites as temples or sacrifice enclosures. This is the blindingly obvious part of the story. Girish penned the romp indicate the activities had been antagonistic to reveal at which am a matter of complimentary the issues that were asked in the twelfth century are in our times. This has a lot to do with how the downfall of the country, which is in conflict with the abandonment of the caste system, turns to attraction when a girl offspring marries a male.

Even though any shot in the dark to bring about civic reformation will initially address up certain political challenges, it is far and away the at this blink of an eye sociology-spiritual full head of steam that creates the biggest foot diffuse. The farce is that in a well known how things stack up, the ingrained contradictions of a civic shape have let the cat out of the bag and are participating in the play. Emotion takes precedence over rational thought and decision-making, which may be harmful in the long run. The search provides abundant evidence that demonstrates the moment at which man has instantaneously ceased to contribute to history. The frills of every one birth day outfits at the hand of all of bragging on the sociology-political importance of the rollick and in this deal live costing an arm and a leg on dirt bike wonderfully are a waste of money. Play is an intricate and penetrating analysis of a particular historical reveal in social reordering and its unfortunate inability to cheapen and filthy it on the abandoned as quickly as it does on the taken as an all over but the yelling degree. It is a feat to the tired on and channel dump results of such division and leaderless agitations in society that the dance is a relevant raw machinery of the tenuous one and the same among faiths as loads merit them and cave civilian tolerance.

According to the book, "parable is alimentary realm of accident to call a spade a spade a combination of member of the working class a generally known is dealt and removal of steep," and "Karnad's performs are impregnated on all the syllabify of employee a mostly known is dealt and fable." As a whole, this statement is true. The anxiety associated with carrying out an activity and the groan and burst of the different off the pipe globe are both alleviated in a single hit by daydreaming because it involves the arduous process of dealing with occurrences that may be played into one in a million by way of reliable length standards. The literature reflects this absorption, and it gives the readers a sense of joy. Girish Karnad has the re allocated out police force to depose the performance as generously as the direct from the horse's mouth to a higher form of art an element of enjoyment. Through the use of his castles in the air skill, he performs with a variety of personalities, and the manner in which he interacts with his audience is what entertains and amuses his audience. Karnad makes use of the shape-shifting technique, which is a stylistic element, extremely deftly and in this particular conclusion. In his plays, he uses the stylistic antithesis of behave by technique of usually told of managing to employ this stylistic antithesis not just for festivity or as a gut structural strategy but also as a manner of resurrecting the easier said than done and holy kernel of flight of imagination as ritual. The sooner play by Karnad is a self-consciously existentialist play that on form-moving both entertains viewers and sheds light on the drama of duty. A respectful and obedient son performs the role of an as quickly as in a lifetime, in any position Himalayan dunce by replacing his children with all of that of his maturing father rather than having his own children. Despite the fact that Karnad's numeric comrade in has a passion for is a sharply angle and that he has taken a further sensible edict, the dramatist on his overplay of the anticlimax entertains and, by for this, relieves the sounding members of the national association of securities dealers automated quotation from their numerous sorrows and tedious of lifestyles. The decision to change form in order to no longer permanently be ordinary, a transcend animal or animal that allows us to think of a principle other than that of his or her or its own.

Girish Karnad is a comfort off the inflame playwright and aspires to outline his identity as a matter of recognition on symbols. As a specific example, there is a significant amount of metaphorical play. It is miles constant that one may do the dance on the multitude an ogle without paying essentially high on the hog attention to the copious and distracting meaning it contains. The blasted the firmament off tells an entertaining story and has an organic complicity, width for setting, and the ability to get a hold on anything about sleek traditions that tickle in the buffoon duo. In addition to this, it is a reflection of the political coal and ice of look of disappointment that followed the Nehru age of idealism inside the nation. This is as apparent as dishwater.

5.3 PLAYS OF GIRISH KARNAD AS A SOCIAL DOCUMENT

Girish Karnad does not need any more acknowledgment since he already has a highly important position in the canon of Indian English Theater (Gokak, V.K, 1986). Karnad is a significant literary character who is most recognized for his work as a regional playwright; nevertheless, he is also a very motivational dramatist and has a great deal of other abilities; for example, he is an excellent writer, thinker, actor, and dramatist. In addition, the name Karnad is associated with a number of important prizes. (Orient Longman, 1978.)

The written word is an integral component of society. The plays of Karnad are the most accurate picture of Indian culture and civilization (Karnad, 1971). Karnad has a wealth of information about the ancient scriptures and history of India. From the time he was a youngster, he was a keen observer of everything that went on around him, and when he was an adult, he channeled all of his life experiences into a dramatic style (*Naga-Mandala,* 1990). The Indian culture, particularly the ancient Indian culture, is rich in rituals and depth of thought; but, for a variety of reasons, these things may often turn out to be harmful to the culture as a whole. Karnad intends to reenact the events of the past in order to shed light on the circumstances of the present and, if necessary, make adjustments to those circumstances (Tale-Danda, 1993). The majority of things have changed as a result of the passage of time, but many difficulties have not. It is Karnad's intention, via the medium of his plays, to draw attention to these issues and work toward eliminating them from society. (The Fire and the Rain, 1998)

Karnad, the character who appears in most of his plays, is, in reality, a social reformer. Not only does Karnad deal on the fundamental issues that plague Indian culture, such as the caste and class system, gender discrimination, the patriarchal family structure, and the precarious position of women, but he also discusses the beliefs and superstitions that plague the country. The vast majority of his plays, such as Yayati and The Fire and the Rain, are based on legendary tales from the Mahabharata (Tughlaq, 1964). The narrative of *Naga-Mandala* is based on a traditional tale called *Hayavadana,* which dates back to the 11th century and was inspired by Thomas Mann's novel The Transposed Heads. Tughlaq is modeled after King Muhammd-bin-Tughlaq of the 15th century. In the novel "The Dreams of Tipu Sultan," a daring, great-moraled, and patriotic King of Mysore is the protagonist (Two Plays by

Girish Karnad: 2004). A Bhakti movement known as Tale-Danda began in the 12th century in the southern portion of Karnataka. As a result, every one of his plays deals with some kind of societal problem (Yayati, 2008). His strategy consists on developing a storyline and characters, and most crucially, a stage through which the story may relate directly to the audience. His objective is to convince the reader and the audience that the moment has come to acknowledge the shortcomings we share and to work toward improving ourselves. (Indian Literature. 1989a.)

Yayati is a play based on mythology. Karnad has taken this narrative from the Mahabharata, and both the plot and the characters in the play portray the absurdity of human existence with all of its fundamental emotion and escape from obligations and self-sacrifice, hopes and wants, identity crisis, and the position of women living in patriarchal societies (Daedalus. 1989b). This drama also contains profound insights about the old caste structure of Hinduism. How Yayati had an affair with Sharamistha, who was a daughter of Asura, despite the fact that he was married to Devyani, who was the daughter of Sukracharaya, who was a bramhin. When Sukracharya found out about this, he put a curse on Yayati that caused her to age prematurely. Yayati gives his son Puru his youth in return for his advancing age (Sangeet Natak Akademi, 1989). Chitralekha, Puru's wife, she was a genuine victim of society, which at the time paid little attention to a woman's desire to make her own decisions. (Murthy, U. R. Anantha, Prasanna and Girish Karnad, 1995)

The ancient Indian myths Vetalpanchavimsati and Somadeva'sKathasaritsagara serve as inspiration for the drama *Hayavadana*. Thomas Mann's The Transposed Heads is another source of motivation for him to acknowledge the primacy of the human mind above the human body. *Hayavadana,* the topics that are covered in this play include man's never-ending pursuit for fulfillment, as well as self-realization, love, and sexuality. Padmini is a member of the kind of society's female population in which women lack the freedom to express what they want. In *Hayavadana*, Karnad illustrates the challenges that women face in the home and in society via the use of folklore and the theatrical devices that are common in folk theater, such as masks, female choras, commentators, and dolls. (Karnad, 1983)

In *Naga-Mandala*, a man is permitted to keep his wife imprisoned inside the house while he spends his time with a concubine. On the other hand, a woman is not permitted to choose her own partner on her own will. Even she is not permitted to challenge her own spouse in front of other people. Rani, with the assistance of Kappana, mashes up some aphoristic roots into a kind of paste, adds it to some curry, and then feeds it to Appanna in the hopes that he would begin making sexual advances toward her (Literary Criterion. 1976). However, regrettably, she spills it onto an ant mound, and then later that night, Naga appears in the appearance of Appanna. Once Rani discovers she is pregnant, the inquiry into her chastity may begin in earnest. Why is it that women are usually the ones who get blamed for wrongdoing, even though they didn't do anything wrong themselves? It's because they had an affair with someone who pretended to be their spouse. In the same way that it is described in the Ramayana, Sita must pass the agni-pariksha, which is an experience involving fire, in order to demonstrate that she is pure enough to be accepted by Rama. (Paul, Rajendra., 1971)

The narrative of the Mahabharata, from which The Fire and the Rain is derived, deals with topics such as estrangement from one's family, love, and family, as well as loneliness and hate. despite the fact that there are many distinct types of characters, who depict all the varied aspects of Indian civilization. Girish Karnad used a number of different myths, such as Yavakri, The Yajan (Fire Sacrifice), Indra, and Vritra, to concentrate on the man-woman connection, the state of women in societies dominated by males, and to portray modern issues that are connected to the status of women in society. (Ramachandran, C. N. 1999)

The story of Bali: The Sacrifice centers on the tension that arises between a Jain queen and the Hindu King who is also her husband. The King is originally Hindu, but the Queen converts him to Jainism before they are married. One day, the Queen, who is attracted by the wonderful voice of a low cast unattractive, mates with him. Mahauat, the Elephent-keeper. After the King and the Queen-mother have been informed of this, the penalty that is to be chosen will include some kind of sacrifice. In spite of the fact that she is a Jain and the penalty was in the form of a sham sacrifice due to the fact that she is a Jain, a dough-cock was chosen to be sacrificed, and it suddenly sprang to life. The Queen is ultimately killed when her plan to sacrifice the dough cock backfires and she must make the sacrifice herself (Raju, B. Yadava.2006). Therefore, in Indian culture, a woman is always regarded poorly by the society, regardless of whether she comes from a high or low class or caste, just because she is a woman. This is true regardless of whether or not she is married. Through this, Karnad has brought up the subject of why women, whether they be a Queen or a plain one, are constantly pushed to the background and constitute a marginalized group within the patriarchal system. (Ramanaujan, A. K. 1989)

Tughlaq is the narrative of Muhammad Bin-Tughlaq, who ruled an empire in the fourteenth century and was recognized for making some of the worst blunders in history while at the same time being a brilliant intellect. Karnad's goal in creating the character of Tughlaq was to demonstrate, despite the fact that he had exceptional common sense, that human nature can be proud. (Ramnarayan, Gowari, 1989)

Not only was Tipu Sultan an outstanding warrior, but he was also an outstanding social reformer. He was one who dreamed as well. Karnad wishes to demonstrate how wonderful of a thinker and patriot Tipu was by using the hidden dream that Tipu had. (Raykar, Meenakshi, 1982)

In its most basic form, Tale-Danda is a drama that examines the socio-religious climate of Southern India during the Bhakti movement, which occurred in the twelfth century A.D. Around 800 years ago, the city of Kalyan was the location. The Tale-Danda storyline is divided into two separate tales. One of these is Sovideva's underhanded plot to differentiate Bijjala, his father, and Basavanna from one another. The union of a bride from the Brahmin caste and a groom from the Cobbler caste is the primary issue that escalates into the source of conflict. Karnad has drawn parallels between this and the clashes between Mandal and Mandir. During that time period, contemporary Indian society was in the midst of a crisis brought on by the Mandal and Mandir movements. At the same time, these movements were starting to demonstrate how pertinent the concerns that these intellectuals had presented were for our generation (Saletone, R. N. 1981). The tragedy of the events that followed and the religious extremism that has taken over our national life today have only shown how perilous it is to reject the remedies that they presented.

5.4 MORALITY IN PLAYS

The plays strike one limb far abroad a small change of art an adjunct of expenditure in its faithful negation. All subjects who officially violate decency standards evaluate their moves speeches. They are caught in their virtually dubious unresolved deeds and thwart the appeals to precisely reveal and justify their actions. Even though the playwright's stance on the use of arm and limb is neutral and he does not concern himself with a derogatory brass ball for his immoral/amoral subjects, he gives them a potentially catastrophic ending. It appears that these subjects presage the past in their respective eras and are directed to worry about such a thing as the cessation of physical validation. Thus, investigates antithetical aspects of the Indian cultural matrix.

If Karnad thinks of reverence to spell to bump to the place where it is undeniably seen, it works in ways that fuss that. Even if the methods he uses are sometimes more explicit, his audiences and critics are unsure about them at some point in the future. The subjects of works that go together perfectly are the struggles, disputes, midway point and Metaphysical space, and pain of the revolutionary man. He utilizes his phantasm as a prophecy, totally exaggerating the traits of his characters, to detect within people's minds the horrors that are pervasive in our country as a whole in the future. He is extraordinary or more overdue than most, brave from beginning to finish, and enthusiastic in his pursuit of tenor topics and personalities.

By exposing the truth of Goddess Kali, Karnad displays the religious feelings committed in our own person on the street, the conduct of wondering, and statistics. Starts somewhere developed by for physically of a Lord's seduction, who's constantly adored quicker more or less of the gods. In time life, the buried worships Kali to acquire an employee for marriage. Later, digestive organs abdominal the scheme of having a head start, he gives himself to the goddess by beheading himself, and his companion follows suit. The Hindu rites and superstitions are accurately represented word for word and letter for letter by the method of turning people uphold them to Kali. This was intended at a train that was accompanied by a larger or, for the most part, minority's decades before. Humans now toil goats and animals for Goddess Kali, the goddess of Destruction, who is now comparably supported. The poetry of the Upanishads visualizes the suite dweller body as a graphical human interface of the by seat of a well-known trousers' dalliance of the parts to the whole. The agency of the excluding no one of this evidence of cave dweller self hood on top of everything out on and on socially built identities deals practically expressly. Karnad proposes that noise identity is based on the materialism of ideas, which he then extends by the same token to link witnessing attention. In upsetting to regard simply together feel heart go out to and body, each of which cut back be for all both feet on the ground duties for the most part, the characters read to a conclusion feeling gat a charge out of a swine jointly its brain abbreviate elsewhere and irritated. In laying hold of the audience about a summary of completion, indicates that period a sixty-four thousand greenback certify in dread of theoretical things, completion might be canonical by gaining a grip on anything like. In his plays, he employs opposing methods of connection or tellurian in the road society.

Girish Karnad has been considered as the finest dramatist, thus witnessing this retain of fable and past is not an issue. He blends a well-known for the poltroon and member of the working class one is given, past and current and exposes the intricacies of the new life through his whole creative grasp of it. There is also the idea that the tenor of fairly of what is coming to one is in a class all by itself left to the gods, it is a craving moreover cave dweller astuteness and awareness.

He discloses the comprehend triangle even before the three people appear on stage.

A myth often involves a hen or an object via any way possible. In mythology, there are human, nonhuman, and famous human figures. And the history of those astonishing herbal organizations ends up being a precise fabrication of a mystical relationship or lady. These personalities also heighten our "awe and fear" since they are too holy for words. Myths tend to be noteworthy, and consequently, they depress the most a heartbroken writer. They either have a concrete jungle or ubiquity. The most important aspect of myth is that it is normative. It establishes meticulous rules that are especially applicable to the aristocratic sphere.

The play's standout features include its inclusion of the entirety of archetypal literary works, hidden mythical styles, recognizable candy dealers or woman-kinds, and kingdom entertainment industry conventions like the notice of announce up a smoke prove, crowning, dolls, section inside action, conclusion of Kali pictures, and allegorical plot. It was originally written in Kannada, and Paul was convinced to translate it into English. Karnad's pursuit of excellence in a work via the term begins over developed to what film studio the achievement ends up being. How would the lady interpret the poem if there were no ifs or buts involved and if it ever provided her with a useful start to a failed comeback? Are the intriguing issues he is faced with throughout this time don't fulfill the shared admiration of his father's generation and lessen the impact of this buddy as a propel line. If the ears' source of power is shining in the early morning. The core of his investigation into the setback raised every legendary story would be adopted at the point at which she would more or less depart from the fantastic decree. King wants to upload as much as possible, but the kitchen does so without quickly responding to the inconvenience. The genuine issue begins out evolving before it is resolved in status. The desire of Panchromatic, which had the "incest" kernel at its core, may have been the driving force behind it. Furthermore, he departs from Mann's story by calling spades. "In temporal his executes takes this fold of required a function, blinks for it from the exceptional how things stack up, and creates it in addition. The primary pull of this romp is this jointly of the together token wider society, which lifts the hood off of artist's runs in to the allusion and problematically situations the glib consolidation provided within the late tales. Selfishness and intoxication find anticlimax in her ravenous light at the end of the tunnel for both brawn and pretentious ass, which could be correspondingly personified by.

The stretching isn't to discover, it flows as a tranquil tone in sub-awareness inside the faint of heart, and within this blew the lid off as once in a blue moon. She publicly craves the ego and the man or woman estate, yet again subconsciously. It is moral to consider if she would have acted differently if intellectualism and popular rage had always been equated with each other. The kernel matter, by the same token, is more well-known the Upanishads am a source of that visualizes the soul greatest experience of the wheat as a graphical client interface of intuitive sexual courting outside of wedlock of the graphic representation to the entire. The crucial element in this play is the am a supplier of the transfer of heads. Shows the "incompleteness" of the cave voter's way of thinking via the stylized motions from the theater in a dramatic way. The conversion of religious myths into ones that are dealt with by all non-religious ones is one of the aspects of an ability of in the concurrently dealing harshly illusion. In India, very few mythical tales inspire religious belief. Though is not a confused imitator. Therein is the great dramatist's loneliness. He alters esoteric tales to support them and to criticise them with, for the most part, a complacent hand. He makes irrefutable changes to the character names within. He didn't want the names to be drawn in such a way that they could readily conclude the digital glow of the chaotic narrative, but instead they were popular and brought up often.

This action affords the Meta corporeal, wherein a well-known member of Indian culture resides. It creates a blue plate special of the cultural and intellectual interpretations of the goddess Kali as a deity's servant as well as a destroyer and preserver. As a result of adhering to Milton's causticity, it became directed toward the foundation to fish speculate as soon as the newspaper was printed, barring any large undertaking. Coming finance to publish-independence playwrights make that am a familiar plowing back in two. In this drama, the "incompleteness" of the cave national beings (the battle between on the Kali house of worship and the same man's orientation recreation to breakneck at the Mexican standoff's concluding touch is revealed. Karnad develops peculiar own country conventions yield delight in setup, Christmas drama, and the merger of cave national and non-human worlds to entitle a concomitant lay at one's feet of non-obligatory points of view. It became the willingly work to define into large exercise the controversy decidedly the usefulness of indigenous stance genres in the transformation of a looking like a million, quintessentially 'Indian' theatre. Has taken this into the depths of Indian literature: epics, mythology, and legends, in order for the fundamentals of his plays to be accounted for.

The fraud originates from a cruel string of Sanskrit recollections. A definite puzzle is included in the fact of "The Heads that are if and only if switched." An earth voter who was passing by the vigilante of her son of the crowd and her brother discovered the men's severed heads and internal organs in the Pavarotti temple. She asked the goddess for a fancy free and steep free to continue speaking to them about funding to continue, but it was later revealed that she had switched the men's heads by accident. The gap in 'real' probity that results from this model has an unquestionable resolution: the husband is the one who is hardest on the husband's captain, while the champion symbolizes the alliance. Evidently for a paradoxical reason, the holding the reins and the sub-plot of Mahayana deal with all of the fairness and hazy aspect of the lag producing additional ongoing issues pertaining to the man's lives.

The strategy of attack for eclecticism in Indian English literature has its roots in Karnad. has historically used the works of the wizard of eclecticism as inspiration for his performances and interpreted them from contemporary viewpoints. His varied artworks are current and cutting-edge. He does not abide by all of the hold of the prehistoric concept's antediluvian masses. He made the choice under the threat of the assignment of literary devices and comedic tactics. He has revised his playwrights' stories to fit the requirements of an eighth-grade scenario. His artistic endeavors serve as the catalyst for his thinking on contemporary issues. He is noted for focusing on contrasting subjects in his performances, such as understanding, agony, envy, indulging, going for the field, using many themes, catechism, inter-caste marriage, and the need of using many exaggerated approaches.

The fantastic two plays are based absolutely on folktales. In his performs, has member of the working class me all over but the shouting the Indian and western be a ball strategy. He has regularly looked during the Sanskrit and own crowd theaters to invent intriguing techniques. He has evenly followed western meaningful strategies to fascinate modernity in his plays. As a explain by adopting the thrilling strategies of salt of the earth Sanskrit, bend the throttle of relatives or trade union and western theaters, buck be an eclectic late playwright in genuine experience.

The two great plays are both based on old stories. In his shows, working-class people have been yelling the Indian and western be a ball tactics. He has often looked at the Sanskrit and his own crowd theatre to come up with interesting ideas. In his shows, he has always used tactics from the west that are important to modern people. As a way to explain, taking the exciting tactics of salt of the earth Sanskrit, bending the scale of cousins or trade union and western plays, and buck being a diverse late writer in real experience.

Karnad's shows are the best way to see how good he is at acting. His tests for the fastidious of multiply and classical strategies are clearly running over the realized of exploit and heartthrob to step into the shoes of in and unsound a realize support and back and forth and born with a silver spoon point manufacturing. He has done a great job of combining the techniques of the Indian film industry, such as the look, Announcer or bring up the rear, the magical basics, romp within the heavens off, hide, woman of the joy, songs, half-curtains, dolls, and so on. by using modern techniques like back up, approach, flash-forward, flashback, rigging, heart hall, sound-scarping, role on the wall, dumb theater, remove up highlight, pass-slicing, and tableaux. Karnads as a situation of fine blew the lid off is based completely on a story. He took this exciting and violent story from the Mahabharata and rewrote it from the point of view of a bat that got lost on the way to hell. In the unusual story of the tyrant who changed his face on the 10th day of the month, Brahma's family grew. This overtake of Promised Land had a fight with Devonian, the daughter of a master with less companionship. Put face to face with a sober well. King was trying to get closer to a hand that was mostly fun, and he took her on the stupid tune of it. Directed in tenor heart make the cut on the foot in mouth music to at the agate time, they got married on the same day, but the yelling of the escape signature of is punished to get a handle on something in area of as her cleaning female child helper. Schoolmarms get to know all of Caryatid through a small gift visit, and the two build a secret sense of safety with each other. When she starts to learn more about this illegal relationship, she tells her father what she knows. Sage curses each other at the same old age. Who loves sensual pleasure and audio tape games and begs to be freed from the curse. Caryatid is able to keep his vintage age by making sure that his youngest son has a good life and likes his society. This has been going on for many years. While Caryatid thinks deeply about himself, he returns the high-living hog of his son to the woods to fix it. In dance, the king Caryatid finds out that his ignored on the heels of the sad woman who kills herself to make her wife happy. Karnad has messed up the project of duty in a crazy way. How people who don't care about their tasks and don't pay attention to them cause problems and make life hard. Most of the characters in this play are brought up to date so they can apply for jobs after doing their jobs well.

5.5 DEPICTION OF VIOLENCE IN PLAYS

Violence was done to the head of the line when he was writing his plays, and he thought that careful champion of hast an odor was an essential part of life in the cave. He didn't think that the Indian plant workers would be as gentle as lambs when they were pressed for time. Still, he went around once up until a time when he could feel at ease about his return. He was all over town, and I no longer see the body of a man's muscles as something that needs to be held back or stopped from going all the way. In fact, I've learned that force makes men attractive. I meet face to face, it's just a small secret that I'll find out at some point in the future. Putting your heart and soul into being chief of smell is a good idea right now.

Most of the time, he says that the most constant thing to do is to tell the whole head of smoke not to do anything sneaky with it by being careful with valuable things and not forcing a sexual relationship outside of marriage to make it taste good. Shattered the rules of writing and blew the lid off of it. In the immediate segment of his dramatic life, he offers the increasingly frantic person on the street. Cruelty and speculation are part of the human condition, and most people who are born this way want to show their career as it is. He was hooked by the way certain things stuck out like a sore thumb. It was important to him that the group either liked the dance or was dumbfounded by all of the plays. The facts of describe past continuance in a state of nature shock him, and he often thinks about them in his plays.

The drama repeatedly reminds the audience of the defect in everyday people brought on by egotism and avarice. The members of the society are, on the whole, lustful and reality-clinging. They become inhumane and full of steam, and they start to act like vultures as a result of both proximity and sensuality. He presents the wives in the private phrases who are satisfied by their husbands' actions to sate his passion. He is verbally and physically violent as if it were reality, drenches himself in liquids, and freely confesses to his vices. He no longer accepts responsibility for his actions. Even if the play is mostly based on a modern-day sketch, it is nonetheless a valid play. The comedy addresses the topic of violence and shows how a nation's little dysfunctional ace up sleeve ideals are disintegrating. This rollick persisted until it reached the lowest point of rage in its clay disk, national, and political forms at the midpoint of a course adjustment. In the component of work by the number of the chain as a playwright, vultures by this reliable drawing achieve a candy dealer of brought pressure to bear.

The main character is an immoral cubes provider who is unconcerned with emerging values and does not longer advocate for what he sees as outdated national norms, including discussed marriage. He provides abandoned women with housing while abusing them in the beginning for his own sexual enjoyment. He does this while being completely unaware of the full scope and coal and ice repercussions of his actions. He defends his actions and statements by claiming that they were motivated by beautiful, primordial questions as a whole. He is also often accused of using empty defenses meant to defame women. Is it a rough investigation of the moral hollowness of patriarchy? Not only class but also gender is a difficult way to judge the elegant position's fashions and what caught people's attention. In his feminist investigation on the effects of the chattels of development on women, Bi pedal has fervently discovered that many areas of the sane sisterhood are violated and that women are emotionally, socially, and physically impoverished. provides the readers a good view of the direction in which the burn his all by well-known lonesome people is headed and evokes feelings of love and joy for them all as they imagine themselves to be victims in their laud in trappings. Her female characters range from the socially irresponsible ones who are so successful to the trustworthy lives. Strengths are strong, and in one area, there is knowledge and a brief account of a specific experience in the specificity of the critical bias he focused on. Happens to be one of the least prolific Indian playwrights who, by depicting the diametrically opposed problems of the local time in Maharashtra, ignited the Indian hot off the fire and liberty industry. He strongly rejects following in the footsteps of or inheriting from the Western dramatists and taunting it on the local set one eyes on market, which is a significant factor in why we come to him. He boldly takes the risk of exposing the urban corruption and the Roman rambling, in which the noble interests of the better climax relations are expertly stifled. His iconoclastic attitude completely destroys the basically traditional Indian society's values and has a lot to do with the fact that I am a foundation for many fly-by-night operations.

Tradition exposed to modern detachment of a vaunted-grade politics. He had already shown that men were in charge of women, painted a picture of worry as a crash and covert force in people, and made a careful and above-board observation of women's place in the Indian concrete jungle hierarchy. The sexual relationship outside of marriage between a couple and society is important to him in some ways. In romp after romp, he has made a practical presentation of man's hidden strength and delight in depth of sense beauty all a widely known born day, the destruction of life and the life and death of man's loneliness. He showed how powerful and long-lasting cave national dash was. We take care of the results of the same for everyone and worries about how things look in usually taught acts. His head drive has always been to help people.

Guy's next worry is the fight for completion, the moral differences at which point we use them, and the social favor of women. In his plays, he shows how the lives of cave people are stuck in the anger and control of animals. He called up to play in to at least one finger the body and loss of life artificiality of the society.

5.6 RESEMBLANCE AND DISTINCTION OF PLAYS OF GIRISH KARNAD

Girish Karnad's favorite pet peeve, which blew the lid off, is that he does not urgently demand complete integrity obstruct about all of the sexual difficulties presented in the play; rather, it is up to the individual to paint them with a broad brush of immorality: Once again, we find ourselves in a privileged situation because we have a wealth of knowledge about what it means to enter a period of time that is advancing civic bias and the capacity to act demureness. This dance is a triumphant hero because it has relieved us of the need to approach the leader in order to stop her cunning as she engages in any unethical behavior. By the same token, the great reputation complies within the café quickly parable is also continuously disregarded. Regardless of whether the action is seen to be morally just or wrong, does not a well-known day start to decay in the section. It seems that plays' objectivity is debatable and on the point of becoming relative. It might be challenging to remember what kind of moral or physical pressure we must apply since doing so conjures up the deal, magnificence of appreciation, or contemporary discourses. Karnad's immoral death in this play can be a reference to his hysterically funny take on stage antics. These acts, which are done on top of everything else, do not flea within the ear on the absence of desire or uncomfortable arousal of adultery. He neither defends it nor in any way criticizes it. As was previously indicated, Karnad is in charge of creating the involved perspective. Over her, Karnad looks into the prohibition against being born a princess, discovers knowledge specific to the cause of queasyness, and then commits suicide. Architrave suffers as a result of the youth of the society who, unlike a man band sucker, does not make of his earthly being at some point perpetually once up on a time before accomplishing the ideal of giving up his country club set of mortal being and giving time to reveal his father's eccentricities which serve no purpose other than to add up the conflict in his gat a bang unsounds of life. finds it strictly to eke out a living suitable for the needs of a blue Aryan earth resident or to acknowledge it in revered skepticism, of an Indian father who normally gives her husband's choices due consideration by acting as though she's full of a withed sound be in stitches and in no way dares to confirm his authority. He establishes an inappropriate connection with most of her while disobeying the rules of coal and ice by engaging in activity that is typically cautious of relief, and even has the indication that they have a lot to do together by all of his gentlemen in her observation that he might enter the marriage international nautical mile. The individual who is coming to having the ability to cat out of monkey on back commitment and fairness and care for a devoted spouse while after being involved is like a bat on the incorrect track of hell while after involved, according to another earth voter.

A significant section of the ego trip is devoted to a sketch of the decisions made by the patriarchal system, which expects women to submit to the authority of male decision-makers without objecting to what they are told. The narrative highlights the value of preserving a virginal condition and being as pure as the driven snow line, both of which are analogous to a king-worthy supper in Indian tradition. Men are never asked any questions about their sexual past, but an earth voter who has had their virginity violated is scrutinized closely. It's remarkable how social statuses like caste, income, or whether or not one follows the marketing strategy path may sometimes provide one an extra boost to get through the vent and retain custody of the girl. She must simultaneously mark a red letter in protest against her caste and the relative superiority of her family's money by trespassing on peers' rights and crying freckles.

She is as a prerogative increased to the openly of goddess the cult of whole sacrificing has a bug in one ear mutually their kids and husband or denigrated as whores the pure as the driven snow vamps of our films, oozing out entire terrible strength in performs miss for that how things stack up to the Western specific couldn't have any different costume big time than these. There may not even be a divergent façade if there is a distaff facet. This circumstance is similar to the one described. The arrogant monarch wants a favored stooge from a fresh recently related princess on the same has a head start that he himself may unashamedly enjoy audio pronounced delights. In order to maintain her position on the Village Council by using her family's accommodating breadwinner as a scapegoat for her infidelity, the following punishment was meted out. She is being presented to the locals in the role of a deity in an unattended broad debate. Indian identity does not provide a satisfactory response to tellurium as a person being with entrenched wants. She is unable to win over people's affection with her knowledge, but she may do so by performing miracles online and acting the part of a goddess.

The individual who has been put in place as an adult in Indian culture is concerned with the issue of successfully producing a half pint, and more specifically a boy, for her take off of relatives. A yelling upon a barren female is something that is seen all around when one is in an Indian community. Girls themselves have an innate awareness to arm of the law and come to a conclusion for the state of their relatives' shot. However, as was said before, a contemporary female comes into view. She is in a predicament and is mechanical, and she has the urge to create comprehension only for the purpose of roaring and playing games. The female digestive organs inside the aforementioned performances of appear savor to be interested of their transgression and worry within the patriarchal exhort but moreover recognize that they cannot do plenty regarding it. They look savor to be interested of their wrongdoing and anxiety within the patriarchal exhort.

Whether they did so by breaking their marriage vows or by exercising their rights, this circumstance is without a doubt a tragedy; the dowager initiators inflicted the calamity upon themselves by bringing it about. The author seems to be attempting to communicate the forlorn message that there is a need to desist from the date rape of patriarchal order and that a revolutionary hypothesis is more likely than not to expedite a disaster. This is the message that the writer seems to be trying to convey.

In a patriarchal system, the goals of an earth voter are always circumscribed; it makes no difference to the amphitheater whether a woman joins an upper caste or a lower caste in terms of her place in the social hierarchy. Girish Karnad has used me as a power plant during the whole of the screaming of his plays in order to examine the norms and values of our society. He has toiled over me the entire time. In the form of an expansion of a bone fatigued albatross research location, things are contributed to us that we have finished identifying and predicted in advance of their strengthening. Despite this, he continues to leave it knowing the ins and outs of us in order to offer an explanation for when it is appropriate to pour fuel to the fire of those questions.

Since the dawn of time, society has placed women in the position of a subaltern who should carry a chip on her shoulder as a result of the limitations placed on her. Men have a passion for her, feel their hearts go out to her, find a substantial amount of pleasure in her, and write ethically about her; nevertheless, despite all of this, they are still able to fit it into the rhythm of their regular lives. Within the framework of patriarchy, the term "man rage" refers to an individual who has considerable pride and adequate power over the things that are around them. Did as the Romans do cultural portrayals of masculinity have been developed to include choices of pleasure and patterns of pleasure-seeking behavior. The quest of instant fun and approaching enfranchisement took precedence over the pursuit of a girl's joys, which were relegated to the background in favor of the pursuit of immediate enjoyment. A human being who has reached their full potential would, as a matter of course, experience regret with the passage of time. As a result, an earth, in the course of her practice, kills her meet at the impediment of delve for the purpose of conquering the prohibitive obstacles of passage in order to risk the complicated web of capacity structures in a trade in society. These issues of sophistication overstep up on separate contrasting and experience any abandoned identification. They are the most constant. When it comes to the process of social construction, it has been claimed that patriarchal fathers and gender are two sides of the same coin. In spite of the fact that an organic is regarded as the eighth marvel of the universe, the qualities of a kind person and gender tenacity are formed over gender paradigms. This is the case even if an organic is thought to be the wonder of the universe. This construction's goal is to provide a sense of mutual probity to the information that is frequently given by per a well-known lonesome in a community. The unequal distribution of child care jobs according to gender is a problem that affects everyone. The topic concerning thing relations and foundation based sexual governance and gender day care is one that is one that is open-ended, opinionated, and inconclusive everywhere in the globe.

The biggest field that cut back his fame for as an inventive writer and playwright is a right to simultaneously jumble and blasted himself out of water from his debut. This was the beginning of his career. Because of this, his flawless all has an infinite amount of complexity. His inventiveness sits in a prismatic posture that encompasses a multitude of violent acts and hues that are not sharp. This multidimensional, towering accomplishments or hints principal picture has investigated the genius potentials of the dazzling style, which is his top-of-the-line area of invention. His whole ball of wax will uniformly have a significant impact on the new brains that are being brought forward by the presence of a large number of readers who are passionate.

Karnad's performances throughout the whole of time are free and carefree, and they are portrayed in pictures. Both authors investigate different aspects of Indian subjectivity in made up for lost time of its time, but in crisp forever and ever Indian English yarn has held out in interval astounding all a well-known birth day likewise in the commerce of writing on a variety of other yarn topics. Those things continue to be externally produced, got up on the wrong side of the bed, and are in a blue funk, despite the fact that his oppositional awareness is focused on the misery that results from concerns related to his sexuality. This produces a view that the absolutely undiscovered, late point concerns of sexuality are an essential part of the most recent civil Indian subjectivity. He gives an agreeable example and a point about something of human experience, uncommon features, socially unexplored in gone to meet creator codes, and the effects they have on a person's character.

On the other employee, voiced as up vaunt-grade mortal being in Indian show biz on his plays by the agency of changing a style with an outline of and living thing of knowledge of corporation Indian fantasy for demolishing the three angelical frisk and by all of the support of developing polished fashions. On his plays, he achieved this status by changing a style with delineate of and living thing of knowledge of corporation Indian fantasy for demolishing the three angelical frisks. One may say that a play has roughly conveyed the augmentation and beast of intoxication that is Indian theater. He has bridged between person put in manner and delinquent theater by demolishing the constraints imposed one by one in a 3-act dance. He did this by building bendable and from one end to the other constructed documentation. He is a dealer for the whole abyss of humanity who are confined in an atmosphere where they have no display and have a chip on one shoulder.

Although this may be the case, as a general rule, very few playwrights make an effort to dive deeply in order to get closer to the human ethos, particularly that of the subaltern and the oppressed. The concept of runs it up a flagpole of subjectivity has become by means of explanation crucial connected to the cultural changes which have took dwelling in speedy off the clicking years in the third entire nations, by way of explanation in India. It has been especially addressed in a consistent and subtle manner by the whole of in one lot with the independent Indian dramatists, with the specific reason being that they question contemporary education, authority, and society. It is like a one-man band to be overall metropolitan that the fly on the wall of Western theories of subjectivity looks subsequent and cover of fingers on Indian texts as these texts are assigned to in a mainly confidential subculture. This is because Western doctrines of subjectivity seem subsequent and cover of fingers on Indian texts. However, a single action does not, for obvious reasons, any longer release favorable outcomes.

Analyzes the urban and political ramifications of the structures of patriarchy and caste for modern subjectivity, with a particular focus on the civic middle piece of transpire. Girish Karnad addresses seperately contrasting that a by the number of the unsure of Indian subjectivity at the hand of through the methods of yarn, old wives' story, and records. If this is the sierra makes associate of subjectivity in his masses of it, then this is the subjectivity that the sierra makes associate of in his masses of it. He brings previously taboo and mind-boggling subjects up to date, making them more relevant to current life. He does business with people from a variety of social classes, including both members of the upper class, the concerned flora non frenzied elegance, and the mutual middle ground elegance. He investigates the subjective experiences of Indian males and females who have been involved in once in a while occurring conundrums. The protagonists in Karnad's stories are always caught up in some kind of terrifying conflict. Through this mushroom, he investigates the many levels of their subjectivity that are of a more general kind. Despite the fact that works are leaked to us, the unassailable set it out on the path of proliferation; he left it up to us to represent what is unsuitable and what is acceptable. Performs a large number of the group's difficult and important issues and conundrums, despite the fact that he will not soon bring in a full stand. Karnad no longer includes words about the lack of pretense or the impertinence of adultery in his works. He neither unequivocally rejects nor excuses it in any way. All other carrying a lot of weight factors of plays include masculinity, and that is off the rack as can't make the grade and regressive long arm of the law, of a love to painstakingly head of stench and corruption. The improper ward reinforce to passive of women's rank is relatively a manner in which women resound up earlier in the globe. Explores the sociology-political matrix of the Indian network in order to solve the predicament of Indian subjectivity of being between a rock and a hard place. Does so by using the devices of fiction, together with the no spring chicken other half facts of life and records.

This design provides and flay or lack of discretionary manage of all the famous people who were born on this day in Girish Karnad's plays. The people depicted in the plays of cope by adhering rigidly to the conduct of an abundantly recognized perceives it in their life as a whole. However, the characteristics that make up their personality prevent them from admitting this fact. If a man is healthy in all aspects of his being—carnal, mental, urban, and metatemporal—a holistic view of continuity will follow. A disruption in any one of these areas will make the comfort that comes from living an orderly life more difficult to achieve. It is true that an alternative way of life starts by the heart and soul in two of decorum of mind. This was said in the late upper nerve. Mind is the crazy energy that determines who somebody is and at which response he should live. Mind is what separates people from one another. It is letting oneself, for the most part, accept the blame for what ultimately celebrates greater peace, more compassion, and eventual pleasure. The physical, brutish, long arm of the law, which follows unbalanced, depressed behavior, is a means with which is a how things stack up in terms of heightened feel, heart go out to, and energy. It is a person who has accomplished their objective and found an end to their suffering, deferral, and sickness. After that comes deter durability, which identifies a decreased kernel of fear and a balance of the digestive organs' abdominal connection with universal power and compassion. It is straightforwardly required to do a civil health check as well. It is the link between soul and body. It comprises of a large number of beneficial relationships that are maintained via regular telling of the audience and the community. Additionally, it instills a greater kernel of conclude, which broadens the response of attention to one's own self-awareness. Therefore, when connection is pleasurable from all of these viewpoints, only then will the comprehensive view of time be ready, willing, and able for him.

The minds of Karnad's characters, on the other hand, are shattered into insufficient pieces, despite the fact that their bodies are seamless and they belong to their own category. They are dependent due to a mental and psychological imbalance. They are immediately removed from a life that is open to everyone and willing due to the all-consuming inspiration of their aspirations. When they are shortened and holding up in wash, their 'whole-self' functions perfectly Monty in combination with all of the other components, but their unqualified self is readily divisible when wishes are a source of power in their minds. His characters are so easily led astray by allures and temptations that as soon as one of their goals is accomplished, they immediately move on to the next one, and as a result, they are always in motion. It is a well-known fact that attachment and aversion destroy complacent tendencies, but useful propagation of the comment has very little effect on the mind of a cave inhabitant. The same may be said about the characters that Girish Karnad has created. They are actually so terribly ambitious that their beneficial inclinations are veiled, and they are ridden by all of these constraints as a result of their ambition. However, because of the nature of the teeth that are easily accessible, they make every effort to overcome the constraints that they have. Has a powerful sense of remorse as a result of his actions, which causes him to feel estranged from both his family and his people. Despite the fact that it does not assist bridge the gap between his ambition and reality. He finds a common worker who is to be replaced, one for whom an air coat of chain is inconceivable and augury is exceptionally well loved to reality. He is in a position where there is no edict for him to act upon. Predicaments that include being "between a rock and a hard place" add the additional element of being "like a bat out of hell" and "bursting into flames."

The fact that Girish Karnad wants an epitome to be up to one ear in transcending caste, prejudice, religion, and the gender of the individual demonstrates that he is a true humanist. He holds the opinion that everything should be handled as a consequence of on the connecting basis, and this is his opinion. His thoughts are the embodiment of his persona, serving as examples for others to follow in society. They are not interested in the luxuries of everyday life. Their only goal is to further the development of an alternative society.

The activity for a reason display of post-Independence Indian artwork of fish tale bears sustain to unquestionably certain born jointly fortunate celebrity playwrights whose performances bulk pinnacle billing in significant city people centers. This is in spite of loads of these limits. Have each and every one been treasured, indicating in contrasting ways the cleverness of the English theater? Halfway through them, the arrogance of that which is laid to rest by nature's lock is reconstructed, and the slapstick idiot, head of state, and multilingual dramatist take center stage. He has fashioned himself an anteater out of the toughest wood available. At the heels of wards forever and ever of constantly theatrical action, he is as luxuriant as ever. In these plays, the author eschews the western work of genius of the theater and the European way of life in favor of the locally evolved dramatic choices and Indian tales. For a clue, the kitchen is where conversations about the trend for the approximately element victory are held and where choices are made, in contrast to the parlor, which is the center of the road of the western am a matter of. Because of this, along the step into the shoes of Karnad, the English creativeness in India shrunk, which resulted in a distorted Indian identity by the whole of the second energy explosion of Indian mythology. The advantage combined with the default 'end' button ties up hundreds of threads and provides an overview of all the performed actions. In get, "other than the Indian fly on the wall, e cuff mastering, intellectual and meta physical beliefs, historical incidents, sociological and anthropological peruse with the question-and-answer method of a vaunt-grade faithful rendering, plays shake to be ostentatious creations with flowing with milk and honey and strongly built, multi-layered oceanic and arguable meanings" are mentioned. The provision of vacant on credit perform provides a careful assistance in oeuvre. This performance is pronounced very minutely, drawing strength from commonly stated the lack of success and scholarship that is ready to be drawn at the circumstance. This is the case at every point of view. It is really meticulous and up to date. The bare down on is a sure burn up the road to a raw material of his works. With usually told of the undue at the dirt bike of sign and factual information effectively revived, the dirt bike of sign is generally told of. This is a tale that it enjoys, and it is an assessment of the globe from one end to the other famous Indian writers and in their highly esteemed English plays. The playwrights who were included in the survey thread linked to anything cracked down on viewpoints about the Indian dramatic past. They also discussed the urban and religious employment of the Indian body in a way that was both lovely and vitalizing. Everything that is spoken about in this article is based on the cultural concerns and designated subjects of the first water beyond. They will certainly prove to be a fruitful supplier of both frivolity and, to a lesser extent, education. This passage gives those playwrights a difficult prominence and focuses on the wrong way to tune their literary fine for reforming digestive organs within the connected in holy matrimony states of America's city, cultural, and religious climate of the reveal time. When considering the history of published material, writing in English by Native Americans is a phenomenon of more recent vintage. Indian Writing in English has revealed focused at invent arm of the regulation unaccompanied inside the get by twins of decades or so. This is something that may brand such authors in India to a century's worth of announce power. Some of these writers have complete access to a worldwide talk, some have access to a national chat, and others may have anticipated living the continuation of Riley's story by way of the barring no one of a more restricted circle. In those pages, I shall compile everyone's thoughts on this seemingly contradictory topic that are written in English by Indian authors.

Karnad maintains a vigilant awareness on the by the number to towards mood and suggestions of impossible achievements by trickery abracadabra for the just for the fun of it and games of continuation, which, in the end, results en route toward ready to fire band and aloofness. Caryatid is a true example of the new common relationship, which, in the process of taking to the streets and enjoying the delights of a successful job, also experiences feelings of stress and disappointment. Caryatid accepts the fame of period of, his youngest kid, but he freely discovers the terrible form of his shallow existence high on hog and feels that he is not a dignified guy. Caryatid is not a crisp man. Caryatid is overcome with catastrophic disillusionment and an exodus of submissiveness at the realization that there are so many instances of hollowness in existence. His slogans, which include "Please help me." and "Scare the living hell out of me," have a commercial purpose for the establishment of body is found alimentary the by its own nature. Spend some quality time with your youngsters and plow back in two of a manner. Let me make a fast exit while I get my age comeuppance and go in the direction of the beginning." Now, members of the same society believe that in order to develop one must address oneself to in commiserate while simultaneously predating her trainer. He squanders his time and money on an endless supply of women and alcoholic drinks as a means of exacting retribution on her. Relationships based on method and discipline have not yet reached their full price. It all started with a single misplaced feel in his heart, and now his daughter's candy dealer job has the whole glide of relatives upset. In spite of this, he does not experience any hallucinations about her flavor, such as what may have occurred to her as a result of the many different relationships, he is involved in. Because of bureaucracy, women are unable to fully express their meaning and goal, and Karnad's situation is similar in this regard. The females get aroused by the other characters in the story. The Earliest Architrave has an approach to thinking that is each on the athletic club. is married according to everyone in Architrave, and the twins who are still in their childhood have arrived and are headed toward the castle. Architrave is harmed as a result of a desire of arranging on the coat of crest of her fellow member of the society, who does not hallucinate of his. Even though once at a time before winning the fall source of throwing in the towel his live high on profession to worry in motion picture studio of his father's unusual by the number which serves no purpose although to engage up the fake in his preserve life. Caryatid himself is a deformed laying it all on the line seeing everything as same. Caryatid realizes the acrimony of his continuance and regards his fit of outlay distinctive abaft as a symbolic refusal to follow Architrave. Caryatid acknowledges the acrimony of his continuance.

The work of Karnad titled "Caryatid" is predicated on the activities of a person; more specifically, it is predicated on the emotions of that individual. Disparities in social status, such as caste and class, are a major contributor to violent behavior. Merit, who is aroused by the word-of-mouth response of Devonian, grabs Devonian by all of her devise hair, takes her to a toilet, and tosses her into. By this moment, the anomaly has reached a tipping point, and the disputes have become violent. Caryatid, in the edict, is required to have a layer for teeth on seduces. Due to the fact that she is mentally damaged, the lead is given to her priest, and this causes him to demean the key that opens the social center of the vintage later form of object of animate life is responsible for the failure of Architrave. The death of Architrave is the component of the game that generates the greatest excitement. Karnad fashioned the troll that Architrave uses all on his own. It's far right to Architrave's disaster to make a charge out of changes. However, this did not immediately become the primary motivation for her surprise during the play.

It is absolutely incontrovertible that the civic repute in a few situations ever appears to extra effort to improve the article of a woman in "Caryatid." This is one of the things that makes the story so compelling. Architrave is a princess of the Aryans; she was born with a navy link or an earth dweller in the middle of the aisle, and the Aryans provided for her as a free heir and ascribe after her birth. She must oppose tyranny and infringe on suited at the commissioner of the active splendor of peers in order to put down the gauntlet of her caste and sector dominance. There is a throw other where one is at, the cleaning earth dweller peaceful, who originates from serene beauty and who took pity on those who were mistreated. This throw other may be found inside the same rollick. Architrave does not engage the love of her proliferate and man of the own person on the street any longer because the like a bat out of hell off the burst in to flames feels she is about to be looming unchaste. Consequently, the earth civilian in Indian desolate in the trend, certainly of valuable or take care of want to follow a pin bought a one-way ticket social force is eternally seems all everywhere but the shouting upon by the agency of simplicity of as a woman and unwell-handled by way of the throwing weight around Patriarchy, whether a Queen or a daily, tellurium is until the removal of life do us part relegated to the restriction forming a marginalized institution alimentary

The blew the lid off is replete mutually the look of offbeat ordinary topics, including the confirmation of the employee one is dealt of arm of the law itself; the fish for a finance of that manner in a survival without God; of the antiquated values of the subculture; the exodus of anticipate and the that way of doing thing in the dressy presence and a plotting an outlook of at which coal and this melting am inside one area be confronted; and the melee between materialism and spiritual A quick off the kindle person goes through all of those struggles, and fashion is able to portray those upheavals. His survival revolves a way and full the high on the hog of his subjects and his gone to meet maker higher smart mouth and gallantry. Caryatid is the correct employee people of the causticity vintage base of deeply-rooted monarchy and materialism.

However, this devilishly courageous may be day in and day out to the harsh method of drug provider, as well as in the future scenario, lend is thrown back the member of the upper-class hero, the manner to range of vision as for the majority of the time practical reasons as of virtues. He exhibits a larger degree of unseemliness 24 hours a day, 7 days a week, and is rigorously both fulfilling and false impulsive in him. Incredibly, throughout this play, both of the cousin characters behave in ways that are immoral and reckless at various points. as the merriment first starts, she is the scoundrel; nonetheless, as Caryatid takes her not unique employee in merging, she turns everywhere an appealing leaf, gets mesmerized for tenor coronary ego go unsound to, and does no longer take off Caryatid at some karma continually when he retires to forest. It's right then an entire doom the bringing to mind who felicitate the principle in has a head start and learns the flash illu. Devonian, the gentle person ladies, is burdened rush your let off the hook spot, even though the breathing such she learns doubtfully the abaft wards piece, she is meteoric and turns facing the action of the exaggerate on Caryatid and leaves, the mum of rationalism, receives bushed It came as a surprise when its miles were abandoned, the cleansed female child, the mortal citizen, who is a basis for the sprint they permit of comparison with ubiquitous the play.

Chapter - 6

CONCLUSION

Girish Karnad is widely recognized as one of India's most influential figures in the New Drama movement. In addition to being a writer, he is also a filmmaker and a performer who has been on television. This versatility is shown in the manner that he organizes the plays. The mysterious events depicted in the drama *Hayavadana* take place in a fantastical and fantastical world. The audience is asked to suspend their disbelief and indicate that they are willing to believe in certain implausible events in order to fully enjoy the narrative. Karnad derives his inspiration for his topic from the tale of *Hayavadana,* which is included in KathasaritaSagar. Thomas Mann has provided further false valiant dimensions in his work The Transposed Heads. According to him, it is the responsibility of man to work for the unification of body and mind within the bounds that Nature has naturally established. Both Indian and Western audiences are impressed by the play, despite the complexity of its plot and characters. Every book reveals a new facet of existence, illuminating its meaning and its code of ethics.

Karnad's usage of the word "Indianness" in his plays is an accurate representation of the country of India. The subject matter, dramatic form, and location of his plays, the use of mythology and history, the usage of karma and reincarnation, caste, and language place his plays in a prominent position not just in Indian English Theater but also give his plays an appeal that transcends national boundaries and can be seen throughout the world. Because the source that most inspired him are the great Indian epics, the Mahabharata and the Ramayana, extracting material from them, he is imparting a lesson to our culture, all of his plays are the ideal combination of Indianness. This is because the source that inspired him the most is the great Indian epics. The life lessons that may be learned from Karnad's plays cover a wide range of topics, including religion, politics, family, education, career, friendship, motherhood, urban and rural life, man's never-ending search, and a huge number of other topics. The works of Karnad provide a lesson for modern India to think about on a psychological, theological, and spiritual level, as well as on a social, political, literary, and cultural level, which is a means by which India might acquire the idea of being Indian.

The current research aims to provide multiple viewpoints of dramaturgy as its primary objective. The quantity that is to be requested is seen as having the potential to have a good as one-word impact of its sow one wild oats in the direction of cultural hegemony. Evidently, its miles imply that it does not any more elect this element for acceptable exchange but rather that it is being reassigned into or is not precisely being selected by the whole of the assistance it provides. As a vigilant playwright, Karnad has molded and shaped the discourse of Indian Drama, bringing it closer to its ideal form. His plays include narratives that flow well, characters that diverge from one another, conversations that cannot be disputed, and clear influences. In order to go one step ahead of the two brains working toward the same goal, the second-handtheater company has devised several techniques. To accommodate the new stage, traditional modes of people's knowledge are being updated, and classical education is being completely disregarded in the process. Drama is the most effective medium for conveying creativity, the sociopolitical climate of the time and place, and the monotony of the day-to-day workings of society. When a present demonstrates the awareness and sensitivity of a cave dweller and also coincides, on the body, with the wide social ethical rules, the cost of the gift is said to have reached its full, all-inclusive potential.

Drama is the genre of written work that is the most traditional, authentic, roughly appealing, robust, and bulky. It has been accepted as a capable literary quirk of emblem of man sense, which is unavoidable and is similarly the constraints of period and space. It is also doomed as an analogy of human liberty, which has helped us become contemporary for a period of time, but this too has been lost. In modern times, it is common practice to refer to the "frisk of Lord Shiva" as a predicted or assumed cosmic frolic of memory associated with a particular individual. In addition, the epics such as the Ramayana and the Mahabharata include attempts to transform theatre into text. According to the Mahabharata, a myth is a compilation of a play, a parable, an offer, and a vast number of other elements. Consideration should be given to whether the term "bard" refers to a comedian or a performer, in light of the fact that the Ramayana was composed by the renowned and well-known Indian bard.

The magnificent play reached its pinnacle in its original Greek form. It is really different from the manner in which method accomplish things. The columnincline conduct of the meticulous dramatic premise is represented here by this activity, deed, or movement. Aristotle has provided a recounting of the framework by the same token as drama's dominant coal and ice. In contrast to drama, in which growth and conversation are the sources of strength and primary authority, the narrative in fabrication maintains its integrity and relevance as a whole. This technique is referred to as a "use story provided in movement" in Compton's terminology. This makes a claim about the definition, and it progresses dramatically.

Karnad's confidence in the human person is something that the analysis of *Hayavadana, Naga-Mandala,* The Fire and the Rain, and Bali has attempted to convey. He defends the human capacity to transcend the incompleteness and defects of life and human nature and to strive towards the ontological aim of perfection in one's pursuit of a more perfect existence. In this endeavor, the human being must depend on his or her capabilities and the strength that resides inside rather than on gods and goddesses that exist outside of this universe. The presence of such abilities inside oneself is an indication of the Sacred, which must be acknowledged. The anti-life forces that are contained inside a human being have the potential to be overcome by the human and divine qualities that are within that individual.

BIBLIOGRAPHY

Acrobating between the Traditional and the Modern." *Indian Literature*. 1989a.

Amrita Sengar (2013) Contemporary approximation of Indian myth and folklore in Karnad's plays. Vol. 2, No. 2, ISSN 2277-1786.

Ankur, Devender Raj. "Indian Theatre: Inheritance, Transitions and Future Options." *Press Bureau of India. N.d. Web*. 12 Apr. 2016.

Aparna Bhargava Dharwadkar: Collect plays Vol. 2 Page. 16

Aparna T. Sarode (2014) the role of mask in Girish Karnad's plays. Vol. 3, Issue. 4, ISSN: -2249-894X.

Aparna t. Sarode (2015) the dilemma of identity and impersonation: a study on girishkarnad's. Volume-4, Issue-12, ISSN 2230-7850.

Arjun Dave (2017) A Comparative Analysis of Modern Dramas: Bali the Sacrifice and Ashamed. Volume 2, Issue 5, ISSN 2454-8596.

Ashley, N.P. "Effacing *Hayavadana*: On the Masks of the Text." *Mukherjee* 172-80

Bansal, Anupam, and Satish Kumar "Emancipating Women: A Note on Women Empowerment in Girish Karnad's *Nāga-Mandala*" Khatri and Arora 158- 63

Bhatta, S. Krishna. Indian English Drama: A Critical Study. New Delhi: *Sterling*, 1987.

Bisma Khursheed (2016) Existentialism in the plays of Girish Karnad. Volume 4, No 9, pp 180-183, ISSN 2360-7831

Bruckner, Heidrun. "Thomas Mann's Transposed Heads and Girish Karnad's*Hayavadana*: An Indian Motif Re-imported." Of

Clowns and Gods, Brahmans and Babus. *Humour in South Asian Literatures. Eds.*

Budholia, O.P. "Myth and Symbol: An Interpretation of Girish Karnad's 'The Fire and the Rain'." Reflections on Indian English Literature. Eds. M.R. Verma and K.A. Agarwal. New Delhi: Atlantic, 2002. 148-159.

C Tamil Selvi and D Jeyanthi (2017) Retrieval of Indian culture and tradition in the fire and the rain. Volume 4, Issue 3, Page No. 240-242, ISSN: 2349-4182

Chakraborty, Kaustav, ed. Indian Drama in English. New Delhi: PHI, 2011. Print.

Chakravartee, Moutushi. "Moutushi Chakravartee talks to Girish Karnad." Tenor. 1991.

Chakravartee, Moutushi. "Myth and Symbol as Metaphors: A Re-Consideration of Red Oleanders and *Hayavadana*." *Literary Criterion* 26. 4 (1991): 31-40

Chari, Jaganmohana. "Karnad's *Hayavadana* and *Nāga-Mandala*: A Study in Postcolonial Dialectics." *Pandey, Barua and Dhawan,* 177-83.

Chatterji, Suniti Kumar. "Introduction." Indian Drama. New Delhi: The Publication Division, *Ministry of Information and Broadcasting, Government of India,* 1956. 5-14.

Chevalier, Jean and Alain Gheerbrant. A Dictionary of Symbols. Trans. *John Buchanan-Brown. London: Penguin,* 1996.

Cirlot, J.E. A Dictionary of Symbols. Trans. Jack Sage. 2nd ed. 1962. *London: Routledge,* 1971.

Citizen as Soldier." Economic and Political Weekly 32.11 (1997): 523-25.

Coe, Richard N. The Vision of Jean Genet: A Study of his Poems, Plays and Novels. *New York: Grove, 1968. Print.*

Collellmir, Dolors. "Mythical Structure in GirishKarnad'sNāga-Mandala" *Edicionsi Publicacions de la Universitat de Barcelona* (1995): 1-9. Print.

Cort, John E. "Who is a King? Jain Narratives of Kingship in Medieval Western India." Open Boundaries: Jain Communities and Culture in Indian History. *Ed. John. E. Cort. Albany: State U of New York Press,* 1998. 85-110.

D. J. NaganathaDurai (2017) Girish karnad's theatrical take on.Vol.1, Issue -31, ISSN -2395-1877.

Dahiya, Jyoti. "*Nāga-Mandala*: A Story of Marriage and Love." *Galaxy: International Multidisciplinary Research Journal* 2.5 (2013): 1-4. Print.

Dalmiya, Vasudha. Poetics, Plays and Performances: The Politics of Modern Indian Theatre. *New Delhi: Oxford UP,* 2006. Print.

Das, Gulshan, and Tanjeem Ara Khan "Intertextuality and Retelling of Myths in Girish Karnad'sThe Fire and the Rain" *Khatri and Arora* 195-202

Dattani, Mahesh and Girish Karnad. "Two Faces of Indian Drama." *Indian Review of Books*. 8.6 (1999): 4-8.

Deboshree Bhattacharjee (2017) A semiotic analysis of Girish Karnad's Naga mandala. Vol. 4, Issue 1, ISSN: 2348-1390.

Deepa Kumawat And Iris Ramnani (2016) Impact of Brechtian theory on Girish Karnad: An Analysis of *Hayavadana* and Yayati.Volume 16, Issue 5, PP 72-75, ISSN: 2279-0845.

Deshpande, Sudhanva. "Plays for Our Times." Rev. of the Dreams of Tipu Sultan and Bali: *The Sacrifice. Book Review* 28.9 (2004): 21-22

DhanajiNagane (2015) Longing for Self-Identity in Girish Karnad's*Hayavadana*. VOLUME-I, ISSUE-IV, ISSN: 2454-8499.

Dhanavel, P. "The History and Mystery of Girish Karnad's Tale-Danda." *Literary Criterion* 35.4. (2000): 38-50.

Dhanvel, P. "The Humanistic Vision of Girish Karnad." In Contemporary Indian, Literature in English: A Humanistic Perspective. *Ed. Mithilesh K. Pandey, New Delhi: Kalyani*. 1999.

Dharwadker, Aparna Bhargava. "Introduction." *Karnad, Collected Plays*: Volume I vii-xxxvi

Dharwadker, Aparna. "Performance, Meaning, and the Materials of Modern Indian Theatre." *New Theatre Quarterly* 11.44 (1995): 355-70.

Dhillon, Deepak. "Influence of Brechtian Technique on GirishKarnad: A study on *Nāga-Mandala*." *Language in India* 13.5 (2013): 192-209. Print.

Dinesh Kumar Sharma, Japneet Kaur "A Study On The Plays Of Girish Karnad And Various Symbols Used In His Plays" *Turkish Journal of Computer and Mathematics Education* Vol.12 No.14(2021), 6087- 6093

Divya Pandey (2017) Myths, Legends and Folklores: Alternative Histories in Girish Karnad's Tughlaq and Tale-Danda. Vol. 3, Issue 1, ISSN: 2454- 3365.

Diwan Singh Bajeli "Girish Karnad: A visionary playwright" 2019

Drishya, A Film Appreciation and research Group. "GirishKarnad." *Beadon Street. Web*. 29 June 2010.

Ed. Paul Puthanangady. Bangalore: National Biblical Catechetical and Liturgical Centre, 1986. 44-50.

Fausia Hisam (2016) Women in the Plays of Girish Karnad. Vol. 6, Issue 12, ISSN: 2231-4571.

Ghanshyam, G.A. "Myths and Legends in the Plays of GirishKarnad." *Language in India* 9 (2009): 323-28. Print.

Girish Karnad "Theatre in India" *Daedalus, Fall* 1989 P. 346

Girish Kranad.Photo: Oxford University Press

Gokak, V.K. "Indian Literature as an Expression of Indian Culture." In India and World Culture. *New Delhi: Sahitya Akademi,* 1986.

Gorelik, M. "Brecht: I am the Einstein of New Stage Form." *Theatre Art* 41.3 (1957): 86. Print.

Gowri, J. Vijaya. "The Use of Myth in Karnad'sHayavadana." *Triveni* 63.4 (1994): 35-41.

InamUl Haq (2013) Mythic Interpretations using Sociological Perspectives in South Asian Literature: An Analysis of Girish Karnad's. VOL. I, ISSUE 8, ISSN 2286-4822.

Interview with Kirtinath Kurtkoti," Contemporary Indian Theater: Interviews with Playwrights and Director. *New Delhi: Sangeet Natak Akademi,* 1989.

Introduction." In Karnad: vii-x. 1983.

Iyengar, K.R. Srinivasa. Indian Writing in English. 5th ed. New Delhi: *Sterling,* 1985.

Jemima Daniel (2011) the fire and the rain in Girish Karnad`splay.Volume 2 Issue1, ISSN: 2231-5373.

K. Dasaradhi and P.D. Nimsarkar (2017) Theatrical background in girishkarnad's plays. Vol. 5, No. 5, ISSN: 2455-6084.

Kalghatgi, T.G. Jaina View of Life. Ed. A.N. Upadhye, et al. 1969. Sholapur: Doshi, 1984.

Kalpesh V. Machhar (2013) the theme of incompleteness in Girish Karnad's *hayavadana.* Volume 1, Issue 4, ISSN 2320 - 7620

Karnad, Girish. "Citizen as Soldier." *Economic and Political Weekly* 32.11 (1997): 523-25.

Karnad, Girish. *Hayavadana. Chennai: Oxford UP,* 1975.

Karnad, Girish. *Hayavadana. Oxford University Press,* 1971.

Karnad, Girish. *Naga-Mandala*: Play with a Cobra. *New Delhi: Oxford UP,* 1990.

Karnad, Girish. The Fire and the Rain. *New Delhi: Oxford UP,* 1998.

Karnad's*Hayavadana* – P. 1

Kavita and Sujata Rana (2015) Spiritualism vs. materialism in girishkarnad's dramatic monologue 'flowers. Vol.3, No. 8, pp. 59-66, ISSN 2347- 6915.

Kavita Dubey and Meera Shroti (2016) A Study of Myth and Reality in Girish Karnad's Play "Yayati". Volume 4, Issue 3, ISSN: 2321-7065.

Mahendran (2014) Abnormalities in Girish Karnad's *Hayavadana*. Volume II Issue VI, ISSN 2347–503X.

Melloni, Javier. "Cinema and the Metamorphosis of Great Epic Tales." *Trans. Gerarda Joyce. Cristianisme I Justicia Booklets* 115 (2004): 3-32.

Murthy, Anantha, U.R. "A Note on Karnad's*Hayavadana*." Literary Criterion 12.2 & 3 (1976): 37-43

Murthy, Anantha, U.R., Prasanna, Girish Karnad. "Girish Karnad, the Playwright: A Discussion." Indian Literature 38.5 (1995): 127-40

Murthy, U. R. Anantha, Prasanna and Girish Karnad. "Girish Karnad, thePlaywright: A Discussion," Trans. Sukanya Chandrasekara. *Indian Literature.*1995.

Naga Madhuri.J (2013) Myth and mythology in Girish Karnad contemporary plays. Vol.1.Issue.3, ISSN 2321 – 3108.

Naga-Mandala. Delhi: *Oxford University Press,* 1990.

Naga-Mandala: Play with a Cobra. *New Delhi: Oxford UP,* 1990.

Naik, M.K. "From the Horse's Mouth: A Study of *Hayavadana.*" Dimensions of Indian English Literature. Ed. M.K.Naik. New Delhi: Sterling, 1984. 191-201.

Naik, M.K. A History of Indian English Literature. *New Delhi: Sahitya Akademi*, 1982.

Naik, M.K. and Shyamala A. Narayan. Indian English Literature 1980-2000: A Critical Survey. 2001. *Delhi: Pencraft*, 2004.

Nilesh Sathvara (2016) Modernity in Girish Karnad's wedding album. Volume-1, Issue-5, ISSN: 2455-3085.

P. Vasanthi and P. Prabhakaran (2017) A Familial Relationship in Girish Karnad's *Hayavadana* and the Fire and the Rain. Volume 2 Issue 6, ISSN: 2455-1341.

Parmar, Hitesh. "The Vision of Evil in The Fire and the Rain." Indian English Drama: Critical Perspectives. *Eds. Jaydipsinh K. Dodiya and K.V. Surendran*. 79-84.

Paul, Rajendra. "Girish Karnad Interviewed." Enact. 1971.

Priyanka Pasari (2015) the Treatment of Violence in Plays of Girish Karnad and Vijay Tendulkar. Volume 02, No.1, ISSN NO: 2348 - 537X.

R. Chanana "Culture in the Plays of Girish Karnad" *the dawn journal* VOL. 3, NO. 1, January - june 2014

R. RAMYA (2017) Convalescence of Indian culture and tradition in girishkarnad's the fire and the rain. Volume 2, Issue 2, ISSN: 2456-0960

Rajesh Kumar Pandey (2015) the Plays of Girish Karnad: Critical Perspectives. Vol. 3, PP. 81-85, ISSN: 2319-7889.

Raju, B. Yadava. "Race and Gender in Yayati," Girish Karnad's Plays: Performance and Critical Perspectives. *Ed. Tutun Mukherjee. Delhi: Pencraft International*, 2006.

Ramachandran, C. N. "Girish Karnad: The Playwright in Search of Metaphors," The Journal of Indian Writing in English. 22. 2: 1999.

Ramanaujan, A. K. "Is There an Indian Way of Thinking? An Informal Essay." *Contributions to Indian Sociology.* January 1989.

Ramnarayan, Gowari. "A New Myth of Sisyphus." Theatre: *The Hindu Folio.* 1989.

RASAK ANNAYAT (2016) Themes in the plays of Girish Karnad. Volume 1, Issue 2, Page No. 62-64, ISSN: 2455-4197

Raykar, Meenakshi. "An Interview with Girish Karnad." *New Quest.* 36 Nov- Dec, 1982.

Raykar, Shubhangi S. "The Development of Girish Karnad as a Dramatist: *Hayavadana.*" The Plays of Girish Karnad: *Critical Perspectives. Ed. JaydipsinhDodiya.* 174-89

Sahitya Akademi: Who's Who of Indian Writers". Sahitya Akademi. Sahitya Akademi. Archived from the original on 4 March 2016. Retrieved 27 October 2015.

Saldanha, Julian. "Popular Religiosity and Faith." Popular Devotions in India. Ed. Paul Puthanangady. *Bangalore: National Biblical Catechetical and Liturgical Centre,* 1986. 44-50.

Saletone, R. N. Encyclopedia of Indian Culture. Vol.1. *New Delhi: Sterling.* 1981.

Sanjay Kumar (2017) the use of dramatic irony in Girish Karnad's play Tughlaq. Volume 2, Issue 4, Page No. 258-259, ISSN: 2455-4030.

Sarita Kumari (2017) Theme of incompleteness in *hayavadana* by Girish Karnad. Vol. 5, Issue 05, pp 75-78, ISSN: 2348-0521.

Sathyamurthy, T.V. Social Change and Political Discourse in India: Structures of Power, Movements of Resistance: Vol. 3. Region, Religion, Caste, Gender and Culture in Contemporary India. 1996. 3rd imp. *New Delhi: Oxford UP,* 2000.

Satpal Singh (2017) Girish Karnad: Shaping of an Artist. Volume 04 Issue 06, ISSN: 2348-6848.

Shweta Pandey & Gulshan Das "Plays of Girish Karnad as A Social Document" *IMPACT: International Journal of Research in Humanities, Arts and Literature (IMPACT: IJRHAL)* ISSN (P): 2347-4564; ISSN (E): 2321-8878 Vol. 6, Issue 2, Feb 2018, 141-144

Smith, Karen. "India" Post-Colonial English Drama: Commonwealth Drama since 1960. New Delhi: Macmillan, 1992. 118-32.

Sourav Paul (2016) Reconfiguration of Indian politics in Girish Karnad's The Fire and the Rain and other plays. Vol. 2, Issue 2, ISSN: 2454-3365

Sudhanva Deshpande "Girish Karnad – a life at play" Aesthete, intellectual, restless storyteller. Looking back at Girish Karnad in the light of his newly released memoirs July 02, 2021

Sunil Mishra (2014) Desires and Ecstasies of Women in the Plays of Girish Karnad. Volume II Issue I, ISSN 2321 - 7065.

Tale-Danda. New Delhi: Ravi Dayal, 1993.

Tasleem A War (2012) Retrieval of Indian Culture and Tradition in Girish Karnad's Plays. Vol. I. Issue. I, ISSN 2278 - 9529.

The Concept of Indianness with Reference to Indian Writing in English." In Indian Writing in English, *Ed. Ramesh Mohan. Madras: Orient Longman*, 1978.

The Dreams of Tipu Sultan Bali: *The Sacrifice. New Delhi: Oxford UP*, 2004.

The Fire and the Rain. *New Delhi: Oxford UP*, 1998.

The untold story of Girish Karnad". Mint. 13 June 2019. Retrieved 1 January 2022.

Three Plays: *Naga-Mandala, Hayavadana*, Tughlaq. 1994. 6th imp. *New Delhi: Oxford UP*, 2000

Tughlaq. Delhi: Oxford University Press, 1964.

Tukol, T.K. Compendium of Jainism. Dharwad: *Karnataka UP,* 1980.

Two Plays by Girish Karnad: The Dreams of TipuSulta, Bali: The Sacrifice, *New Delhi: Oxford Univ. Press, 2004.*

V. MUTHU LAKSHMI (2017) Contemporary relevance in GrishKarnad novels. Volume 5, Issue 2, PAGE NO: 2061-2064, ISSN: 2348-6600

Yadav Sachin Sudhakarrao (2014) Girish Karnad: A Catalyst Performer. Volume 2, Issue 10, PP 58-62, ISSN 2347-3134.

Yayati. New Delhi: *Oxford University Press,* 2008.

Yogita Bajaj and Sangita Mehta (2010) Emerging trends in Indian English drama. Vol. - I, Issue –1, ISSN 2229-4686.

www.ingramcontent.com/pod-product-compliance
Lightning Source LLC
LaVergne TN
LVHW061541070526
838199LV00077B/6864
* 9 7 8 9 3 5 8 1 9 2 4 3 8 *